MY AUTOBIOGRAPHY
JOHNNY BRIGGS

WITH PAT CODD

BLAKE

Published by Blake Publishing Ltd,
3 Bramber Court, 2 Bramber Road,
London W14 9PB, England

First published in Great Britain in hardback 1998

ISBN 1 85782 206 4

British Library Cataloguing-in-Publication Data:
A catalogue record for this book is available
from the British Library.

Typeset by BCP

Printed in Great Britain by
Creative Print and Design (Wales), Ebbw Vale, Gwent

1 3 5 7 9 10 8 6 4 2

Pictures reproduced by kind permission of Granada, LWT, News International and John Paul. Every
effort has been made to contact the relevant copyright holders, but some were unobtainable. We
would be grateful if the appropriate people could contact us.

My thanks to Pat Codd
without whose persuasion, pressure, patience
and perseverance this book could never
have been written. My grateful thanks, Pat,
for persuading me to write this through you.

Prologue

THE RAIN WAS HAMMERING AGAINST THE WINDOWS as I slid out of bed at 5.00am on that dank autumn morning, hoping the miserable weather was not an omen for the day ahead. Heading for the shower before slipping out of my warm Midlands home at 5.30am to drive the 90 miles to Manchester, my mind was racing as I once again rehearsed the date that was to change my life ...

Roaring along the roads, the windscreen wipers beating in relentless rythmn with the pounding of my heart, I was keyed up on a heady mixture of expectation laced with the inevitable flutter of nerves. For this was my first day on *Coronation Street* — and my opening scene was to be a sexy embrace with Julie Goodyear, already adored by millions as fiery barmaid Bet Lynch.

But the tension that had built to a heady adrenalin rush as I finally drove through the traffic-choked streets of Manchester, turned to an icy chill when I finally pulled up at the heavy steel gates of the Granada Studios at 7.30am.

I had expected to be ushered straight through to the car park, so I could nip into make-up to be at my very best for my 8.00am date with the delicious Julie. After all, I had been brought in to boost the London ratings with a three-month on-screen fling with the blonde bombshell. But that didn't cut any ice with the surly security guard. He wasn't having any flash London git sweeping in as if he owned the place.

'You can't park here,' he barked, suspiciously eyeing me up and down.

Turning on the Briggs charm, I gave him a winning smile, explaining that I was joining *Coronation Street* and was due on set at 8.00am to start filming.

'Oh are you? So what!' he sneered dismissively. 'Well, you can't park in here. There's a public car park down the road, you can park there,' he added with a malicious smirk.

With the rain lashing down and the clock remorselessly ticking away, the fear of being late was making me break into a worried sweat, as I asked the guard if I could leave my bags with him. He truculently agreed. But, just as I started to dump my gear down beside him, a gust of wind blew my script away …

In a blind panic and with arms flailing, I chased after it across the forecourt, finally retrieving the soggy mess from the middle of a huge puddle.

Running back to my car, I leapt in and raced up the road, looking desperately for somewhere to park. Finally, having found a spot, I rushed back, picked up my bags and tore into make-up with just five minutes to go.

As I sat there, soaked by the rain and with sweat beading my forehead, Julie Goodyear breezed in.

'You're Johnny Briggs, are you? Well, you'll never get me into bed,' she coolly greeted me.

Talk about an entrance!

I warmed to her, however, as, with a bright smile, she added, 'But I can be a very good friend.'

'I can always find someone to make love to,' I assured her with equal candour, adding with a broad grin, 'but good friends are hard to find.' She smiled back, we shook hands and then walked on set — and into the scene where I had to kiss her in a car.

Without another word, she looked straight at me and, suddenly, her huge lips were wrapped around my face like a vacuum cleaner.

It was one of the most memorable experiences of my life ...

What a welcome to Weatherfield!

It was also my introduction to Mike Baldwin, the smooth-talking, womanising rogue everyone loves to hate. That was 22 years ago and while my career has spanned 50 years of films and television in which I've played my share of both crooks and coppers, I could have been a bigger real-life villain than Baldwin could even dream of ...

I knew the lads and had the opportunities, but I preferred acting and instead have enjoyed a career crammed with some amazing highs, like having the pick of the most beautiful topless dancers in London and boozing with legendary hell-raisers of the calibre of Richard Burton and Peter O'Toole.

But I have also been banged up in a tough army nick and known devastating lows in a life that began in South London in the Thirties.

1

I WAS BORN IN A MIRROR IMAGE of *Coronation Street* — a red-brick, two-up, two-down terraced house in a close-knit working-class community. But instead of the neat rows of homes of the mythical Weatherfield (in reality the Salford, Greater Manchester, of the Sixties) my home was in Lavender Hill, Battersea, in the South London of the Thirties.

Our home was a little grander than the cottages of Coronation Street as our house, number 11, Lavender Sweep, was bow-windowed and we had a tiny front garden, but when I was a lad the atmosphere was similar to that of the original Coronation Street. People were neighbourly, and if they didn't know everyone else's business, they wouldn't rest until they did! But you could rely on them in hard times. No one locked their doors, which were always left open. There were never any burglaries and crime was at a minimum.

If that sounds too good to be true, well, that's the up side. In reality, times were very hard, people scrimped and saved and money was always tight. I was luckier than most because my father, Ernest John, was a master joiner and carpenter, and earned relatively good money. I used to play in the streets with the other kids, but from a very young age, I was a bit of a loner, a trait that was to accentuate as I grew older.

Although my family were South London born and bred, unlike most of the other children, I didn't have many relatives. The First World War had devastated my family. My father was the only man surviving from both my father's and mother's families. Both my grandfathers and my father's three brothers had died in the war. My paternal grandfather and three uncles were killed on the Western Front, while my maternal grandfather had died from sunstroke while serving in Mesopotamia, modern-day Iraq. Having neither a brother nor sister at that age increased my loneliness, but my first real memories are from the the early days of the Second World War.

As a child I thought it was all rather thrilling, especially as my father had joined the RAF, and I spent countless hours playing war games in the streets of Battersea. And in the war years the sense of community grew even stronger, with everyone inclined to help each other. Sadly, that changed afterwards.

But in 1940, the war lost a lot of its glamour as far as I was concerned when I was evacuated from Lavender Hill to Guildford, in Surrey, because my parents feared for my safety in the air raids the German bombers were starting to launch on Britain.

I don't remember much about my time in Guildford as I was only five, but I hated being separated from my parents. I missed them desperately and became so upset that, I must confess, I wet the bed on one occasion. But I was lucky to have been placed with a charming couple called Smith, who were very kind and didn't say a word to me about it. They understood how unhappy I was and, instead of scolding, comforted me.

The biggest thrill for me in those days were the visits by my father, who was then training to be a pilot. I was so proud of him in his smart sky-blue uniform and gleaming boots. In those dark days of the Battle of Britain, everyone admired the pilots who were keeping the Germans at bay. The Smiths were always delighted to see him and regarded him as very much a hero. But it was my father's boots that held a special fascination for me. They glistened so brightly that I could see my face in the toe caps, but he was none too pleased the day I scratched one of his highly bulled boots while poking it in childish awe!

Even leafy Guildford was not safe from the German bombers, however, and after a year, with the raids getting increasingly closer, I was sent back to rejoin my mother, Rose, a pretty, natural blonde, in Battersea. I was thrilled to return home, although my father was away in the RAF. But my mother, who was working in a munitions factory, became increasingly worried that I would be harmed. Night after night bombers would fly over our home and I would be rushed to the nearest shelter. At other times we would crouch under the kitchen table until the all-clear sounded. But, with childish confidence and a complete lack of fear as long as my mother was there, I found it more exciting than frightening.

My three aunts would call round and I particularly enjoyed going to see my paternal grandmother, who lived in Tooting. By then rationing was strictly enforced so whenever we went to see my gran we always took a bit of tea or sugar with us. She kept it in a big biscuit tin, and in the end I reckon she ended up with more tea and sugar than anyone!

In 1942, however, the German Blitz became so bad that my parents decided I should be evacuated again. But this time to real safety — in America. I didn't like the idea of leaving my mother yet again, but going to America was a young boy's dream come true. I had been brought up on American films and believed America was just like a Hollywood movie!

Nowadays, I spend much of my free time in the States with my own family at our home in Florida, but I never made it back in the Forties — because of yet another air raid.

I could hardly contain my excitement as the day finally

dawned when I was to start my journey to the land of real cowboys and Indians. My mother packed my little suitcase and, dressed in my best — and only — suit, we caught the bus to Waterloo, where I was to catch a train that would take me to Southampton, where, along with hundreds of other children and quite a few mums, I was to board the liner that was to take us to safety across the Atlantic. My mother, naturally, was upset to be sending me away, although it was for my own safety, but I was by then keyed up with excitement and I can still vividly recall travelling across London in the bus with my gas mask, my little suitcase — and my name tag around my neck.

My mother had just tearfully kissed me goodbye and left me with the officials who were looking after my party of evacuees, when disaster struck. German bombers swooped in and bombs rained down on the station.

I was absolutely petrified. The noise was deafening with the crash of bombs and the screams of women trying to protect their children. And there was I, a skinny little seven-year-old kid, standing on my own in the middle of a platform as everyone else dived for cover.

It was absolute chaos, but although I was terrified, I had the wit to try and find shelter, as my mother had taught me so many times before when we had dived under the kitchen table or into the shelters back home. Throwing aside my case, I leapt off the platform and crashed down on to the railway tracks below. I caught my knee with an almighty thump, grazing my legs and hands, but I didn't even notice the pain. Total, complete and utter panic had taken over. I didn't even think about the danger of being crushed beneath a train's wheels, realising, even in my terrified state, that the bombs were far more lethal than any train that might still be moving.

Fortunately, they had all ground to a halt and, more importantly, the trains gave me the protection I so desperately craved. I dived beneath one stationary train and, curled up like a ball, lay between the railway tracks sobbing with fear, my face pressed to the oil-stained wooden cross ties. And that was how the police eventually found me;

filthy, blood-smeared and very, very scared — but safe beneath the coaches.

Although I didn't realise it at the time, that was the end of my hopes of going to America, but it was not the end of my adventures that day. I was hauled out from beneath the train, brushed down, comforted and given a mug of sweet, steaming tea, as the rail staff, air raid wardens and police started to get the station back into action.

It was still pandemonium and the priority was to get me, along with scores of other evacuees, out of the station and away to safety as fast as possible. The officials weren't worried about where we were all supposed to be going. This was war and speed was all that mattered, in case there was another raid. I wasn't allowed even to try and find my case, which had probably already been destroyed, and I was popped on the first train leaving the station.

With the resilience of youth, I had now completely got over the shock, and revelled in the train journey, which seemed to last for ever as we were shunted into sidings and halted several times because of threats of more raids. Instead of heading south-west for Southampton, our train weaved across country.

I was fascinated and stood for hours with my face pressed to the grimy windows peering out in wonder. Eventually, the train chugged into Winsford, deep in the then Cheshire countryside, where the local residents were asked if they would take us in. They were as surprised as we were as they hadn't even been expecting any evacuees, but the local school board inspector, Clement Jackson, persuaded them to help.

That was quite some feat, because not only were the locals asked to take in 30 or so evacuees, they were also asked to clothe us. All we had were the clothes we stood up in, as everything else had been lost in the air raid.

Lots of the other children were going to America with their parents, brothers or sisters, but I was by myself — and no-one wanted to take on a young boy of seven. And I don't suppose I looked much of a winner: a bedraggled, soot-smeared, filthy little lad, streaked in blood and looking for all the world like a nightmare version of Just William in my tattered suit with only my label and a gas mask in a cardboard box hanging around my neck on a bit of string. So, in the end, I was left standing on the platform, all alone. I don't think I have ever felt so lonely and unwanted in my whole life as I did on that draughty platform …

But, ironically, that misery turned out to be a terrific break for me. For Clement Jackson, who had an adopted daughter called Bertha, persuaded his wife, Alice, that they should take me in until he could find someone who would take over caring for me.

Happily, that never happened. And, surprise, surprise, in view of some of the characters I was to go on to play, I was such an endearing little fellow, that they decided to keep me, and I stayed with them until the end of the war.

On my first day, Mr Jackson set about transforming the grubby little horror, washing off all the filth and marching me round to the Salvation Army hall to be kitted out with fresh clothes, supplied by the locals who had rallied to Clement's appeal to help by handing over their unwanted clothing.

The Jacksons — I called Bertha 'Aunt' because she was much older than myself — became a second family to me and, although I missed my mother, I had a truly happy childhood with them. Having been brought up in Battersea, I had no real experience of the countryside, or even farm animals like cows and sheep, until I arrived in Cheshire. Although Guildford was then quite a small place, it wasn't rural.

But Winsford in the Forties certainly was, and Uncle Clement, as I called him, introduced me to this wonderful new world. He taught me how to play football and cricket, how to fish and what bait to use, and he taught me to love and respect the environment — lessons I have never forgotten. He introduced me to the mysteries of bird-nesting; how to take just one egg so the birds would return, and a score of other, to me, fabulous country pursuits.

I missed my mother terribly, but I loved my new family dearly. They were wonderfully kind. But I found it very hard to be accepted by the local children. To them, I could have come from the moon with my South London accent, and they mercilessly took the mickey. So when I wasn't with Uncle Clement, I spent hours alone fishing or going into the woods and climbing the highest trees. Eventually, I lost my London accent and took to the Cheshire way of life like a duck to water. I even started talking like a northerner and pestered Uncle Clement until he bought me a pair of wooden clogs to wear like all the other lads.

I can still remember the thrill when he finally agreed. And what clogs! Clement took me to see his friend the local blacksmith, who put horseshoes on the soles so that my clogs threw out sparks every time I hit the ground. I was in my element.

I became so at home that when the war finally ended and it was safe for me to return home to London, I didn't want to go and missed Uncle Clement very, very much.

But home I went — and my northern accent soon earned me my first brush with authority.

My family had by then moved to a flat in Colliers Wood in South London and I became so fed up with the local lads teasing me because of my accent that I bunked off school. I just couldn't stand going there to face all the aggravation and bullying. I was only a slightly built lad and, with my northern accent, was once again a perfect target for the school bullies who would set about me, making my life a complete misery. I became so desperate that I persuaded Keith Smith, a teenager who lived opposite, to forge a letter saying I was in hospital!

That worked a treat for a whole term, until my mother received my end-of-term report, which simply said, 'Cannot comment on his progress because of lack of attendance.'

I had skived off lessons for practically the whole term and my mother was absolutely furious. But I was so bullied at the school that she eventually moved me to another — Singlegate Secondary. That wasn't as bad as the first one, but I still found it pretty horrible as I struggled to get to grips with the three Rs.

My father had been invalided out of the RAF, suffering from duodenal ulcers, while I was in Cheshire and after working with a building firm as a carpenter, he eventually palled up with a guy called Gallagher to start their own firm, Gallagher and Briggs.

Things were really looking up as there was no shortage of building work in bomb-shattered London. But when they were doing quite well, Gallagher went away and left my father with a lot of debts. This made it quite hard for my parents and the last thing they needed was me playing up at school.

By this time, however, I was thoroughly fed up with school and loathed sooty London with all the bomb sites and dirt. I yearned for the green Cheshire fields and was planning to hitch back to Uncle Clement's when my mother struck gold in the pages of the London *Evening Standard*. She spotted an advertisement for boy sopranos, and thought this might prove the perfect solution to my problems.

As luck would have it, while I was living in Cheshire I had been marched off to chapel three times every Sunday, and while, like any kid, I had found that a real drag, it proved crucial in launching me into showbusiness. Uncle Clement had discovered that I had quite a good voice and I became a member of the choir, where they taught me breath control and how to make the best of my voice. So when, towards the end of 1947, my mother saw the advertisement from the Italia Conti stage school, seeking boys aged about 12 with soprano voices, she put my name forward — and I was one of 105 initially chosen.

We all went to the school for one day a week for a month while they selected the six who would go into a season of Italian operas at the Cambridge Theatre. And I was determined that I was going to be one of those six. We had to learn Italian phonetically and although I had found ordinary schoolwork tough, I was finally in my element and surprised myself at the speed with which I picked it up. And, happily, I was one of the six chosen.

The Italia Conti were offering us a wonderful deal, for we

had all our stage tuition — ballet, modern ballet, tap, fencing, ballroom dancing, and so on, free of charge. The school, however, charged £8 a term for tuition in the three Rs until we were 15 — and that could have spelt the end of my fledgling showbusiness career — my father refused to pay it!

That could have been an absolute disaster as far as I was concerned, and he wouldn't budge an inch despite all my pleading. I suppose it was a worrying time for him for he had bought a bungalow at St Mary Cray, near Orpington, in Kent, which had been taken over by squatters.

He had been told the only way he could get them out was to move in himself. He was reluctant to leave Colliers Wood, because of his business, and the fact that the bungalow needed a lot of work on it. This was a course he eventually took, but at the time he was in no mood to part with any money to pay for my education. Fortunately, however, my mother took a longer view, realising that this was the break I needed. She was eager to get me into showbusiness, so she got a job as a cleaner to earn the cash. So while I was learning the theatrical ropes, my mother went out at the crack of dawn — usually at 5.00am — every day with a gang of girls cleaning newly-built houses. It was a wonderfully supportive gesture on her part which I didn't really appreciate at the time, but it launched the Briggs career.

I hated doing ballet and tap-dancing, and when they said I had to wear tights I was horrified and was practically sick every time. I did, however, enjoy the ballroom dancing, as I fell in love with the tutor, a Miss Keys. I adored her as only a young boy can, and that made it all seem worthwhile. The fencing was pretty good, too. That was real man's stuff!

Eventually, we went into the Italian operas for a season in the bitterly cold winter of 1947. It was the worst winter I have known, with the country gripped by snow and ice for months. Even in London it was freezing and I was always cold. Inside the theatre was OK, but my teeth used to chatter the moment I stepped outside at the end of the performance. Fortunately, my father, a dashing man with a Ronald

Coleman moustache to complete his jaunty air, used to come and meet me at the stage door. As I stepped out into the biting night air he would sweep me under his long, thick overcoat to keep me warm. And it worked a treat although we must have looked a funny sight walking to the tube station. I was completely blind, but I didn't care — I was gloriously warm.

By then, however, I was used to privation. The war had hit me and a lot of children very hard, and although we were forced to take our cod liver oil and malt extract, I still suffered badly from the poor diet. I was chatting to Des O'Connor one day and we started comparing notes as lads brought up in the war.

'I had double pneumonia,' I said.

'So did I,' echoed Des.

'I had rickets,' I declared.

'So did I,' retorted Des.

'Well, I'm still here,' I added.

'So am I,' laughed Des.

But I have always protested that if it hadn't been for the rickets, caused by a vitamin D deficiency, that made me bandy, I would be 6ft tall!

But even in my earliest days in showbusiness, a certain friction was growing between me and my father, because of the money I was earning. I think he felt demeaned that while he, as a master carpenter, was earning £3.50 a week, I was bringing home £8.50. The sums seem ridiculous in today's money, but in the Forties my wages were very grand, especially for a small boy. And my father was not happy about it.

It was during my stint at the Cambridge Theatre that I had my first sensational — and extremely painful — introduction to the dangers of showbusiness. There was I, a green 12-year-old appearing in *La Bohème*, when one of the men in the chorus took me on one side and told me I should wish the diva, an international star of her time, good luck with a special Italian phrase, which he then taught me.

So, green as I was, I did just that — and was rewarded

with a spectacular slap across the face that rattled my teeth and really made my eyes water. That was some introduction to showbusiness!

What I didn't realise at the time was that I was being set up, and was making an outrageous sexual suggestion to her in Italian. I burst into tears as the furious diva raged, and I thought I was for the high jump. Fortunately, I wasn't, but when the truth came out, the chorus singer was sacked on the spot.

That taught me to be very careful in future.

2

IF THAT INCIDENT TAUGHT ME ONE LESSON, I soon learned another as my showbusiness career started to take off.

8 April 1948 is the day I shall never forget. It was the day after my younger sister Barbara's birthday, but what made it so special was that it was the day I had my first proper part in a film, called *Quartet*. I had a little scene with George Cole in one of the movie's four stories, called *The Kite*, which we filmed on Wimbledon Common.

George was lovely to me and made me feel completely at home, as did Dirk Bogard, who was also in the film. That was when I first met Dirk, who was to have a major influence on my career as he swept to stardom, and it was the beginning of a friendship I have always treasured.

The previous year I had been in the Ealing comedy classic *Hue and Cry*, directed by Charles Crichton and produced by Michael Balcon and starring the magnificent Alastair Sim and Jack Warner, which culminated in hordes of boys of all ages flocking to the bomb-ravaged wastes of London's docklands to round up a gang of crooks. I was one of the boys, and it was tremendous fun, but in *Quartet* I had a proper scene of my own.

I was to learn a key lesson in showbusiness life from the renowned and much revered actor Fredric March the following year,when I had a little scene with the delightful David Tomlinson in the film *Helter Skelter*, which we were shooting at Lime Grove. March was also at the old Lime Grove studios, filming interior scenes for the then spectacular Gainsborough Technicolor movie *Christopher Columbus*, in which he had the title role.

His dressing room was next to mine and I was determined to get his autograph. So, clutching my autograph book, I knocked on his door, which was opened by a very aloof gentleman who, looking down his nose at me, said imperiously, 'Yes?'

'Could I have Mr March's autograph, please?' I asked, flashing my best smile.

'I'm afraid he's resting, you'll have to come back later,' he said dismissively, starting to close the door in my face.

'Oh. OK, I'll come back later,' I replied, adding hopefully, 'but if he wakes up, I'm next door.'

As I turned to leave, I heard a voice call, 'Just a moment.' It was March, who added with a smile, 'Come in little fella.' Eagerly, I stepped inside and March, dressed in his Christopher Columbus outfit, said, 'You're an actor, too, are you?'

I told him what I was doing and he said, 'Oh, lovely,' and signed my autograph book — which, sadly, my first wife, Caroline, lost — 'To John Briggs [as I was then known], a fellow actor. May you be successful.'

I walked out of his dressing room with my chest puffed up with pride, feeling as if I was walking on clouds. And as the door closed behind me, I heard March, with a sharp edge to his voice, tell the aloof gentleman, 'Don't ever do that again.'

I took that lesson to heart and if I am asked for an autograph, no matter how annoying it may seem at times, I always give one, hopefully with a smile. For I have never forgotten that the fans are the people who have helped put me where I am today. Some people can be nasty, but the nice ones cancel them out.

Those early years were good ones for me and I had plenty of work in plays like *The Winslow Boy* and *The Browning Version*.

And then there were the films. In 1948, I was in David Lean's then sensational adaptation of *Oliver Twist*, in which Alec Guinness gave his revoltingly faithful portrait of Fagin and Robert Newton was considered a natural as the brutish Bill Sikes. It also featured my chum Anthony Newley. There was always scope for a young boy actor and I was lucky to be in another memorable film, the Ealing classic *The Lavender Hill Mob*. That was a great comedy, which I took a special delight in doing, having been born in Lavender Hill!

Like *Hue and Cry*, it was also produced by Michael Balcon and directed by Charles Crichton, but had an even bigger impact, with the brilliant Alec Guinness playing the mastermind in a £1m bullion theft, along with Stanley Holloway.

We also had a lot of fun at the Italia Conti stage school, which in those days was in Archer Street, off Piccadilly, and opposite the famous Windmill Theatre, where I was later to land one of the most envied jobs in theatre!

It was certainly a lot better than boring old school, and my mother could scarcely believe her eyes when she met me after I landed my first stage play at Northampton Rep in 1949. It was *Life with Father*, in which the whole family were redheads. But I was drafted in so late that there wasn't time for them to get a wig made for me in time, so they dyed my hair red.

They made such a good job of it that when I walked down our street, everyone started shouting 'Hey, Rusty,' or 'How's it going, Ginger?'

But I never let being in the theatre or making movies go to my head, or turn me into a precocious theatrical brat. I always remained a bit of a lad, and formed an instant dislike for the lady who played the piano in the orchestra. She didn't like small boys one little bit and, as I was certainly small, she had me marked down as trouble from the moment she first clapped eyes on me. She was right. I decided that if she didn't like me, I might as well get up to some mischief at her expense.

And as luck would have it, that proved remarkably easy — and spectacularly successful, with the prank I planned outshining my greatest expectations. She might have been a right battleaxe as far as young boys were concerned, but she suffered from claustrophobia and when she was playing in the interval she used to leave the orchestra pit door open to avoid feeling trapped.

This was a heaven-sent opportunity as far as I was concerned. So, one day, as she was playing her interval piece, I nipped down to the orchestra pit and closed — and locked — the door from the outside. She didn't notice anything amiss until she finished her stint. Then, when she went to leave and found the door was not only closed, but locked, there was pandemonium. She banged and pounded at the door as if her life depended on it, her huge bosom shaking with fear and fury. But the door wouldn't budge, and then she really panicked. With the audience looking on in open-mouthed amazement, she finally ended up heaving her huge frame out of the orchestra pit and clambering, like some great whale, into the stalls. It was magnificent and I was curled up with glee, laughing at her predicament. I wasn't very popular, to put it mildly, but she never bothered me again.

I had even more fun, however, when, during my stint at Northampton Rep, they produced a live parrot to go on stage in the play *Peace Comes to Peckham*.

That was just asking for trouble, and I duly obliged. I spent hours backstage with that parrot painstakingly attempting to teach it to swear, and eventually I succeeded, training it to chirp 'Bugger off'. My training was so successful that whenever someone approached the bird it would squawk, 'Bugger off ... bugger off ...'

As a result, the parrot was absolutely useless on stage, and no one could get near it without setting off an avalanche of swear words. In the end, the theatre management had to get rid of the parrot and used a stuffed one instead!

I thought it was hilarious, but, once again, the management were not so pleased, and I thought I was for the high jump when, one day, the director took me to one side. But instead of scolding me, he paid me a back-handed compliment over the success of my pranks, which had made an even bigger impression than I imagined. The director told me that they had not had so much trouble with anyone in that Rep since Errol Flynn had left. Flynn, the then legendary hell-raiser, notorious for his boozing, womanising and general bad behaviour, had been leading man in the Rep for two years before he moved to Hollywood. As Flynn, with his great movie adventures, was a screen idol for boys like myself, I was thrilled at the comparison, feeling I was in very good company.

I had a great time travelling around the country and 1949 was a vintage year for me.

Post-war Britain was pretty grim, with shortages and rationing, but that didn't bother me one jot. For that was the year I had my first crush on a girl — and, incidentally, when I managed to supplement my meagre sweet ration.

I was in *Sauce Tartare* at the Cambridge Theatre in London's West End when I fell head over heels for the most stunning girl I had ever seen — Audrey Hepburn. She was a little bit older than me and in the chorus, but her dressing room was next to mine and I thought she was the most beautiful thing in the world, with lustrous dark hair framing her elf-like features and huge eyes. I was absolutely captivated.

To add to her attraction, she used to be sent chocolate from Holland, which she was only too happy to share. And that was a real bonus for a lad like myself, with sweets and chocolate still rationed. But the relationship never got beyond my puppy-dog-like adoration for such a beautiful girl. I was still only a lad of 14 or 15, while she was already a young woman. She was quite out of my league, but I used to hang around the theatre hoping to catch a glimpse of her or engage her in casual conversation. We worked together for several months, for when *Sauce Tartare* finished, we started a new production, *Sauce Picante*. And I wasn't the only one besotted by Miss Hepburn.

Cecil Landon, who staged the reviews, was very fond of her, too. It wasn't really that surprising, as she went on to become a major movie star captivating millions around the world. But no one really had a chance, as she was going out with a French singer, Marcel Le Bon. And when the reviews finished, the pair of them toured France singing and dancing. I didn't completely lose out, however. I did get to kiss her — three times; at Christmas, on Valentine's Day and on my birthday. They were very treasured kisses.

In the same year, Italia Conti staged a pantomime, *Where the Rainbow Ends*, featuring their up-and-coming stars like Edmund Purdon and Donald Houston, who were the leads. But I had my moment of glory as a lion cub and the biggest thrill for me was being presented to Hollywood stars Tyrone Power and Linda Christian, who came to a gala performance. I was quite overwhelmed and madly in love again — with Linda!

When I wasn't touring, I lived at home with my family and, paradoxically, that meant I didn't really have time to make that many real pals outside the Italia Conti. The days were very long. I used to walk down the road to Colliers Wood underground station with my father at 7.30 every morning, to catch the Northern Line tube train to Leicester Square. I would then walk through Leicester Square to the school in Archer Street. After a full day at the Italia Conti, I didn't get home until 6.30 at night. But in those bleak, pinch-cheeked days of rationing, I used to give myself a bonus.

There was a guy who used to sell hot jacket potatoes outside Colliers Wood tube station in four price sizes, ranging from a halfpenny to two pence in old money! And he would give you a dab of butter, free. I would eat one of these potatoes on my way home and sometimes that would be my supper.

But I did make pals at the local youth club, The Capstan.

It was there that I first met Gareth Hunt, the coffee advert king who starred as Mike Gambit in *The New Avengers*. He lived in Phipps Bridge Road and I lived in Runnymede, a couple of streets away, and every Guy Fawkes night we would have a competition between three gangs of lads to build the biggest bonfire. Gareth's gang were the youngest, but they always won. So I thought, 'Blow this,' and my gang nicked their wood and old tyres and piled them on to ours. They kept scurrying around getting more and more wood and rubbish, but their bonfire continued to shrink as ours grew substantially. Gareth couldn't understand what was happening, but I thought it was sweet revenge. For even then he was such a good-looking blighter that I hated him. As he grew older he pulled all the girls and I loathed the sight of him. Years later, Gareth and I were playing golf at Wentworth with Sandy Wilson and Dennis Waterman, and it was an awful game for Sandy because Gareth and I kept chatting about old times.

When I was about 16, I had a black-and-white dog — a real Heinz 57 varieties — called Whisky, of which I was very fond, but I didn't seem to spend that much time at home. Which was probably just as well. I adored my mother and, once I was working, was happy to be able to pay her back for all the sacrifices she had made to send me to drama school. But the friction intensified between my father and myself over the relatively large amounts of cash I earned.

Basically, he was jealous because by the time I was 16, I was regularly earning more than the £8 a week he was bringing home. With my work on films I was on £13 10s. If you convert that into today's money — £13.50 — it sounds pathetic, but that was a handy pay packet in the late Forties and early Fifties. My father found it difficult to cope with this and he got a bit funny about it. On one occasion, he said he couldn't afford the phone and he made me pay for all the calls I made. And he used to moan if I put on both bars of the electric fire in my bedroom, insisting that one bar was sufficient. But my mother was always on my side and when he went out she would say, 'Put it back on.' But then mums are always like that with their sons, because no matter how old you are — and you can be 50 — to your mother you are always a little boy. Thank God.

Then in 1950, the inevitable happened — my voice broke. I woke up one morning speaking in a much lower, mature male voice, and my days as a boy soprano were gone for ever.

That could have been the end of my showbusiness adventures as it was my voice that had got me into the theatre in the first place. But by then I was hooked, and while I could still hold a tune I did, fleetingly, consider trying my luck as a popular singer. But I decided to carry on acting, and went to Dewsbury Rep with Anthony Newley. That was a real eye-opener for me. I grew up on that stint at Dewsbury, discovered pubs and found I was pretty handy at snooker and darts. But then, I should have been, as I spent most of my time practicing!

I had never been that successful with girls, although I was surrounded by them at the Italia Conti, and wasn't bad looking. I was very fond of Millicent Martin when she was at the Italia Conti, but she took absolutely no interest in me whatsoever. Neither did Jill Gascoigne, with whom I used to dance before she started laying down the law on TV as copper Maggie Forbes in *The Gentle Touch* and *C.A.T.S. Eyes*. I also had an affectionate spot for Nanette Newman, whom I also thought was gorgeous, and very nice, too. But all Millicent and Nanette did was teach me to swim. No kisses, just the breast stroke, and I mean as in swimming, sadly! I wasn't even very successful at that. All I managed was the doggy paddle and even today I am a most reluctant swimmer. I find the sea awesome and am not even comfortable in a bath. I will always have a shower where possible.

The girls used to call me 'Little Johnny Briggs' and give me a kiss on the cheek. It wasn't quite what I wanted, but it's all I got. The bloke who pulled all the birds at drama school was Anthony Newley. They all fell for his good looks and he was never without a date.

It was when I was at Dewsbury Rep with Tony that I learned the classic excuse for when you forget a line. We would just say, 'Sorry, but I knew it on the bus,' because we used to learn all our lines while we travelled on the bus to the theatre from our digs. As it was a repertory theatre, they used to change the plays with breathtaking frequency to keep pulling in the punters, and it was quite a slog learning the different parts, and not to mix them up. We certainly never bothered to look at our lines when we finished at night. Then, we had only one priority — getting to the pub before closing time. And in those drab, dreary days in the provinces, all the boozers closed at 10.30pm sharp. And you needed a drink after a night working under the lights. So Anthony Newley, myself and the rest of the cast used to run over our parts as we trundled into the theatre by bus.

At Dewsbury, Anthony had lost none of his pulling power, but, even then, I was more of a man's man and would rather be in the pub than have a bird stuck on my arm. I played snooker and darts and any other pub game going, revelling in the smoky, boozy atmosphere. It was heady stuff for a young man.

But bigger thrills were heading my way. When I finished at Dewsbury, I landed my first major film part — as Skinny, one of a gang of hooligans in the hard-hitting crime drama *Cosh Boy*.

It was the first X-rated film to be made in Britain and caused an absolute sensation. Like most of the films of that period it was in black and white, but that only added to its realism. It was the first major film by director Lewis Gilbert, who had made his name with stunning documentaries, and he knew how to make the most of the stark material. It was retitled *The Slasher* in America and became a major talking point. But it didn't seem particularly tough and exciting when we were filming it. Although it was a big career boost for me, it was just another movie and I was more fascinated by Joan Collins, who played the girlfriend of the gang leader.

She was two years older than me and had just married

Maxwell Reed, a big hunk of a fellow, who was 6ft 2in tall and very good looking. Joan had beautiful eyes, but at the time I thought she was a trifle chubby and quite plain. She had just been to Spain on honeymoon with Maxwell, and had been badly bitten by mosquitoes. She was covered in bites and was not that glamorous. Maxwell was the one exuding the glamour as the English Tyrone Power! Joan was quite friendly, but Maxwell was on the set all the time because it was very much a case of young love.

I could never understand how, in later years, Joan could become six years *younger* than me, but there you are! She was, however a lovely girl and all of us young guys were very impressed.

This was the sort of break I had been dreaming of, but fate, in the shape of National Service, cut my career short at that vital breakthrough point in 1953.

That September I was 18 and was liable to be called up for the armed forces at any moment, which meant I couldn't really take on any serious work.

This could have been a disaster to a young actor who was just getting the breaks, but, by a quirk of fate, just having to kick my heels for a few weeks gave me a fantastic opportunity. I landed a job that every red-blooded bloke in the land would have fancied — working at the Windmill Theatre.

The Windmill was then the most sensational theatre in Britain, with its saucy revues and stunning nude showgirls, all at a time when even the hint of something a teeny bit sexy was frowned upon. Those were the days when the Lord Chamberlain could close a theatre if a show was considered too saucy, censor sexy books, and comedians could be axed from the BBC for a too-risqué joke.

So to get a job at the Windmill was my idea of heaven — and what a job! I had the eye-popping task of taking the dressing gown from the fan dancer as she slipped out of it, and then handing her a fan, before she went on stage to tantalise the punters with her sexy nude routine. Then, when she came offstage having sent the audience's collective blood pressure soaring, I simply reversed the process, taking her fan and helping the naked goddess back into her dressing gown!

It was incredible, and I was being paid to do it.

It was at the Windmill that I first met Bruce Forsyth, who, as the resident comedian, was doing ten shows a day. Working at that phenomenal rate, it's not surprising that Brucie, at 70, can still do a week of one-man shows at the London Palladium and soft-shoe shuffle with the best of them. Brucie had all the girls after him. But I, allowing for my youth, also had a superb time. I also did ten shows a day, so had plenty of opportunity to chat up the girls. I might have been only 18, but there was never any problem getting a date.

Surprisingly, it was quite easy, because although the girls were appearing topless on stage at a time when that was considered very daring, they didn't see many men beyond the footlights. They also did ten shows a day, and when they weren't performing, they were rehearsing for the next show.

I don't think the girls really had such a good time, so it was quite easy for a bloke like myself to take them out, especially if you had the cheek to ask them in the first place. The girls were always happy to go for a drink — and the punters were discouraged, thank goodness! And while some of the girls just thought I was sweet and treated me rather like a gofer — 'Johnny, darling, fetch me a cup of tea, there's an angel,' and that sort of thing — I had a marvellous time.

Even as a teenager, however, the novelty of working with scantily-clad girls soon wore off. In the end, it was just another job. You just get used to seeing all the flesh.

But it was still exciting and pushed the thought of joining the Army to the back of my mind.

Like all good things, however, it didn't last. That October, I had my army medical. At my interview I said I wanted to join the RAF Repertory Company, but I was told that I would have to sign on as a regular to get into that élite band. So I settled for the Royal Army Service Corps at Aldershot, as that was the nearest unit I could get to London.

But when my call-up papers arrived, I was informed that I wasn't going to the RASC at Aldershot, but the RAC — the Royal Armoured Corps — at Catterick! Horrified, I rang up and said that there had been some mistake. But the army authorities wouldn't even listen to me, let alone do anything about it, and at 9.00pm on 5 November — Bonfire Night — I ended up in the Royal Armoured Corps at Catterick Camp, in the bleak, freezing wilds of North Yorkshire.

3

So there I was on a bleak November night in the middle of the Yorkshire countryside, drawing a mattress, blankets, sheets and pillows from the stores before setting off into the darkness in search of a bed for the night.

Catterick Camp was a grim place at the best of times in those days and in mid-winter it was a real hell hole.

Talk about a culture shock! This was more unpleasant than I had imagined in my worst nightmares — and it only got worse.

It was absolutely freezing but I eventually found the wooden billet to which I had been allocated. I then thought my luck had turned. Sitting unoccupied was a bed slap bang next to the radiator. I leapt on it like a drowning man — only to discover that it didn't work and it was as bitterly cold as the rest of the billet.

Totally browned off, I palled up with a bunch of other new recruits and we set off in search of the canteen — and some hot grub. We soon found the cookhouse, but all that was on offer was some cold pie, some dry, curling bread and a mug of the most revolting tea I had ever tasted. We were all used to hearing tales of how the Army put bromide in the tea to dampen the ardour of young lads, but I couldn't believe, bromide or not, how disgusting that swill tasted.

We had been sitting there for about five minutes when the orderly officer — the duty officer of the night — breezed in with a sergeant and asked if we had any complaints.

'Oh yes, sir,' says I, and told him that the pork pie was revolting, the tea was awful and, to be honest, I didn't think very much of it at all.

That took him back a bit. Soldiers weren't really meant to complain, especially raw recruits, but he told me to report to the cookhouse at 7.30 the next morning and make my complaint to the cook sergeant. He then strolled off and I and the other lads went in search of the NAAFI canteen for a few beers before finally heading for bed in our freezing billets.

The next morning, I duly went down to the cookhouse and saw the sergeant in charge. He eyed me up and down before barking, 'Ah, you're the recruit who complained are you? Right, get some breakfast and then report back to me.'

When I returned, I learned my first lesson about the Army — never complain, never explain. For the moment he clapped eyes on me, he marched me to the back of the cookhouse where there was an enormous cauldron full of potatoes.

'Right,' he snarled, 'get a knife and start peeling.'

You didn't argue, I can assure you, so I did as I was told and set about peeling, realising that if I didn't do a good job of it, he would soon find something far worse for me to do.

I managed to peel about half the flaming things by lunchtime, when I had a break to sample another truly disgusting meal, and then it was back to the spuds. I finally finished at half-past four in the afternoon. By then my hands were covered in blisters and I thought, 'If this is the Army, you can stuff it.'

To make matters worse, I discovered to my absolute horror, that *Cosh Boy* was being shown in the camp cinema. You would have thought that appearing in that as a right little thug would have given me some street cred, but not a bit of it. Instead of admiring glances and blokes thinking I was a real tough guy, the lads took the mickey out of me something awful. I really took some stick over that, as everywhere I went I was sneeringly called Shirley Temple or Lana Turner!

So it didn't take long for me to realise that the Army was not the life for me. But I didn't know what to do about it. You couldn't buy yourself out of the forces in those days so I had to think of another way of getting my ticket out.

Suddenly, like a bolt from the blue, I remembered a conversation I had had with an actor on *Cosh Boy*, who had told me that both he and another actor had got out of the Army by pretending that they were gay. He told me that they had done it by going to the doctors and telling them, 'I can't live with all these lovely men, I want to kiss and cuddle them all the time.'

He told me that the doctors then sent you to see a psychiatrist, who stamped you out of the Army as 'unfit within the company of men'.

I decided to try that trick myself, although I was a bit worried that they might put me in a room with a big homosexual sergeant who would say, 'Prove it!' But as I decided that was very unlikely, that became my plan of action.

That night I rang my parents and explained in detail to my mother what I planned to do. She was delighted and said, 'That is wonderful, son, come on home.'

But two minutes later, my father came on the line and he was furious. 'I did my bit for my country in the war, and if you can't do yours, don't bother to come back home,' he roared down the telephone.

He also pointed out that I might find life very tough after telling the world that I was a homosexual — and slammed the phone down. He was right, of course, because it was illegal in those days and gays went around in fear of being reported and possibly jailed.

That really shook me as I weighed up the pros and cons and thought, 'Blimey, what do I do now?' I was a very unhappy lad as I crawled into my chilly bed that night.

And the Army had a lot more unpleasant surprises in store for me.

The next day we were marched to the camp barber for the ritual army hair cut. And it was every bit as bad as I had feared. The barber asked me what I fancied, but took not the slightest bit of notice of what you said, running the electric clippers up the back of your neck while insisting that what was under your beret was yours, the rest was his.

By the time he had shorn me up the back and sides, I looked like a bleeding coconut. It was so awful I decided to have the lot chopped off, and must have been one of the very few people in those days to have a crew-cut.

We were then marched off to get our uniforms and that was another pantomime as I was issued with clothing that would have fitted Arnold Schwarzenegger. It was so big on me that I could get my chin inside the collars of the shirts while they were buttoned up! But the quartermaster simply said, 'Don't worry — you'll grow into it.'

Some hope!

I was just 7st 7lb when I joined the Army, and if I had been an ounce lighter they would have sent me on a toughening-up course. As it was, I was so slight that the medical officer put me on multi-vitamin pills, and I have taken them ever since.

I was then issued with boots and though I told them I only took size five or five-and-a-half, they slung me a pair of size six boots. They were far too big — I felt I was slipping around inside boats. But those hideously uncomfortable boots proved to be a life-saver.

After struggling around in the huge boots for a couple of days, my ankles swelled up like balloons. I went to the doctor and was excused boots for a couple of days.

The moment I put the boots back on, however, my ankles swelled up again. So, eventually, I was permanently excused boots, and was issued with a much prized little chitty which I carried everywhere in case I was challenged for always wearing comfortable shoes.

That was magic because, as a result, I didn't have to go on parades and was excused the much hated guard duty.

In view of the tough characters I was later to play, it was ironic that in the Army I ended up wearing women's shoes. Not high heels, of course, but the flat, lace-up shoes that were issued to the Women's Royal Army Corps. They were wonderful and I was the envy of most of the guys in the barracks who called me a 'jammy bugger'. I can't think why!

But while my small feet might have landed me with a cushy number, I wasn't exactly rolling in money.

I was paid just £1 a week — yes, one measly quid — and while it went a lot further back in the Fifties it wasn't very much, especially as the Army deducted two bob (10p) of that for so-called 'barrack damages' — a sort of fine for the natural wear and tear of soldiers living in their far from comfortable billets and barrack blocks. In addition, the Army took another two bob in compulsory savings.

So I was left with the magnificent sum of 80p a week to spend on myself — for cigarettes, booze and the very occasional night out, if we could save up enough to be able to afford even to go to the local pub or cinema, let alone take a girl out.

Like most people, I smoked in those days but couldn't afford cigarettes, so my mother used to send me an ounce of Virginia Gold tobacco every week in a registered envelope to make sure it wasn't nicked.

Always a reluctant soldier, one afternoon I was forced to become involved in regimental sport. You had to take up sport in the Army and I used to do Egyptian PT, which was lying on your bed having a kip. But not that afternoon. Suddenly a big, hairy sergeant came up and, kicking my bed, told me I was playing rugby — as scrum-half. I'd never played rugby in my life, but I quite enjoyed the first two games. Then, in the third match this big guy — he must have been 6ft 6in tall — jumped on me, and I woke up on the touch line with a splitting headache and a split lip!

It didn't take me long to decide that I had had quite enough of that and I put my brain on overtime working out how to skive off any more rugby. As an actor, I used to earn a bit of extra money playing snooker, so I volunteered for the regimental snooker team instead. I played every Wednesday afternoon and we did quite well until we played the Woman's Auxiliary Air Force — and they won everything. They even beat us at table tennis as well.

The Army certainly wasn't my cup of tea, but I was determined to make my life as easy as possible. It was while I was finishing the tough basic training that a pal tipped me the wink that the cushiest jobs going were as instructors, and suggested that I should have a crack at landing one. And it really was the life compared to being a squaddie. As an instructor you got sergeant's stripes, and while you didn't get paid for them, you enjoyed the glory.

So I put in for a tank driver's instructor's course, and passed. After that little success I put in for every course I could think of — wireless operative's instructor's course, gunnery instructor's course, and passed the lot.

Now life was really starting to look up and I set about getting the best possible billet I could in the Army. After the freezing horrors of Catterick, I was determined not to go anywhere cold again. So I dropped the posting clerk a couple of quid and he promised to send me somewhere hot.

He did, but it wasn't quite what I expected. I had landed a posting to Benghazi in Libya, where we still had troops in those days. I was given all the innoculations against tropical diseases, issued with light-weight clothing and sent on embarkation leave. It was while I was on leave that the shine was knocked off my little plan when some pals in the TA warned me that Benghazi was the grottiest dump on earth, and unless you wanted to live in tents in a place infested with snakes and scorpions, you gave it a wide berth.

Naturally, I didn't fancy any of that, so I nipped back to camp a couple of days early and dropped the postings clerk a few more quid to get out of it. As a result some poor unsuspecting guy was transferred from Germany to Benghazi and I, with all my hot weather kit, was sent to Paderborn in Germany, which, when I arrived, I discovered was so awful it was used as a punishment posting for the German Army! Not such a smart move after all but, it seemed, better than Benghazi, and I stayed there for the next 15 months.

When I first arrived, the guys in the camp were inclined to take the mickey out of me because I was an actor, but I was lucky that the tough nut of the Regiment, a guy called Paddy Brennan, took me under his wing and defended me. With Paddy and another pal called Fred Downer, I jogged along doing various Army schemes with the 8th Royal Tank Regiment, and working a few scams to boost our pay. It was quite interesting and I enjoyed roaring over the North German plains in tanks on major exercises, as no one in those days seemed to care how much damage we caused.

And to be honest, the major exercises in main battle tanks were very exciting when we started blazing away with live ammunition. I loved all that. The Korean War had finally ground to an Armistice and we were locked in the Cold War with the Soviets, which meant that we would have huge battle schemes to let the Russians know we meant business. The battle schemes also gave me the opportunity to charge across the open countryside in scout cars at break-neck speed, which was right up my street. But the Army wasn't my idea of a career.

As an actor, I was used to having a stand-in, a stuntman and a guy to go and do things for me, and suddenly I was up against a tough senior sergeant whom I shall call 'Smith', a burly hard-case who loathed me on sight. 'Briggs, you are like a septic spunk bubble,' he snarled at me. 'I could step on you and lose you under my boot!'

As I was also a sergeant, although unpaid, and a mate of Paddy's, we tended to keep out of each other's way, but eventually things came to a head. I had finally had enough of his taunts and took him behind the guardhouse, where we had a real set to. I am not a big guy and he towered over me. He was also an extremely tough, 30-year-old regular soldier, and was soon knocking lumps off me in a brutal, dirty fight. He didn't know what a clean fight was, but, fortunately, I had a trick up my sleeve, or rather my boot, too. Just as he was dishing me some real punishment, I kicked him between the legs and he went down as if he had been pole-axed. That took the wind out of him and and we agreed to call a truce.

I thought that was the end of Smith's vendetta, but I couldn't have been more wrong. He nursed a grudge against me from then on, waiting for his chance to even the score and really hurt me.

I might not have wanted to make a career of the Army, but with my pals I was having a good time. There were such huge shortages that you could get almost anything you wanted, including girls, for coffee and cigarettes. We used to buy our rations of incredibly cheap cigarettes and then flog them at a huge profit on the German black market. It was amazing what you could get away with. We even recycled our used coffee grains after an exercise. We would dry them off, put them back in the boxes, seal them up, and flog them. I could never resist smiling when the racketeers used to complain that a lot of our coffee was very weak! But you could get a camera or a watch for a packet of coffee.

You had to be tough to survive the Army in those days. The conditions were fairly primitive for the squaddies and, compared with today, there were huge class barriers between the ranks that were rigidly imposed. This was really brought home to me one day when I drove my commanding officer, a Lieutenant-Colonel Ramsey, to a gymkhana.

I got on well with Lt-Col Ramsey, although we could hardly go out for a beer together, and I enjoyed the day out. He was partial to his gin and tonics and, having had a good lunch, was a bit the worse for wear when we arrived at the gymkhana. It was then that the difference in ranks was really hammered home.

There were three entrances to the event, suitably signed. The first said 'Officers and Ladies', the next,'NCOs and Wives', the third, 'Other Ranks and Women'. I was so amazed, even in those days, by such blatant discrimination, that I took some photos. Sadly, the pictures never survived. I was parking the car after dropping Lt-Col Ramsey off, when a Royal Military Police officer came up to me and demanded my camera. Then, despite my protests, he ripped the film out and destroyed it. I was furious at the arrogant way he pushed me around, ruining my film, but that's how the Army was then.

Germany was wide open in those days and if you had the right posting you could have a ball, but it wasn't the case where we were stationed — and Smith was always lurking, waiting to pounce.

While I was quite pally with another officer I used to drive around a lot in a Jeep or scout car — the absolutely charming Lieutenant Jarlath Finney (now a High Court judge). It was then that Smith thought his chance had come on a couple of occasions.

We were all pretty young and if we weren't out scoring with the local girls, we used to get involved in some pretty heavy boozing sessions.

And they could be lethal, literally. We all thought we could handle any amount of beer or spirits, but one night out ended in disaster when we ran into an American on a major war games scheme.

He boasted he could drink anyone under the table, and there were plenty of lads only too happy to take him on. He really could knock it back, but, sadly, he killed himself downing a whole bottle of Jack Daniel's. That sparked a huge row and we all ended up before a court of inquiry. But I was cleared, much to the fury of Smith.

Another time he thought he had nailed me was when a gang of us were drinking in a Hamburg bar during a rest and recuperation break in the middle of a major army field exercise.

Surprisingly, it was when we were on major army schemes that we had the most fun. Paderborn was a total dump, so we pushed the boat out when we hit Hamburg, which was a really wild town, where anything went. The sex acts would make your eyes pop.

We would head for the red light area and boast about how many women we would score with. But, truth to tell, I was always a bit frightened of catching something. The Army venereal diseases films were so horrible I wouldn't take a chance.

And while there were some lovely German girls, and I eventually dated one called Brigit for a while, Germany was still so poverty-stricken and shattered from the war that you could buy a girl for just a few marks — we got 12 to the pound in those days. You could get anything you wanted for some tea, and they would give you a car for a camera. So, naturally, some of the lads were always peeling off with the local hookers. But it was risky and one NCO who worked as a medical orderly used to claim that he always gave himself a shot of penicillin to make sure he hadn't caught anything after a night out.

Woe betide you if you did catch a dose of VD. The Army had a strict system to ensure soldiers didn't — and it put most guys off. If you planned to have sex with a girl, you had to report to the medical officer before you booked out of camp. You would then be issued with condoms, and had to sign a register. When you returned you were supposed to hand in any unused condoms and then put a tube up your penis and squeeze it. Then, if you caught VD you were in the clear and would be treated for it. But if you caught VD without signing the book and taking precautions, you were charged with self-inflicted injury and could end up in prison.

You could even be slung in the nick for sunbathing. One of our boys went sunbathing on an afternoon off and got terrible sunburn. He was also charged with self-inflicted injury and was given seven days' detention; we were going on a scheme and he couldn't drive, because he couldn't lean back. But the Forces were normally far tougher about VD. The local girls were eager to oblige, but our Regimental Sergeant Major used to give us pep talks and he had this motto: 'If she is easy she has got it, and if she has got it, you will get it!'

So I kept well clear when we went into the big cities like Hamburg, where literally anything went. Instead of scoring with the girls, we would hit the shows — and the bottle — big time.

We got so boozed up on one occasion in the red light district that we decided we would each have a tattoo. They were ten marks apiece and we all picked a design. As Fred Downer was the biggest, the toughest and the bravest, we reckoned he should go first. Fred swaggered in, rolled up his sleeve and told the tattooist that he wanted a bird with a banner trailing from its mouth bearing the legend 'Mother'. But the guy never got any further than making the outline of the bird's wing with the needle before Fred keeled over. He was out for the count, having fainted with fear. So the rest of us thought, 'Sod that for a lark!' and fled!

We then piled into a nearby bar where an army lorry was due to pick us up and take us back to the exercise. As we hurled down the beers, a military policeman poked his head round the door and bawled, 'Eighth Royal Tanks, your truck is here.'

I had this huge stein of beer and was chatting to the bar owner as the MP continued to shout, '8th Regiment, out, out, out!' As I called out that I wouldn't be a minute but wanted to finish my beer first, the landlord sportingly told me I could take the beer, tankard and all.

I couldn't believe my luck, so grabbing the stein I sauntered out of the bar and over to the lorry, just as Smith came round the corner. When he saw me with the beer glass he beamed with evil delight.

'Got you at last, Briggs, you little bastard, stealing a beer glass,' he snarled. 'I have been waiting for this.'

I told him not to be so stupid and tried to explain what had happened. But he wasn't having any of that.

'Oh, bollocks,' he shouted, 'you stole that glass and are going to be charged with theft!'

He then insisted on arresting me, but at that moment a regular military policeman turned up and asked what was going on.

I told him the story and he marched into the pub to check it out. He spoke perfect German and, after chatting to the landlord, told Smith I was telling the truth. Smith was beside himself with rage. His face was a picture as he clenched his jaw so tight I thought his teeth would crack.

I laughed it off, but Smith had the last laugh when I went on the beer on another night out.

My army career really hit the skids when I went drinking with a bloke called Vowles. As an NCO, I didn't have to be back in barracks before 6.00am, but he had to return by midnight. Well, we were having such a good time that we didn't notice the time until, suddenly, Vowles realised it was a quarter to midnight. He flew into a panic, abandoned his drink and raced from the pub. He was in such a state that I, naturally, ran out with him to try and catch a taxi. As luck would have it, we couldn't find one and he was very worried, realising he would be up on a charge if he was late back.

Well, we had downed a few over the evening and, emboldened by booze, we thought our prayers were answered when we finally spotted a motorcycle parked outside a guest house. We looked inside for the owner, but couldn't find him. So, as things were now looking very serious for my chum, we decided to borrow the bike. We jumped on and the pair of us scooted back to camp.

We made it in the nick of time, with Vowles signing in at the guardroom just before midnight. As we were the last back, we went off to bed. But not for long. I had only just dropped off to sleep when the guard came round, hammering on my bedroom door. Then, without any ceremony, I was ordered from my bed and marched off to the guard room, where I and my pal were accused of stealing the bike.

The owner had turned up at the guardroom and was kicking up an awful fuss. I couldn't believe it. I explained that it was totally untrue to say we had stolen the motorcycle as we had only borrowed it — and planned to take it back in the morning.

But the furious owner wouldn't accept my explanation, and neither would the orderly officer. We were charged, much to the delight of Master Smith, and put on orders.

The next day we were marched in before the Colonel,

who was equally unsympathetic and we were both sentenced to 28 days' detention. That was an expensive ride home.

But worse was to come. I could have easily handled serving 28 days' detention in the regimental nick, but my luck was really out this time.

The Regiment was going off on another major war scheme, and because of the bad blood between Smith and myself, the Colonel was reluctant to leave me to Smith's tender mercies. Both he and I realised that would have been tantamount to signing my death warrant — and I am not being dramatic.

No one today can imagine just how brutal some NCOs could be. It was a tough life at the best of times, but the Smiths of this world could make it hell. The colonel knew I wouldn't have survived 28 days while the Regiment was away on the scheme. I would probably have been found hanged in my cell or Smith would have beaten me to death, and said I had attacked him! And Smith would have got away with it. It wasn't unusual for prisoners to be dealt with extremely savagely if they stepped out of line. And it was always carefully covered up from the officers.

So I was sent to Bielefeld nick for my own safety. But it was my bad luck that the nick was one the toughest prisons for Army personnel in Germany.

That nick was a nightmare. I had only seen them in films and thought it would be a bit of a joke. How mistaken can you be! The minute we arrived we were marched to the barber who shaved our heads completely. And that was the easy bit.

Your name no longer existed, you were just a number and were always shouted at as a number. And the screws made it very clear that if you didn't behave, you would be in there for ever. And that wasn't an idle threat. In the Army, they just kept adding to your sentence for any misconduct, even the most trivial offence. And the time you were in the army 'Glasshouse' didn't come off your National Service time. They just added it on, and if you didn't knuckle under you could be there for years.

There were a couple of real hard nuts who ended up in solitary. They thought that if they were in for life, they would be sent back to England and dishonourably discharged. But it didn't work like that. You couldn't beat the system and if National Service hadn't ended, those guys would probably still be in Bielefeld nick!

When I wasn't running everywhere at the double — you were never allowed to stand still, but had to keep running on the spot — I spent the rest of every day on my hands and knees scrubbing a 50-yard-long corridor. And when I got to the end of the corridor, I was marched back to the beginning to start all over again!

The food was equally awful. Breakfast consisted of a bowl of porridge and a mug of tea; lunch was a bowl of German stew; while our tea meal was two slices of bread and a wedge of cheese and onion the size of a golf ball, and a cup of tea. And that was it.

It was horrendous. The screws were harder than Smith could ever have dreamed of and we would lie in bed and pray we would break a leg, or get appendicitis. Anything to get out and into hospital. Fortunately, I didn't put a foot wrong and after three weeks I was released, having been given a week off for good behaviour. I was then given a shilling and a rail warrant, and sent back to my Regiment.

So it is hardly surprising that I couldn't wait to be demobbed.

Fortunately, after Bielefeld, I escaped from Germany. I was sent to Bovington Camp in Dorset to instruct officers on a new gas turbine tank they were trying out. It was so hush-hush I had to sign the Official Secrets Act and couldn't talk about it for 25 years. But that was a bit of a joke as the tank was a complete and utter flop.

After the 16-week course had finished, they asked me if I would like to go back to Germany or stay at Bovington. There was no contest as far as I was concerned. I was having too good a time in nearby Poole.

In addition, I had also had girl problems. Naturally, when I had been posted to Poole, I had left my German girlfriend Brigit behind. She worked in the camp cinema and was a nice girl, but I didn't want to get involved.

Germany was such a depressing dump, and I had landed a new girlfriend in Poole. Well, a couple to be precise, plus all the ones I picked up casually on nights out on the town. After Germany and all the regulations about girls, I was determined to have a really good time again. And I did.

At Bovington, my best pal was a guy called Don, who was the head cook, and we had a partnership. I was quite a good-looking lad while he was a bit chubby, so if I went out with him and we pulled the birds, when we returned to camp he would cook us a couple of the juiciest steaks from the Officers' Mess as a little 'Thank you'. We generally found a couple of beers and would liberate a little of the officers' cooking brandy. As Don also cooked for the Officers' Mess, he knew all the tricks and we used to really indulge ourselves. It was a splendid way to round off an evening.

We seldom failed to pull for a kiss 'n' cuddle in Poole, much to the annoyance of the Royal Marines who were based there. They hated the tankies and we used to wind them up by lying that we had fought in Korea, but didn't wear the medals as we didn't want to show them up.

I also had a girlfriend who worked in a florist and, as she had quite a bit of money, I would date her when I was skint. When I called round she would always ask, 'Why haven't I seen you?' Naturally, I could hardly tell her I only dated her when I was broke, so I used to spin her some yarn about manoeuvres. Amazingly, she always seemed to fall for it. But she was very generous. Too generous on one occasion, when she bought me a carnation for Valentine's Day and insisted I wore it back to camp. As she drove me to the gates, I had a heck of a job sneaking in so that the lads wouldn't see and start taking the mickey.

While I had been home on leave to my parents' new house in Spencer Road, Clapham, I had met a stunningly gorgeous girl called Vicky Smith. She was a model for Raymond, the famous 'Mr Teasy-Weasy' hairdresser, and only lived two doors down the road. I was really smitten with Vicky and we used to write to one another. I used to take her out whenever I could on my visits home, but as she was always travelling for exhibitions, she wasn't regularly available.

So I stayed at Bovington until I was demobbed. When the magic day came I went to see the Colonel, who told me that they were so impressed with the job that I had done that they were prepared to make me a substantive staff sergeant, which was a good rank with a decent bit of pay.

But I wanted to go back to Civvy Street and finally marched out of the Army on 15 November 1955.

4

THE DAY I LEFT THE ARMY should have been the start of a glorious new life for me, but the next three months were the worst of my life — and the shadow of that time still hangs over me.

For the very next day, the 16th, tragedy struck my little sister Barbara, and I blame myself for her death to this day.

She was a beautiful, vibrant 15-year-old with her whole life ahead of her and couldn't wait to be reunited with her big brother.

Yet her life was snuffed out after what seemed just a simple accident. She was a trainee hairdresser and slipped over on a pile of hair on the salon floor that afternoon, cracking her head on a washbasin.

She seemed to recover all right and didn't appear to have seriously hurt herself. She didn't make much of it at the time as that night she was due to go out with me and my girlfriend Vicky to a cinema near our home in Clapham, South London. And she was really looking forward to that.

To be quite honest, as it was only the night after I had left the Army, I was not too pleased that she came along. I didn't really want my baby sister with Vicky and I on such an important date, but she wanted to be with me, so I said OK.

We went to the cinema in good spirits, laughing at the usual good-humoured banter. But halfway through the programme, Barbara complained of a terrible headache, which grew steadily worse. Eventually, the pain was so bad that Barbara decided to leave the cinema and go home — and I didn't stop her. She said she could manage on the bus by herself and so Vicky and I stayed in the cinema, enjoying each other's company and thinking no more about it,

When I finally got home and walked into the living room, my father greeted me saying that Barbara had been terribly sick, but had then gone off to bed. Like any caring parent, he was sufficiently worried to have been upstairs to check how she was. He had looked into her room but told me that he had left her as she was in a very deep sleep.

'I can't wake her, so it's best to leave her alone,' he said, never realising how ill she was.

Tired after a good night out, I went off to bed, to be woken next morning by my anxious father, his face ashen and his lips trembling beneath his neatly clipped moustache, shaking me.

He had come into my room to tell me that Barbara was unconscious and that he couldn't wake her. My heart skipped a beat, and with a horrible sinking feeling in the pit of my stomach, I rushed into Barbara's room with my father and also tried to wake her. But I couldn't rouse her from her deep sleep either.

Realising that Barbara was seriously ill, I told my now distraught father to call an ambulance and our local doctor. When the doctor arrived, he confirmed my worst fears, diagnosing that Barbara had a brain haemorrhage, and saying that she had to be taken to hospital immediately so that she could be operated on.

My mother's whole body seem to shrink at the dreadful news and, throwing my arms round her, I tried to comfort and calm her, as we anxiously waited for the ambulance to arrive. When it pulled up outside, Barbara was placed on a stretcher and taken in the ambulance to hospital. But instead of heading straight for a hospital specialising in neurosurgery, the ambulance took Barbara to the then St George's Hospital at Hyde Park Corner. There, we suffered another shattering blow, when the doctors announced that they couldn't carry out the necessary operation on her, and that Barbara would have to be taken across West London to the specialist Atkinson Morley Hospital in Wimbledon.

We lived a nightmare as we raced across London with the ambulance, but worse was to follow. When we finally reached the Atkinson Morley Hospital, and the specialists had examined Barbara, they told us that Barbara was too weak for them to operate on. They said there was nothing they could do for my beloved sister and, tragically, on the 17th she died.

Barbara's death devastated the family, my mother in particular. She just couldn't come to terms with it and my father was little better. We had been such a happy family and, because I has spent so much time away from home throughout my teenage years, Barbara had become even more special in my parents' eyes.

My father was so upset that he didn't go to work for six months. And I was equally crushed at the senselessness of it all. One day, Barbara had been a happy, laughing teenager without a care in the world and everything to live for, yet just hours later she was gone. I, too, have found it incredibly difficult to come to terms with her death.

I blamed myself for her death and kept telling myself, 'If only I had paid more attention to her on that fatal night,' or 'If only I had stayed with her, things might have been different.'

Unfortunately, that line of thinking doesn't solve anything; it merely makes matters worse and you become consumed with guilt and sorrow. But trying to be rational about such a pointless death — that of the sister I loved so dearly — doesn't make the tragedy any easier to cope with, even after all these years.

What really hurts me, though, is knowing that Barbara

idolised me. She looked up to me as her big brother, and didn't deserve to be treated like that.

My parents never really recovered from Barbara's death. They just couldn't come to terms with life without her sunny, smiling face, and eventually they moved from Clapham to Staines to try to escape the bitter memories.

But we weren't the only ones devastated by Barbara's death. She had a young boyfriend, Derrick Smith, who was so upset that he jumped off the roof of a house. By an incredible stroke of luck, however, a large pile of coke had just been delivered to the house, and, instead of hitting the solid pavement, he fell on the coke, which broke his fall. He was taken to hospital, but, fortunately, survived.

For three grim months after Barbara's death, I stayed at home looking after my mother, but then I realised I had to go and get a job. I couldn't put my mind to anything and knew I was in no state to try to return to acting just yet. But we needed money and I had to go and earn it.

So I went around to the Windmill Theatre where, fortunately, John Gale was still in charge, and asked him if I could have a job, any job, until I was ready to audition again.

By an amazing stroke of good fortune he gave me my old job back — looking after the topless fan dancers. Talk about luck! And this time, as I was that much older, I really knew how to get on with the girls. And some of them took a real fancy to me.

I became especially friendly with one particular fan dancer and was having a great time, but, unfortunately, Sheila Van Damme, who had taken over as boss of the theatre after the death of her father, liked this dancer more than I did, so I was banished to the back of the auditorium to work the spotlights.

That didn't stop me dating some fantastic beauties, however. We would go to the cinema or for a walk, but more often I would take them to the clubs. They loved that. I knew most of the young actors and I was very friendly with Peter Finch, who was a great guy and a huge hit with the girls.

I was starting to get quite serious with one girl, Perrin Lewis, who looked like Brigitte Bardot, who was *the* film star of the time. But she preferred Micky Most, the record producer, and that was the end of that romance. I was really cheesed off when she went off with Most. But I was at the Windmill, so I didn't take it as hard as I might have otherwise. When you were surrounded by so many eager young girls, you sensibly thought, 'It's just like the buses — miss one and there is always another coming along.'

I soon palled up with another beauty, who, strangely, was also a Lewis. She was called Barbara and we had some good times. But I didn't take any of it too seriously. My acting chums were always delighted if I brought along a couple of the girls on a date. All the guys — and the girls themselves — were very generous when it came to getting the rounds in, which was a nice little supplement to my earnings, as I wasn't paid much.

I had been dating for years, but I suspect that I was still pretty naïve when it came to girls. Girls of 20 are much more advanced than guys of a similar age. I don't think blokes acquire the same polish until they are 30. And men forget that there is no way you can get a girl into bed unless she wants to. But if a girl wants the guy, she'll always get him! At least that's how I've found it works — not that I'm complaining!

I eventually left when I got a job with Bromley Rep, where I met one of the most charming men in my life — Alec Ross, who was married to Sheila Hancock. Alec was the leading actor and we became firm pals from the start.

My parents, Ernest and Rose, were living in Staines and this meant a lot of travelling to and from Bromley.

So Alec invited me to stay with him and Sheila. That was a tremendous help to me and I had some great times with them.

I found the transformation from boy to male actor very tough at first. It is a different world and not many find the switch easy.

The theatre had also changed during the time I had been

away in the Army. Before I went away, I had known all the other boy actors — Anthony Newley, Harry Fowler, John Charlesworth — and if you didn't get the job you were up for, you knew who would. But all that had changed in two short years.

Television was also really getting into its stride, and the Royal Academy of Dramatic Art was churning out actors and actresses left, right and centre, some of them good, some of them terrible. So it was quite difficult to get jobs because some former boy actors just couldn't act when they matured. One particular boy, Neil North, landed the starring role in the film *The Winslow Boy*. We were all after that film, but he got it and he was very, very good, but it was the first — and only — good part he ever had.

Richard Attenborough, obviously, had no problems switching from juvenile roles to adult ones. He was a bit of big-headed swine in those days. But he landed another plum role all of us boy actors were after in the film *The Guinea Pig* — and he must have been in his twenties!

When I returned after the Army, there was also competition from pop stars for film roles. Marty Wilde, Tommy Steele and Cliff Richard were all going into films and doing acting jobs, but we couldn't do the singing jobs. My voice might have once been my key into the theatre as a boy, but I decided that I didn't want to try my luck as an adult — besides, I reckoned the then top music impresario, Larry Parnes, had already got too many lads in his stable, what with Billy Fury and all that crowd.

I did toy with the idea briefly, but decided that rather than trying to pick up singing again, I would stick with my main love and make it as an actor, even if that did mean working my socks off in Rep.

Which is how I wound up playing Danny in *Night Must Fall* at Hunstanton just before my 22nd birthday. We did two shows a night and three on Thursdays, plus a Saturday matinée.

I arrived on the Sunday, days after the rest of the cast, as I had been doing a television slot, and after I had booked into my digs I wandered down to the theatre to check out the girls in the show from their promotion photographs. To my surprise, the doors were open, so I sauntered inside to be greeted by the joyous shout 'He's here', and the director eagerly asked if I had brought my script, as we opened on the Thursday. That gave me just three days to learn my lines, but that was standard for the theatre, as we changed the show every Thursday!

At the Thursday matinée I walked on stage to the worst reception of my life — the buzz of people talking.

'I can't be that bad,' I thought, 'I haven't even opened my mouth.'

The talking continued and, when I came off stage, I asked the assistant stage manager, 'What's the problem?'

'Oh, we forgot to tell you,' he said, 'but we allow the blind in to the Thursday matinées and the noise is their companions telling them what is going on!'

The following week was my birthday, but when the curtain came down at 10.15pm I found I had as much chance of enjoying it as Danny when he is led away in handcuffs. The actor with the key to the handcuffs had vanished. I was furious as I had just ten minutes to clean off my make-up, change and get into the pub before closing time. I summoned the assistant stage manager for the key, but he said he hadn't got it and that the other actor must have gone to the pub.

Hampered by the handcuffs, I scrubbed off the worst of my make-up and was in a right temper when I stormed into the pub just as they were calling time. I asked the barmaid if she had seen any of the cast and she told me they were in the room next door. I was raging by now and kicked the door open — to burst in on the surprise birthday party they were throwing for me!

It was a lot of fun, but really hard work and the money was nothing to write home about, so it was hardly surprising that in those days I seriously thought of packing it in and trying to break into motor racing instead. I had spent two years in the Army teaching other people how to drive at high speed and was confident that I could make the switch. I knew that I was good behind a wheel but, more importantly, I had that essential feel for the vehicle and, I'm happy to say, the nerves to match.

I dreamed of being a racing driver and, as luck would have it, I knew the right crowd to give me a break. At that time I was still living with my parents in Staines and used to drink at a local pub with Mike Hawthorne. Sadly, Mike was eventually killed in a high-speed crash, driving along the dual carriageway across the Hog's Back, near Guildford. That was such a tragic loss because Mike was one of the great grand prix aces. He was also a tremendous bloke and we had some great times. We used to meet and chat for hours and he encouraged me. I really fancied having a go as a racing driver myself, and if Mike had lived he would have helped me.

As an army instructor I used to roar around at 70mph in a scout car — in reverse. I was hooked on speed then and still like smart motors. For years, just like Mike Baldwin, I used to drive a Jaguar, but now I drive a white Saab 900 Turbo convertible — and love it.

It was the danger of high-speed driving that attracted me. I had been in showbusiness since I was a kid, but driving appealed more. I have always liked danger, being on the edge for the sheer thrill of it. I think that is part of the reason Baldwin is a hit, because viewers can sense the danger in him.

I was also drawn to motor racing because the drivers earn a lot of money, and quickly. I certainly wasn't doing that in those days. But I couldn't afford the training, and then the time — and the opportunity — had gone.

Strangely enough, I did get the chance to get my hands on a large sum of money through my driving skills in a way that would have even put the frighteners on dodgy Baldwin.

In those days, I knew a lot of the London villains, as they were always attracted to showbusiness and liked to throw their money about drinking in a lot of the same pubs and some of the clubs we used. But even I was surprised when one day, as I was driving up the King's Road in Chelsea, my car was suddenly shunted up the back. It was only a tiny bump but it was done deliberately to catch my attention. So I pulled over, as did the car behind. Out leapt Gordon Goody.

'Hiya, Johnny,' he greeted me. He suggested we went for a drink and then he dropped the bombshell. How would I like to make a lot of money driving a car, very fast? Well, it was quite an offer, but when I told my mum she told me to keep well clear, insisting that it had to be really dodgy to pay the sort of money Goody was talking about. But I had already made up my mind to say 'No'. I might have fancied becoming a grand prix ace, but in the real world I knew I had a much better chance of making it as an actor, and I told Goody so. That was the end of that for me, and just as well, or else I might have ended up taking part in the Great Train Robbery!

I always found Goody, and people like him, very generous. They were always happy to treat a young up-and-coming actor, and I never experienced any suggestion of pay-back time. If they met a young, struggling actor they would buy him a drink and probably a meal — and that is how you got to meet them.

I met a lot of tough characters in the late Sixties when bosses at the old ATV company phoned me up and said, 'We are doing a boxing play, how do you compare with Terry Spinks?'

'Oh, I am about the same build and height,' I replied.

'Good,' they said, 'because he is going to make his acting début in this play about a rigged fight and we want you to partner him in the ring, playing the boxer on the take.'

'Fine,' I said enthusiastically and they told me to go and see the casting director the next day.

I was delighted, but the casting director wasn't when I turned up. They had got the name wrong and it wasn't Spinks, who is an Olympic flyweight gold-medallist, but Terry Downes, a former middleweight world champion.

'Oh, Christ,' they said, when they clapped eyes on me. 'You're not like him at all.'

So I had to have built-up shoes, and a built-up sweater — and then I had to fight Terry Downes, who had never acted in his life. That was quite hysterical.

But Terry befriended me and, he knew quite a lot of hard men because of his boxing contacts. But to me they aren't hard when you meet them. They are like your elder brother or your father. They don't greet you by announcing, 'Hello, I'm a villain. Now what do you want?' There was none of that. And I was always amazed when I read in the papers that someone I had met had done such and such. I couldn't believe it and would think, 'They are not like that.' To me, they were just nice, happy, generous guys. And I never found that they wanted to call back a favour. If they liked you, there was nothing that you could do wrong — as long as you toed the line.

When I came out of the Army, and not long before Goody tried to shunt me into doing some fast driving for him, I was standing in my new local in Staines, shortly after my parents had moved to the town, when I told one of the 'characters' that I wanted to buy a car, but was stony broke. I wouldn't call Harry a villain, but he knew his way around, and he asked, 'Well, how much have you really got?'

'Nothing,' I replied.

'You know what sort of car you are going to get with that?' he grinned. 'A Noddy car.'

Anyhow, he took me to a garage where I spotted a Sunbeam Rapier convertible I fancied. It was £230 and I had just £30 in the bank, but I said to Harry, 'I fancy that motor.'

'Right, John,' he said, and turning to the owner of the garage said, 'Put that down to me.'

'When are you going to pay me?' asked the garage boss.

'When I am ready,' said Harry, and that was it. Harry and I then went to the pub for a couple of large gin and tonics.

'Look, Harry,' I said, 'I'm getting a bit embarrassed because A, the car's not taxed; B, it's not insured; and C, I have got just about enough for petrol.'

'Don't worry,' he said, 'we'll see to all that, and give it

me back on the drip when you've got it.'

And he did all that. He even serviced the car. And the only thing he ever asked me to do, apart from popping in to see him now and again for a drink — he lived next to the pub — was to give his mother a special treat on her 80th birthday. It was years later, when I was in *No Hiding Place*, and I had dropped in to see Harry in the pub, when he said, 'Will you do me a favour? The whole family, 80 or so people, are gathering for her birthday and we have got a special cake. She's a great fan of yours, so is there any chance of you carrying in the cake?'

I said I would be delighted and, on the appointed Sunday, I carried in the cake for Harry's mother, and everyone burst out singing 'Happy Birthday'. Her face, when she saw me, was a picture, and everyone started crying, including myself. That was quite a moment. But Harry didn't want anything from me, he just liked the company.

So instead of linking up with Goody, I carried on at Bromley Rep and reckoned I was pretty lucky to have a regular job. But I was always confident my big break would come. I stayed there for about two years, fitting in the odd small TV job, film, or going on tours. The nearest I got to a musical was to tour in the thriller *The Rock 'n' Roll Murder*, in which I once again teamed up with René Houston.

René had already been a major influence in my life for she had persuaded me to call myself Johnny instead of John, when we were in revue together back in 1949, when I had been a callow boy actor.

In 1957, I made *Second Fiddle*, the first of four Norman Wisdom films I was to be involved in over the years. It was fantastic working with Norman. I think he is one of the cleverest comedians in England. He had a natural touch as a real clown and was huge in the Fifties. He was fun to work with and we got on very well together. Norman was a perfectionist; he wanted everything right, and generally surrounded himself with people who knew their jobs. But you could always rely on him to clown it up and he never worried about getting hurt in one of his wild routines in which he would bash his head or go flying to the ground. It was if he was made of rubber!

Even now, in his seventies, he is still clowning around with the same wonderful manic touch he had in his heyday. I still meet him on charity golf tournaments and on one trip to the Isle of Man he proved he had lost none of his magic. He pretended to fall on the luggage carousel. He disappeared, and then came crashing back though the luggage exit tube with all the cases on to the carousel crying, 'Ow, ow, ow ... Ooh, Miss Diane ... Ow, ow ...' He was very good. That was the beginning of a very fruitful association for me. Norman liked me, and the following year had me back for his zany comedy *The Diplomatic Corpse*. I was later to team up with him yet again in *The Bulldog Breed* and *Stitch in Time*.

Various Reps were also always asking me to do *Cosh Boy* and so I jogged along, always scanning the trade papers on the look out for the job that would really get me into the big time.

It was during that period that I met Caroline, who was to become my first wife.

As a young man who had knocked about a bit, I had had my share of dates, but had always kept moving, carefully avoiding any serious commitment. I just didn't want to get involved. But Caroline was different.

And, incredibly, I, the guy who used to set up so many dates for my mates when I had the pick of all those gorgeous topless girls in my Windmill days, met her on a blind date!

Caroline was a window dresser and I was drafted in to take her to a bash after she had travelled to London from Swansea for a party without a date of her own. It certainly wasn't love at first sight, but romance followed our first real date after I had escorted her for the evening, and soon we were dating regularly.

That was a pretty unique situation for me. Despite Mike Baldwin's string of conquests on *Coronation Street*, I've always been more of a man's man really. My wife Christine, who knows me better than I know myself, has often joked that while I like the ladies, I would run a mile if they chased me. There is a certain amount of truth in that. I would rather play golf with the boys.

You get too much aggravation with the girls, and women want to tie you up. I've always found women very possessive — and I don't like that one bit. Fortunately, Christine is smart enough to give me room. To be honest, I think she's glad to be rid of me sometimes.

But I met Caroline on this blind date because she was a friend of a former girlfriend of mine called Yvonne, who had just started dating someone else while I had been away on tour. But I was still pally with Yvonne, and she decided that she would help me out and fix me up with her girl chum, Caroline.

But she didn't fix me up — she stitched me up!

I was going steady with Caroline when, in 1960, I had my biggest break — with Granada TV. They were making a series, called *The Younger Generation*. It consisted of 12 plays, which would be filmed over 12 months, using the same cast of six men and six women . The plays were by 12 young playwrights, and each member of the cast would take it in turn to play the leading role. This really was a tremendous break and I set off for Manchester for a year with my head in the clouds. And with good reason. John Thaw, who has become one of our most successful television actors, and Judy Cornwall were among the other members of the cast and the plays, including *Rabbit Set*, *Animals Can't Laugh*, *Our Ted*, *Mating Age*, *Josie*, *Run Away Home*, and *Sucker*, were very successful. That was my real grounding in television and, flushed with success, I became engaged to Caroline, who had joined me up north.

In those days, you didn't play the field on the scale young people do now. If you had a steady girlfriend, people expected you to stay with her. Society was more stable before the swinging Sixties really got under way and if you had been seeing a girl for a couple of years, people would say, 'What are you going to do about it?' Besides, those 12 months were tremendous fun and it seemed a great idea at the time.

John Thaw was very serious then, but a whole gang of actors, actresses and production staff used to meet up in The New Theatre, a magnificent fun pub just off Deansgate in the heart of Manchester, where I used to stay. It was really handy, because not only was it a terrific boozer, but it was only a spit from the Granada studios, and we had some fantastic evenings there. Arthur Gosling, a wonderful man who ran the pub, used to really look after me in my bachelor days. He would say, 'Briggsy, book in, there are a couple of good 'uns in this week.' And there would be a couple of very pretty girls from the Opera House, or somewhere, staying in the pub. Arthur used to always put me right. It was £2.50 a night, bed and breakfast, and it was the best value I have ever had. But you had to like a drink to be allowed to stay there.

I tipped off an actor that it was a really fantastic place to stay, but when he tried to book in they told him they were full up. I was very surprised when I heard this and had a word with Arthur. He soon straightened me out, telling me that the real reason the actor was shown the door was because he didn't drink!

So you can imagine what fun nights we had. Arthur and his mother had another great pub, The Grapes, nearby, and the pubs were always staffed by gorgeous barmaids, who tended to be very friendly with the young bachelors on the prowl. We were all young and every day was like one big party. I must confess that I was more than a trifle sad when we finally finished the Granada plays and Caroline and I moved back to London. Sadly, both pubs were demolished in the rebuilding of Manchester city centre and were no longer open for business when I returned to Manchester in *Coronation Street*. But I could still nip down to see Arthur in Didsbury, where he ran another pub with stunning barmaids, The Royal Oak. And there is a new Grapes pub near Granada, owned, appropriately, by Liz Dawn, the *Street's* magnificent Vera Duckworth.

I was so in my element making *The Younger Generation*, that one day the director Gordon Flemyng asked me to help

Michael Caine get his lines right! It seems ridiculous now, but back in the early Sixties Ronald Lacey and myself were told to take Michael to the pub to help him perfect his part.

Well, I've never said 'no' to popping along to the boozer and while Michael got his tongue around his lines, Ronnie and I poured ale down our throats. After about half-an-hour, I got a bit bored and left, but Ronnie, wisely, stayed — and he and Michael became great mates.

But Michael turned the tables on me a few years later when Lewis Gilbert decided to film the comedy *Alfie*. Lewis took my agent, Maurice Aza, and myself along to see the play, which then starred John Neville in the title role, with a view to me playing Alfie. I was very confident, but told Lewis, 'If I don't get it, I hope you give it to John.' In the end, however, neither of us got the plum role. Lewis decided that I looked too young — in my late twenties, I still looked 17 — and gave it to Michael.

They were great days in Manchester, but I didn't have time to mope after Caroline and I left the heady, party-party atmosphere of the city.

Upon my return to London, I was asked to go and see one of the top directors of the era, Basil Dean. Basil had been head of ENSA, the Forces entertainment company, during the war, and he was now doing an army comedy called *Touch It Light*.

After I had read for him, he said I could start rehearsing on the following Monday, on two weeks' approval. So I joined the cast and I thought I was doing OK, but there had been a few wrangles and on the Friday of the second week I was on tenterhooks waiting to hear if I would get the job.

I was nervously sitting in the theatre when I saw Alfie Lynch stride into the foyer. After we had greeted each other, I asked, 'What are you doing here?'

He replied, 'There is a bloke in the cast and if he is not very good today, then they are going to tell him this afternoon. Do you know who it is?'

'Yes,' I said, my heart missing a beat, 'it's me.'

At which, Alfie, bless him, said, 'Oh, Christ, I'm going' — and left.

The way Alfie rallied to a mate in trouble, by walking out of the theatre without even seeing Dean, sent my spirits soaring, but I was still apprehensive when I finally went up to Basil Dean that evening and asked, 'Mr Dean, will I be wanted for rehearsals tomorrow?'

A chill went down my spine when Dean replied, 'No,' before adding, 'we are not rehearsing tomorrow, we are not working until Monday.'

So, bracing myself for the worst, I nervously said, 'You were going to decide today if I was any good or not.'

And it was a great relief when he said, 'Of course you are good — Monday morning, 10 o'clock.'

I always knew just where I stood with Dean. If he liked me he called me 'son'. If he didn't like me he called me 'Smithy', which was my character's name in the play, and if I was really in the dog house he called me 'Briggs'. Fortunately, that didn't happen too often.

We opened at the Theatre Royal in Windsor and, after touring for a while, we finally went into the West End for six months.

That was very exciting, but when the run finished I had my first taste of being out of work. That's a depressing time for any actor, but one we all have to endure some time. It's known as 'resting.' I knew it as panic!

Fortunately, I managed to get the odd bit of television work here and there. I then heard that Lewis Gilbert had bought the film rights to *Touch It Light*. He changed the title to *Light up the Sky* and signed up a terrific cast, Tommy Steele, Benny Hill and Ian Carmichael, who was a huge box office pull for his comedy roles. But, more importantly as far as I was concerned, he asked me to play the part of Smithy, which I had originally performed on stage.

I was thrilled, and was even more excited when he told me we were going on location in Normandy, before moving into Twickenham Studios to shoot the rest of the film.

'Normandy! Great,' I thought, and raced off to get my

passport sorted out. I then went to Bermans, the theatrical costumiers, to get my uniform, before popping around to the barber's for a haircut. I then bought a pile of French francs, before setting off home to pack my case.

I was sitting at home reading the script and waiting for my first call when Lewis rang up and said, 'Right, be at Twickenham studios at 7 o'clock tomorrow.'

'Yeah, oh, great,' I said.

Lewis had even better news, however, telling me that we were then going on location.

I didn't have a car in those days so I felt very important the next morning when a car came to collect me and I was driven to the studios clutching my case, with my breast pocket bulging with my passport and the francs. But I was puzzled. 'How are we going to get to Normandy?' I asked.

'By car,' said the first assistant director.

'Oh,' I said, 'we are going over by ferry, then?'

'No,' he replied, looking at me a bit oddly.

So I repeated my question. 'How are we going to get to Normandy?'

'Like I said, by car,' he retorted, raising his eyebrows, before adding, 'It's a little village just outside Guildford ...'

I felt a right twit, with my passport, francs and my carefully packed case. I didn't dare tell anyone for fear of making an even bigger fool of myself. Benny would have taken the mickey mercilessly, so I put on one of my better performances as I played it straight.

I had a great time on the film, even if I didn't get the French break I had been counting on. Benny Hill was marvellous fun, he was charming, witty, very open and an altogether lovely man. He also had the last laugh on me the night we teamed up on a double date — and I appeared to be the only one who was going to score.

To spice up our love lives, Benny asked me to arrange a date for him, saying he would, in turn, arrange one for me. We would then all meet at his flat for dinner and party the night away. Well, that was the plan.

I arranged for Benny to meet my old girlfriend Vicky

Smith, who was still modelling for Raymond, and he arranged a date for me. So after we finished filming that night, Benny and I set off for his West London flat, where he had arranged the most fabulous meal — smoked salmon, caviar, champagne, vodka, everything we could possibly want to woo the girls.

But as we walked through the door there was a telegram from Vicky, saying she had to go to Scotland on a modelling assignment. 'Very sorry, but ...'

So I got out my little black book to get a girl for Benny, but to no avail. It was too short notice. 'Love to another time, but ...'

'Don't worry, Johnny, I'll fix it,' said Benny, reaching for his little black book. He then got on the telephone and started going through the pages, but also to no avail. Again, it was a case of 'Love to, but it's too short notice ...'

The evening was starting to look a real frost when this vision of loveliness turned up for me. I may have failed for Benny, but he had come up trumps for me. She was superb, but Benny was left with no one. Shrugging it off, Benny poured the drinks and we set about the sumptuous meal.

When we had finished, the gorgeous girl said, 'Do you mind if I phone my father?' and disappeared into the bedroom, where Benny kept the phone.

As I poured myself another drink, Benny looked at me and said, 'What on earth are you doing here? Go on in to the bedroom.'

'I can't,' I replied, 'she's phoning her father.'

Rolling his eyes to heaven in mock disbelief that I could be so naïve, Benny, started shaking his head from side to side, and in a stage whisper, said, 'No. No. No.' Then, with that famous twinkle in his eye and looking for all the world like a naughty schoolboy, he continued, 'No, no, no,' adding, with a little shooing gesture with his hands, 'Now go, go, go.'

There was only one answer to that, so I went into the bedroom, and there was this stunningly beautiful girl lying in bed, waiting for me. I didn't need any encouragement. Tearing off my clothes I bounded into the bed, but just as we were about to kiss in a heady embrace, I was stopped in mid-pucker by the sound of music.

Benny, who was standing right outside the bedroom door, started serenading us with a love song, accompanying himself on one of those tiny harps he used in his comedy routines.

It was like something straight out of a Benny Hill sketch — and was probably used by Benny at a later date.

It didn't do much for my libido. Benny's warbling with that little harp was the ultimate passion killer. I don't believe anyone could possibly have made love in those circumstances. I know that I found it completely and utterly impossible.

Furious at Benny's prank and beside myself with frustration, I yelled, 'Benny, bugger off! Bugger off for Christ's sake!' But, strumming away on that blasted harp, he just sang louder.

My passion was well and truly doused!

She was an absolute stunner, but I was incapable of doing a thing about it, as Benny knew full well. When we finally emerged from the bedroom Benny, with that feigned look of innocence that was his hallmark, inquired with a cherubic smile if we had enjoyed his serenade of love. Talk about taking the mickey. I reckon the girl and I were prototypes for some of Benny's cheekier sketches down the years!

But while I may have missed out on love that night, that was the start of what I thought was going to be my golden years in films.

5

I HAD IMPRESSED THE STUDIO BOSSES SO MUCH with my performance as Leslie Smith in *Light up the Sky*, that the moment I finished filming, Guido Coen, who was the head of Twickenham Studios, offered me another movie, the hard-edged social drama *The Wind of Change*. This was a fantastic break as I was to play the lead, the brutal Teddy Boy Frank, who hated black people and went around beating them up.

The subject matter was very controversial as it tackled prejudice, but they were lucky to get Donald Pleasance, who had just opened in the sensational play *The Caretaker*, to play my father, while Ann Lynn, who was then Anthony Newley's wife, played my sister. And David Hemmings, who was to become a major sixties heart-throb with stylish and very sexy movies like *Blow Up*, had a very small part as one of my gang of Teddy boys.

I thought I was really on my way when, just as we finished the movie, Coen told me he had another film starting in a couple of weeks' time called *Saturday Night and Sunday Morning*. And he then said, 'How do you feel about playing the lead?'

I was thrilled and told Coen so. But the studio bosses suddenly changed their minds and, for some strange reason, decided to have a northern lead, and gave it to Albert Finney. I was bitterly disappointed. That film, produced by Tony Richardson and directed by Karel Reisz, was to have an incredible impact and set the tone for British films for years to come. It would have opened the doors of Hollywood to me. But, there you go. And, later, when I saw Finney in the role of the hard-drinking, womanising anti-hero who hates all authority, I thought he was absolutely fabulous.

But that set a precedent. Finney was so successful that suddenly the British film industry started using a lot of northern leads in the movies. And I was soon to miss out again.

My pal Eddie Judd starred in a play in the West End called *The Tinker*, about a Londoner going to a red-brick university. When they made a film version, retitled *The Wild and the Willing*, Dirk Bogarde, who was then hugely influential following his years as *the* matinée idol of the Fifties, put my name up for the lead and I was confident that I had clinched it. Because of Dirk's support, I went to see the producer, Betty E Box, and the interview went like a dream. Nothing, I felt, could stop me. But I was wrong. The film bosses rang me back to say, 'We are sorry, Johnny, but we have decided to play it north country.' And instead of using a southern actor, Ian McShane won the role of the Londoner, which they again changed to a northern character.

That was a real hammer blow.

I was so fed up I wouldn't even go out that Friday, which was a 13th, to collect my dole and meet the lads for our normal boozing spree, thinking, 'With my luck, I might get run over.'

But as I morosely sat at home feeling as if I had the weight of the world on my shoulders, the phone rang — and I was offered the part of the Welshman.

My luck had changed. For that film, directed by Ralph Thomas, was a breakthrough for a lot of actors. It was the first film for McShane, Samantha Eggar, John Hurt and Jeremy Brett.

Strangely, as I had been pipped for the lead, Betty expected me to show the others the ropes. Taking me on one side, she said, 'Johnny, you have done lots of films, will you look after them?'

That was a pretty tall order and I told her so. I thought I can't look after them, especially as we were off to Lincoln for a 13-week shoot, which, set in a red-brick university, was about youngsters trying to find their place in society. But I needn't have worried. We all got on famously together and I must have been of more help than I realised at the time.

Twenty years later, Samantha Eggar publicly paid me the highest possible compliment on my edition of the hit television series *This Is Your Life*, when she declared, 'Thank you for being a wonderful helping hand at the beginning of my career.' Forever generous, Samantha went on to tell me in front of all the millions of people watching, 'You were always so gay and always had the jokes on the set. You made me feel responsible and worthwhile. You are a kind, caring and sensitive man.' It was incredibly kind of Samantha to say such nice things and it made me blush furiously. But then she is a very special lady.

Making *The Wild and the Willing* was a lot of fun, but I shouldn't have been so surprised that I was asked to look after other actors. I always tried to do favours for my mates. In the mid-fifties, for instance, I taught Ann Lynn to drive, after Anthony Newley lost his licence.

He had just bought a new Ford Anglia and had lent it to my schoolfriend David Gregory, who shot a red light when the car was not insured or taxed. They were both fined and Tony was banned from driving, which was a bitter blow as he was in the hit West End revue, *Cranks*, at the Duchess Theatre, and he wanted Lynn to be able to drive him to the theatre.

The play was a major success for Tony, who had first triumphed as the Artful Dodger in *Oliver Twist*. *Cranks* was the toast of London — Princess Margaret had seen it three times — and was heading for Broadway when disaster struck for Tony.

One night, he and Lynn, who was pregnant, had a row and she refused to drive him to the theatre. After failing to get a taxi from their Chelsea flat, Tony took the car and drove it to work.

Then, as he got out, a policeman strolled across and said, 'Hello, Mr Newley. Can I see your driving licence, please?'

That did it. Tony was charged with driving a car while banned and uninsured and got a month in Brixton. To add to his misfortune, the cast of *Cranks* sailed for America while he was still in prison, and he missed a date with the Queen at the Royal Performance of *The Battle of the River Plate*, in which he played a radio operator on a merchant ship sunk by the German pocket battleship.

The early Sixties were a good period for me, although the fact that I looked so young did occasionally work against me. When Lewis Gilbert decided to make the naval war epic *Sink the Bismarck!*, I went to see the casting director, Maude Spector, but she turned me down on the spot, declaring that I looked too young to be in the Forces.

'But I have been a Sergeant in the Army,' I protested.

'I don't care, you look much too young,' she said dismissively.

I was furious and told my then agent Maurice Aza, who was Lewis's brother-in-law. When Lewis heard Maude's reason for turning me down, he said, 'That's rubbish, Johnny's in the film.' And that was it.

Later, when we were shooting the movie, Maude turned up and said to me, 'What are you doing here?'

'I'm in the film,' I replied.

'I am the casting director. Who hired you?' she stormed.

When I told her it was Lewis, she said, 'Right, I will sort this out,' and marched over to Lewis, only to be quietly told to leave the set. Needless to say, I was never in another film she was casting!

But I was still getting some good breaks, and it wasn't just in films that I was starting to make a name for myself. I landed the role of Kevin the Irishman in *The Kitchen* at the prestigious Royal Court Theatre and got such fantastic notices that Lewis Gilbert came to see it, and offered me a key role in his major new action film, the swashbuckling *HMS Defiant*.

He told me the cast included Alec Guinness, Dirk Bogarde, Anthony Quayle and Tom Bell, and he wanted me to play a young man press-ganged into the Navy during the Napoleonic Wars. Lewis said that I would be paid £100 a week, which was a lot of money in the early Sixties, adding, 'It is a 16-week shoot, six in Spain and the rest in the studio. Would you like to do it?'

Would I just! I could have bitten his arm off as it was the boost I needed and I told Lewis I would love to be in the film. He then sent me a script, which led to me having a huge bust-up with John Dexter, the director of *The Kitchen*, who was a power at the Royal Court. Dexter had taken a fancy to me and had even chased me around the theatre. It had got so bad that I had only succeeded in keeping him at bay then by telling him, 'If you don't stop, I will give you a real right-hander.'

Dexter was furious when he heard that I had been offered the film. Sparks were almost flying from his eyes as he stormed up to me saying, 'Now listen, what's all this I hear about you going to do this Lewis Gilbert film instead of the play?'

I was completely taken back by his attitude as I was thrilled by Gilbert's offer, and told him so, declaring, 'Sorry, John, but I am going to do the film.'

He then made one final effort to get me to change my mind. 'Luvvy,' he said, 'don't you realise that the Royal Court is a shop window?'

This was absolutely true. I knew actors who would have given their right arm for a leading role at the theatre, but I had made my mind up and I told him so.

'John,' I said, 'I have been in the shop window so long I am beginning to feel a bit shop-soiled! I am sorry, but I am going to do the film. I want to earn some money.'

Dexter was absolutely livid and told me that I would never work at the Royal Court again. That was quite a threat, as such a ban could have been a severe blow to my future career. But it didn't bother me too much at the time as I was only earning £25 a week at the theatre, while the film offer meant not only big money, but also big opportunities.

Dexter, however, got his own back on me years later when he made the film *The Virgin Soldiers*. When Dexter was casting for the movie, based on Leslie Thomas' witty novel about young National Service rookies thrown into action in the jungles of Malaysia during the Communist uprising, my agent rang up and said, 'What about Johnny Briggs?'

Dexter, feigning complete ignorance of my existence, said, 'Johnny who?'

'Johnny Briggs,' replied my agent.

'What about him?' asked Dexter imperiously.

'What about a part in *The Virgin Soldiers*?' my agent said.

'Ah,' said Dexter, adding, 'Oh no, no, no ... He's not a chicken any more.'

So my agent tried once more, saying, 'What about a part as an NCO?'

Then Dexter really put the boot in, declaring, 'No, sorry, luv, but he's not butch enough!'

I couldn't resist smiling at that bit of cheek, but it didn't help me get the film, although Geoffrey Hughes, who played Eddie the dustbin man in the *Street*, did. But you can't win them all. And Dexter was always determined to even the score.

Back in 1961, however, I didn't have a care in the world and was really excited at the prospect of doing *HMS Defiant*. In fact, of all the 50 movies I have made, it still remains my favourite. It was also during that film that I first got to really know Dirk Bogarde. And it was on the strength of my performance in the film that Dirk was prepared to put me forward for the lead in *The Wild and the Willing* later that same year.

HMS Defiant — which was known in America as *Damn*

the Defiant! — was a great action film, real schoolboy adventure stuff, with lots of sword fights, blood, sweat and tears, most of which seemed to be mine. My character was lashed to the mast for allegedly attempting to strike an officer, the sadistic First Lieutenant, played by Dirk, who ordered me to receive 72 lashes! But I loved all the action. The film also had a superb cast and although the conditions under which we filmed were really primitive, I revelled in it.

During the filming in Spain, Dirk and I became quite close and I soon realised that not only was he a superb actor, he was also a charming, delightful man. A lot of the cast were northern and prided themselves on being as rough and tough as the characters they played, while I was willing to listen and learn. Dirk appreciated that as a young actor I wanted to polish my craft and he was only too happy to help me. We spent quite a bit of time together and when Sir Alec decided to throw two dinner parties at the house he was renting in Spain, to enable him to meet the cast informally before shooting began, I was placed in the second party with Dirk and Anthony Quayle.

Sadly, the first dinner party was a disaster — a total and utter shambles. Sir Alec had invited eight of the cast, including Tom Bell, Brian Pryngle and Victor Maddern, to a buffet dinner, but the lads went to a bar first and didn't get to Sir Alec's until 9.15pm, by which time the meal was ruined. Even the ice had melted in the sangria!

Sir Alec was so upset that he cancelled the second dinner party, saying that it would probably be better if he left it until we started shooting.

Needless to say, Sir Alec never held another dinner party once we began shooting. He was too busy. I would have loved to have had a meal with Sir Alec.

He was a very quiet, very nice man and one of the four nicest guys I have met, along with Dirk Bogarde and Roger Moore and *No Hiding Place* star Raymond Francis. They were gentlemen. So it would have been superb to have had dinner with two of that very special quartet.

There was absolutely no side to Sir Alec. When I was

introduced to him, I asked him how I should address him; as 'Sir Alec', 'Alec' or 'Mr Guinness'.

He then asked me, 'What is your name?'

I told him and, with that shy smile spreading across his face from those intense eyes, he said, 'I will call you Johnny, and you will call me Alec.'

He was totally charming, and it was while we were filming *HMS Defiant*, that Sir Alec persuaded me to flash the Briggs smile as often as possible. I was standing on the deck of the sailing ship on which we were filming miles out to sea, when, in between takes, he strolled across to me and said, 'You have a wonderful smile, Johnny, you should use it. Always smile. Remember that no one kicks a dog that comes towards them wagging its tail. The smile always disarms.'

Going to Spain to film was very exciting, too, in those days. People didn't go on overseas holidays in the way we do now, and just to be in a foreign country was a novel experience. So novel, in fact, that it led to me marrying my first wife, Caroline. I was only 26 and far too young really, but in those days of General Franco's hard-line, right-wing regime, you couldn't share a room with a woman in Spain unless you were husband and wife.

Even so, I wasn't completely sold on marriage, but in the early 1960s people married for far lesser reasons than sharing the same bed for six sunny weeks in a foreign land and, besides, I found myself subject to a little emotional guilt.

Caroline and I had been living together and she said she would go back to Swansea and wait for me, but I didn't think that was a very good idea because her former boyfriend was lurking around down there waiting for the opportunity to see Caroline again. So we decided to get married, which seemed a good idea at the time, but there you go. My best mate Alec Ross tried to warn me, repeatedly saying, 'Are you really sure you want to do this?' But I was impetuous, and I wanted to take Caroline to Spain.

So, making light of Alec's warnings, I flashed the old Briggs smile and jauntily told him, 'Well, you know, I suppose we all have to get married some time ...'

We were married in 1961 at St Mary's Church in Swansea, Caroline's home town.

Looking back, I regret that I married so young, for the sake of my two children from my first marriage. It was not like the marriage I have now with my second wife Christine, which is so strong that nothing can break it. I am convinced that if you meet the right person at the right time there should never be any need to marry twice in your lifetime. That, however, is a lesson you only learn with age and the convenience of hindsight. But it upsets me that I had to marry a second time to find true happiness, because of my two eldest children, Karen and Mark. They are my own flesh and blood and I would have liked them to have been with me to share the success I now enjoy.

Caroline was not, however, the big love of my life and I now realise that until I met Christine, I hadn't met anyone I really loved. I didn't know the meaning of that word. Before, what I had mistakenly thought was true love, had simply been infatuation. And, I'm afraid, it was, sadly, really just a case of infatuation with Caroline. But we were happy enough in the early days and the joy of having my first son Mark was indescribable. I was over the moon. There was some celebration booze drunk that night at the Wentworth club house, I can assure you.

I was on the golf course when Mark was born — keeping well out of the way. Not because I wasn't thrilled — I most certainly was — but Caroline wanted me to witness the birth, and I didn't fancy that one little bit. I feel a birth is a very private time between a mother and baby and I didn't want to intrude. And when Karen came along, I was very happy because I had my pigeon pair, and that was it, but I don't think I was ever really in love.

The marriage lasted for 11 years, before it ended in 1972, and divorce followed amicably in 1975. I honestly don't know why it didn't work. I don't think anybody would get married if they didn't believe it was going to last. But when we split up, I had had enough. She's a lovely lady and she liked the good times we had at the beginning: the premières, the parties, but she found it less easy to cope with some of the difficult periods.

That, however, was a long way in the future and Spain was a lot of fun. But it was also a lot of hard work. Tom Bell also had his wife with him and we both agreed that we should have left the girls at home, because we didn't really have enough time to look after them or enjoy their company to the full.

We had to get up at 6.00am every morning to get to the quayside in time for breakfast — which consisted of a cheese roll and a glass of water — before being ferried way out to sea to the sailing ship on which we were filming. It was moored so far from shore that you couldn't see any horizon, no matter which way you turned, and it was pretty grotty when you got there. Dirk later joked that it was as bad as serving on the ships in Napoleonic times, with 400 of us crammed aboard with just one lavatory — and everyone going down with Spanish tummy!

We didn't return to shore until 9.00pm, and then we had to get back to our hotels before we could even think about relaxing with a shower and a meal. I was lucky to be pally with Dirk, as he knew how to make life as comfortable as possible. Already a major star, he had taken his Rolls-Royce to Spain, and it would be sitting on the dock waiting for him when we got off the boat that ferried us to and from the ship. He would then ask, 'Would you like a lift back to the hotel?' and I would gratefully travel with him and Tony, who was his friend and manager. That lift to the hotel in Rolls-Royce comfort was a wonderfully luxurious boost at the end of a long day, but the boys soon started getting a bit jealous. They would make snide remarks, so in the end I had to decline the lifts. That was a great shame as I thought Dirk was a superb, lovely man, and a very good actor. He had a real presence and was completely underrated, despite the success of his films.

When I did get back to my hotel, and Caroline, there was only time for a wash and something to eat. Then I had to learn my lines for the next day, before falling into bed. Some honeymoon!

I also had another chum on the film, Tom Bowman, with whom I was very pally until he died some years later. Tom was an incredible character and had been in the Special Forces in Burma with Earl Mountbatten in the war. But that association led to Tom being slung off the ship and out of the film when his old shipmate Mountbatten came to visit us.

The producer, John Brabourne, was Mountbatten's son-in-law, and he persuaded the earl to visit the ship while we were filming in Spain. Tom was thrilled when we heard about the visit, explaining that they had been together in several campaigns. When Mountbatten arrived we were all lined up along the deck and were introduced to him one by one. When Mountbatten arrived opposite Bowman, Tom said, 'Hello, lovely to see you again. I haven't seen you for ages. How are you?' Mountbatten simply looked down his nose, said 'I beg your pardon!' and then proceeded to ignore Tom. Two days later, Tom was released from the film as being 'unsuitable'.

Back in England, I went to see Tom, who opened a box and showed me photographs of himself with Mountbatten, who had his arm around Tom's shoulders as they stood next to each other!

'There you are, Johnny,' said Tom, 'I wasn't lying. We were in the Special Forces together.'

I thought Tom was treated very shabbily as he was wonderful in the film. Yet they released him and Victor Maddern took his part.

My friendship with Dirk was also given a further boost the following year when I joined him on the set of *Doctor in Distress*. Ever since the fantastic success of the hospital comedy *Doctor in the House*, in 1954, when Dirk had created the character of Doctor Simon Sparrow, then a medical student, the *Doctor* films had steadily rolled off the production line, and I had been in the 1960 *Doctor in Love*. This, like the others had been directed by Ralph Thomas but, with Michael Craig instead of Dirk in the lead role, it had failed to hit the high laughter mark of the other films in the series. In *Doctor in Distress*, however, Dirk was firmly back in control, along with the magnificent James Robertson Justice, as the grumpy head of a hospital who becomes a changed man when he falls in love. It also starred Samantha Eggar as a glamorous model, with whom Dirk, playing James's young aide, had several problems.

But the star on that occasion was never seen on screen, although he made the film the most outstanding of my career. Dirk, as I say, had taken a liking to me from my first days on *HMS Defiant* and tried to help my career. While I never went out with him socially, it was natural for us to spend a lot of time on set chatting, probably because I liked Guinness — so did Dirk. He used to drink Guinness all the time in those days and he was the first person I met who liked it chilled. He was so keen on cold Guinness that he had a fridge in the boot of his Rolls in which to keep it at the right temperature. So when we were relaxing between takes while on location, we used to sit in the back of his Rolls quaffing it down.

And that's precisely what we were doing in Windsor one morning when we were joined by James Robertson Justice, who was also an enthusiast for a glass of chilled Guinness. Dirk introduced the pair of us and the conversation eventually got around to venison. James was larger than life off screen as well as on. And he could be as intimidating — and irascible — as the characters he played. He was also very successful, and he used to roar around in a gull-wing Mercedes. And woe betide anyone who overtook him when he was zooming along at 90 miles per hour. He would promptly report them to the police for speeding. But he was a gentleman, amusing and had enormous influence in high circles.

James used to teach Prince Charles falconry and a host of other Scottish pursuits. So stalking red deer and eating venison were subjects very close to his heart. When I confessed that I had never tasted it, James boomed out, 'Right. We will have to fix that. We'll pop down to the

Brown Bear at the end of the week and have some venison for lunch.' He then added, almost as an afterthought, 'I will bring my little godson down and he can have a look at the set before we set off for our venison.'

The prospect of going out for a special lunch with two such eminent stars was heady stuff and I was really excited when five of use adjourned for lunch in the hotel. Suddenly, James disappeared, to return eventually with ... Prince Charles.

James had taken him round the set and then brought him in to join us for lunch. I was overawed that James should be on such familiar terms with a member of the Royal Family, but it was a very jolly lunch. Prince Charles was quite young and didn't say a great deal, and neither did I. You didn't get much chance with James around. That was my royal introduction to venison. I must admit that I didn't like it very much, but I had to pretend that I did as I didn't want to offend anybody.

When Caroline and I returned to England from Spain, we lived with my mother for a while, but that didn't work out, so I had to go flat-hunting.

That wasn't easy. We wanted to be near the large number of film studios that were then to the west of London and the only thing that I could find that was bearable was a very large bed-sitter in Kingston Upon Thames — one room and use of the kitchen!

But we were in good company, Matt Monro had the other bedroom on our floor, and that is when I first met him. He was just embarking on his singing career after working on the buses. He had a marvellous voice and was very pleasant so that bed-sit — the first of many we were to live in before we finally bought a house — was fine. Caroline and I used to go to the pub with Matt and his wife. I used to smile, though, at the presents he bought his wife. Every time he got into the Top Ten he would buy her a solid copper saucepan! They seemed strange gifts for a pop star, but Matt had fairly simple tastes and I guess his wife liked them.

It was while we were living in Kingston that I gave my

most embarrassing impromptu singing performance, when I was cornered by an over-enthusiastic woman shopper in Bentalls, the big Kingston department store. She pounced as I was out shopping, insisting that I was Frank Ifield, who had just soared to Number One in the charts with 'I Remember You'. The more I protested that she had made a mistake the more insistent she became, declaring, 'You are my favourite. I know you are Frank Ifield.' Eventually, I had to burst into song to get rid of her. And I did, in short order. I may have started my career as a singer, but the moment I started to belt out 'I Remember You', she took one disgusted look, and sneered, 'You're not Frank Ifield, are you!' and stalked off.

In those days, I was part of *the* in-crowd and a whole gang of us — Richard Burton, Roger Moore, Stanley Baker. Peter O'Toole and Richard Harris — used to meet in the Salisbury pub, in St Martin's Lane in the West End, if we weren't working.

It was a regular meet and if you had a job you put a quid in the kitty and if you were on the dole you put in ten bob (50p). Dole day, which was Friday, was always a good day to meet and we usually partied right through Friday to Saturday breakfast time.

We didn't see so much of Roger because he was always working, he was such a good-looking swine. He always looked as though he had just got out of the bath. But he was great fun because he was always sending himself up. He was also very generous and would always get the drinks in. Richard Burton was pretty busy, too. He was making *Cleopatra* at the time, but when he could get some time off he would always join us, and was just a member of the gang.

Sean Connery also used to come along, before he hit the big time as James Bond. In those days, he was just in the chorus of South Pacific and I remember that we could hardly understand a word he said because of his thick Scottish accent!

A lot of the guys later became regarded as hell-raisers — and we certainly had a good time. But we didn't think they were wild days, it was just normal behaviour as far as we were concerned. It was just boozing. But we didn't drink for the sake of drinking — to get drunk. We would just stand around chatting and having a bit of fun as we spent our dole.

It was all very jokey and I remember that when Peter O'Toole came back from filming *Lawrence of Arabia*, he swept into the Salisbury with its glittering mirrored walls wearing his full Lawrence kit for a laugh. It was like a scene from a film as we all stood open-mouthed around the bar and Peter camped it up. He had a chauffeur in a limousine waiting outside in St Martin's Lane. It was a bit over the top but we just had a good laugh. Peter even had an Arab bloke with him who had played his servant in the movie. Peter, who loved to cut a dash, had brought him back to Britain, and he certainly added to the sense of occasion.

When Peter marched into the Salisbury he yelled, 'I'm home, darlings! Home from the desert, dears,' to which I promptly called out, 'Never mind the desert; have you got your bloody handbag so you can buy the beers?'

Burton may have been the darling of Hollywood and his romances, marriages and spectacular bust-ups with Elizabeth Taylor the stuff of legends, but while he liked a drink and could hold his own with the best, we never saw the roisterous side of him. He was always extremely pleasant and I got on very well with him, probably because I didn't crawl and treated him like anyone else in our company. But, fundamentally, he was a very quiet man.

He used to sit in one of the corners of the pub agonising over his lines, and as our laughter grew louder and our voices rose in direct ratio to the booze we sank, Burton would sit there, look at us mournfully and insist on telling us what a serious business we were in. We just used to carry on drinking while he clutched his head and boomed in full theatrical splendour, 'It's so serious.' Then he would clutch his hands to his head and moan, 'Oh, the agony of it all.' We thought it was all a bit of a laugh, but we never laughed when he brought Liz Taylor along after they had fallen in love on the set of *Cleopatra*.

Their romance was the sensation of the year — and many more to follow as Burton spent a king's ransom buying her staggering gems and other exotic gifts in 'the love affair of the century'! But there wasn't a sign of that famous chemistry when they were together in the pub. She was already a huge Hollywood star and an Oscar winner for her efforts in *Butterfield 8* in 1960 — and she expected to be treated like one. But Richard wasn't putting up with any of that nonsense on the rare occasions she would join him at one of our regular booze-ups. And to see them bicker anyone could have been forgiven for thinking they were an old married couple instead of *the* dream lovers.

She was sensational to look at with her long dark hair and those mesmerising violet eyes. She was incredible, but she only joined us because Richard wanted to go drinking with the boys and she didn't want to be left at home on her own. On one occasion they dropped in, Liz foolishly asked if the pub did Martinis. Well, as the Salisbury was one of the smartest pubs in the West End, they most certainly did just about any drink imaginable, but in those days we had a rule that no-one drank spirits — it had to be beer. Later, when they were really coining it and were major stars, O'Toole and Richard Harris would get on the shorts, knocking back large gins and vodkas. But it was still 'beer only' when Liz came in with Richard, and he wasn't going to let a girl start disrupting our boys' club. So, quick as a flash, Richard boomed at her, 'Look, woman, you'll have a bloody pint or a bloody half pint. So whaddya want?' Liz had a half pint!

That was the way it went. But while it was mostly just matey boozing, it could get a bit heavy now and again. There was always an underlying tension, because we were all looking for the next job.

So it wasn't surprising that one night I almost came to blows with Ronnie Fraser. Despite our 'beer only' rule, Ronnie had a favourite drink — a large vodka with a dash of lime and soda — which we labelled a 'Fraser special'. One night he had knocked back far too many of these and got right out of line. The cheeky blighter had the neck to call me a poof — and chucked a pint of Guinness over me — because I was then working at the Royal Court!

I was incandescent with fury. I thought, 'You insolent, stupid idiot,' and launched myself at him. I was determined to bury Ronnie's fat face in the pub floorboards, and the lads had to pull us off each other. Full of bravado, Ronnie and I then challenged each other to a fight the next day, with the loser having to pay for the drinks, which was a tidy packet given the amount of booze we could put away!

Next morning I was up with the lark and, really fancying my chances and still thirsting for revenge, arrived at the fight rendezvous all ready to go and pumped up for action. But I might as well have stayed in bed. Just as I and the other lads, who had arrived to see the action, were thinking of heading off to the pub, a doleful Ronnie eventually limped in clutching his thigh.

'Awfully sorry old chap,' he said to me with an apologetic smile, 'but I seem to have a gammy leg here!'

That was the end of that. What could I say? We had a laugh and, all the best of mates again, we headed off to the pub. We had some really mad times in those days and a session went on for a very long time. We would start in the Salisbury or the Duke of Wellington, and when it was last orders at the end of the lunchtime session we would go on to the Arts Theatre club or the Kismet, a drinking club known as 'The Iron Lung', because it was windowless and very dark. You had to be a bit tiddly to enjoy spending an afternoon boozing in there. By 5.30pm the Salisbury would re-open, and we would troop back there for another session until closing time. If there was a party somewhere we would go on to that, and when the party finished, or if they ran out of drink, we would then head off to the old Smithfield meat market, because the pubs around the market would be open for the porters at two in the morning!

I had a special group of pals with whom I used to go boozing down the markets, Sean Lynch, who married Annie Ross the singer, an actor called Raymond Smith, Jimmy Kenny and John Charlesworth — and others would tag along.

We became a familiar sight in the Smithfield boozers. We would pile into a pub and the landlord would look us up and down very suspiciously before enquiring, 'What do you lot want?'

'Oh, six halves of bitter, please,' we would chorus.

'Oh yeah,' he would reply.

Only genuine market workers were allowed to drink in the pubs that early in the day, so we would then spin the landlord a yarn that we were meat porters — and the real porters used to fall around laughing. Well, it was pretty ludicrous. There was me, all of 7st 7lb claiming to be a meat porter and asking for a half of bitter! No wonder everyone killed themselves laughing at us. If the barman had said, 'Pick up that side of beef,' I would have fallen over. The beef weighed more than me. But it's amazing what you can get away with if you are cheeky enough, and we always got served, although the landlords used to worry a bit in case anyone checked up as they could have lost their licenses.

From Smithfield, we would later head for the fruit and vegetable market at Covent Garden, just up from the Strand, which opened a little later. There we would go through the same routine, only this time claiming to be fruit porters.

We were equally unconvincing, but we always managed to keep drinking all night. When we finally left in full daylight, we used to poke around in the rubbish bins to see if there were any still edible apples, oranges or bananas that had been dumped in them, for when the real porters picked up a load of bananas, some would inevitably fall off and they would just kick them into the kerb, where they would be swept up. So we used to pick up this slightly battered fruit and if you got a really good haul you would then call to the others, 'Fellas, we've got the breakfast.' We would then go back to John Charlesworth's or one of the other lad's flat and get ourselves something to eat — usually beans and banana.

If, after a day and a night's boozing, we still had funds, we would treat ourselves and have breakfast in a working men's caff, before finally tottering off home. It was drinking around the clock, but we didn't go boozing like that every night. We usually went on a real bender on a Friday, because on the other nights we would be either working or learning lines.

We might have seemed a bit of a joke to the real market porters, but I knew all the ladies of the night, because of my days at the Italia Conti drama school in Archer Street, which was just off Piccadilly and a regular haunt for prostitutes. The girls would say, 'Come here, Johnny, how are you? Oh, I saw a film you were in the other day ...' And they would even offer me their services free, which, naturally, I always declined. But they were always good for a laugh. One lady had a marvellously cheeky answer to any punter who turned her down after VAT was first introduced, and she really made me chuckle when she tried it on with me.

'Come on, Johnny, come on, Johnny,' she said. 'I have known you for years. Come on, love. I will spoil you.'

When I said 'No,' she asked, 'What's the matter?'

'Can't afford it, sweetheart. Can't afford it,' I swiftly replied. 'I've never paid for it yet, and I'm not starting now!'

She'd then saucily retort, 'Johnny, well remember one thing, there is no VAT on fanny!'

'Very sweet of you, darling,' I said with a grin, 'but the answer is still no ...' and I beat a hasty retreat.

As I remarked, the real hell-raisers, like O'Toole and Richard Harris, used to drink spirits and they could really knock the booze back. We'd be on our halves of bitter and they would be on their large gins, but, while there were times when Ronnie, Peter and Sean Connery would be earning more than us, it didn't affect the party spirit. They were very generous and they would say, 'Do you want another half?'

'Oh, yes please,' I would reply but there would be none of this, 'I've bought you a drink, now it's your turn.' It was just mates having a drink together and if you were doing better than one of the others, you looked after them.

There were hardly ever any girls involved in our boozing sprees because, basically, it was a men's clique. We didn't generally arrange anything special. You just knew that everyone would be in the Salisbury on such a day and at such a time. It was spontaneous, and it went on for years, from the late Fifties to well into the Sixties.

There would be girls at the parties, but if you didn't pull, once the girls left someone would say, 'Might as well get the cards out,' and we would play poker, brag and blackjack until we headed off to the Smithfield pubs.

I never had any trouble getting a girl and I used to pull loads of them, but I tried to keep my romances fairly low key. In those days, I didn't have that much money and, more importantly, I didn't want to get involved; I didn't want a regular girlfriend. I liked going on a spree with the lads and having a bit of a laugh.

One of the funniest times I can recall was with John Charlesworth, bless him. He was one of my friends who never successfully made the switch from boy to grown-up male actor and, sadly, committed suicide. That was a real blow, for John was a fantastic bloke, who appeared to have everything going for him. I was in the pub one day with another of my old drinking partners, Sean Lynch — who was later killed in a car crash in Spain — when in walked John Charlesworth, who invited us to his engagement party. He was marrying the niece of the Dowager Countess Cathcart.

As John had such a well connected fiancée, I realised that the party was obviously going to be a very smart event and, as Sean and I were only dressed in sweaters and trousers, I tried to cry off, pointing out to John, 'We can't come along dressed like this.' But John couldn't have cared less how we were dressed; he just wanted some mates for moral support, and when he turned on the charm he could be very persuasive. So we went over to the countess's elegant West End London home and knocked on the door. It was opened by a butler who, looking down his nose at Sean and myself, said to John with icy disdain, 'Who are these gentlemen?'

'These are my friends,' said John, airily waving in our direction and, faced down by John's superb nonchalance, the butler retreated and ushered us in to meet John's fiancées's aunt.

As I suspected, it was a black tie party and after the countess had taken one chilly look at us, Sean and I were shown into a private side room on our own, next door to the main party. A footman brought in a trolley of drinks and Sean and I eagerly set to. We hadn't wanted to go to the party in the first place so were quite happy to knock back the superb French white Burgundy, château-bottled claret and the full array of spirits on offer. But John wasn't so sanguine about the way we had been treated when he bounced into the room half an hour later.

'What are you doing in here?' he asked, having finally broken free from his fiancée for a few minutes.

'Well, they wouldn't let us go into the main reception room, because they didn't think we were suitable,' I said, reaching for my glass.

'Oh,' said John, his face like thunder, 'I think I've made a mistake here.'

At that moment, a Siamese cat strutted into the room looking for all the world as snooty as the Dowager Countess. Without another word, John swooped on the cat, sweeping it up and holding it with its head under one arm as he held its tail in his other hand.

'Open that door,' he said, with sheer devilment written across his handsome features.

'What are you going to do?' I asked anxiously, fearing the worst.

'Just open the door,' John replied silkily.

Well, we had had quite a few drinks and I was beginning to feel just a bit fed up at the shabby reception we had received, so I was game for any mischief, and opened the door. A total hush descended on the party as John stood in the doorway like a Western gunfighter, facing into the packed room, with the cat's head still under his arm while he clutched the tail like a bell pull.

'I say,' he called in his best cut-glass tone, 'has anyone heard me play the bagpipes?'

As all faces turned expectantly towards him in a mixture of concern and amazement, he played his party piece — biting the cat's tail! As his teeth sank in, the wretched cat let out a long hellish shriek and exploded out of John's arms, almost leaping through the ceiling.

That did it. As the once so-smart party dissolved into pandemonium, a gang of heavies appeared from nowhere, grabbing hold of all three of us and, with John protesting volubly that he was the guest of honour, we were unceremoniously thrown out on to the pavement. As we dusted ourselves down we almost went into hysterics, too — killing ourselves with laughter. Needless to say, that was the end of the engagement — and John's by-then ex-fiancée later gave him his ring back.

But that didn't bother John, then or later. He just thought it was a huge joke, and he was still bubbling with mischief as we set off for his mother's flat above an exclusive dress shop, near Saville Row police station, where she worked as a window dresser. When we got to the flat, we decided to carry on having a bit of fun, and went downstairs to the shop. We then sneaked into the shop window, where we stood pretending that we were window models. Every time someone walked by we would wink or move — and they would jump out of their skins at the sight. It was hysterical and in the end we had to abandon the prank because we couldn't stop falling around laughing.

One of the great characters we used to delight in running into regularly was the great Irish playwright Brendan Behan. He was a very loud man, but he was also very generous and we used to meet him in The Circus Tavern, The French House and the Duke of Wellington.

I really liked him and, mostly, he was good fun to be with — until he got drunk. Then everyone, myself included, would run for cover. It was the only wise thing to do, for Brendan was totally unpredictable when drunk and would invariably get into fights, or start them, to be precise. He really was a hell-raiser in every sense of the word and if you weren't careful you could find yourself ending up at the end of an evening with Brendan lying face down in a Soho gutter.

He loved to drink and he loved to brawl. He also liked actors and enjoyed meeting a gang of four, five or six of us. He was very successful and I was always trying to persuade him to put me in one of his plays, but he insisted that I didn't speak the right language. But I wouldn't take 'no' for an answer.

'I know I am a Londoner,' I would say, 'but surely you could write a Londoner into one of your plays!'

He would then look at me fondly as we leaned against yet another bar and say, 'Johnny, I love you tons. But, no ...'

He would then kiss me on the cheek — a great slobbering kiss in which you could feel the great gap in his tooth.

But the real trouble with Brendan was that he was always fighting and was barred from a string of my favourite pubs, which could prove very embarrassing. I would arrange to meet him in one of our Soho watering holes and, as Brendan always had the money in those days, I would time my entrance so that we both walked into the boozer together. Then, as we headed for the bar, the landlord would look up, clock who we were and then, thrusting a finger towards us, bellow, 'Out you, out you ... out, out , OUT!'

'What have I done?' I would protest, turning on my best look of innocence.

And the landlord would say, 'No, not you, Johnny, not you, him,' and, stabbing an even more forcible finger in Brendan's direction, would roar, 'Out, you. Out.'

Brendan, bless him, if he wasn't already boozed up and looking for trouble, would shuffle out, and I would go with him, thinking, 'Well, he has got the money. I might as well join him ...'

There was always a fracas when I was out with Brendan. He attracted trouble wherever he went, but I would have had a few too, and it would all vanish from my memory in a technicolour blur of booze and noise. If you weren't careful, you could easily end up getting a thump or two yourself. We used to go to the pubs in Covent Garden in the early hours of the morning and there would always be fights with porters. Brendan used to insult the porters, which was a totally insane thing to do because those Covent garden porters were a tough bunch and were quite happy to start trading punches with anyone who upset them. And Brendan was a past master at that. So I was never surprised when I met Brendan occasionally sporting a magnificent black eye. And it could have happened when he was out with me. We both had dreadful memory lapses after mammoth sessions. But it never bothered him. Oh, he was great fun.

Dylan Thomas, the Welsh playwright, was also very generous and full of fun and jokes. But while Brendan was just a drinker, Dylan was more poetic and very into the arts. He was also good fun, but he had more time for the Welsh actors like Donald Houston. We were all struggling for jobs and usually a bit short of cash so we were always very disappointed when Dylan's wife Caitlin would turn up and drag Dylan out of the pub. We would think, 'Cor, blimey, there goes our money. There goes our next half pint!'

But it wasn't all wild fun and games. People think the hell-raisers shouted and screamed and brought attention to themselves. Well, they did sometimes, but usually they just got on with serious boozing.

The British public imagine that if they see a group of people enjoying themselves they are hell-raisers, but it was not as hairy as people think.

And there was a certain method in our enthusiasm to go drinking. We were all on the look out for jobs and while our lunchtime sessions were generally just a case of relaxing with the boys and catching up on the showbusiness gossip, when the pubs closed and we moved on to the Kismet Club at 3.00pm we were seriously looking for work. We used to hang around the Kismet, which was opposite the Arts Theatre Club, because there we would see the director casting films for the next day, and that could mean work.

We would stay at the Kismet until about 5.00 or 6.00pm on Mondays to Thursdays — and if you didn't get work, you went home.

But I was lucky and usually managed to get work, even if I was once killed off because I was getting too big a slice of a film's budget.

My date with premature death came when I flew into a role in the 1964 war epic *633 Squadron*. The film was based on an RAF bomber unit's successful but costly mission to destroy an almost impregnable Nazi rocket fuel installation in Norway. It was being shot at the then MGM studios opposite Elstree, and I had been guaranteed six days' work at £100 a day, which was a lot of money in the early Sixties.

As a member of one of the bomber's crew, I did four days on the set and on the fifth drove into the studios, went into make-up, and headed for my dressing room to wait to be called back on to the set. And there I sat ... all day. On the sixth day I again drove to the studios, went into make-up, and then headed for my dressing room, where, once again, I sat about waiting all day. On the seventh day, I went through the same routine; drove to the studios, and ended up sitting in my dressing room all day. On the eighth day — the same. By the ninth day I was starting to get worried and I suddenly thought, 'I wonder if they know I am here?' because every day I had simply arrived at the studios and, without speaking to anyone working on the film, had then sat in my dressing room waiting for the call that never came.

With a feeling of mild unease, I thought I had better wander on to the set and see what was happening. As I walked on to the set I spotted the director, Walter Grauman, leaning against the scenery with his head resting against one of the flaps. So, quietly walking up behind him, I smacked him on the bottom and cheerfully inquired, 'Hi, Walter, how's it going?'

He turned round and said, 'Oh, Johnny, baby, how are you kid?'

'Fine,' I smiled.

Then he asked, 'Where've you been the last few days?'

'Sitting in my dressing room,' I replied.

'Sitting in your dressing room?' he asked incredulously.

'Yes,' I beamed. 'How's it going?'

'How's it going?' he snorted, with the blood rushing to his temples, 'I am four days behind schedule. That's how it's going.'

'Why is that?' I asked, realising at once that something had gone badly wrong for the picture to be slipping so far behind schedule.

'I'll tell you why,' said Walter, who by now was almost exploding with anger and frustration, 'it's because we have got this George Chakiris (one of the stars of the huge musical success *West Side Story*), who is supposed to be leader of the Norwegian Resistance because Steve McQueen turned it down. And he's strapped to a chair naked from the waist up with the Gestapo whipping him — and he's grinning all over his face!

'Grinning! I ask you! The bosses have seen the rushes and went absolutely ape. They were so furious that they have ordered me to re-shoot them all. Jeez, I don't know what I am going to do!'

I know when it's time to make a fast exit, and that was certainly one of them.

'Oh, well I might as well go back to my dressing room,' I said, turning to leave.

'No, just a minute,' Walter called after me. 'What was your guarantee, John?' he asked.

'Six days,' I replied, not liking the way this conversation was going one little bit.

'And how many have you done?' Walter persisted.

'This is my ninth,' I said.

'What is your daily rate?' he then asked.

'One hundred.'

'Bucks or pounds?' he inquired.

'Pounds,' I said.

'Today you die!' he said.

And he put me in a plane that crashed into a cliff — and I was not supposed to die. I was supposed to survive the whole film and the swine killed me off!

He made it up to me a few years later when he was making another war thriller, *The Last Escape*. He phoned me out of the blue and said, 'What are you doing from such and such a date to such and such a date?'

'Nothing, Walt,' I replied, my heart skipping a beat as that was during my long lean period and a job offer would be manna from heaven.

'Well, you are now,' said Walter. 'You are doing this film for me in Germany. Come by my hotel in London and pick up your script.'

With that he hung up, without even waiting for my reply. His confidence was well founded. I didn't need to be asked twice. Again Walter was offering me £100 a day, which in 1969 was still very good money, and I knew better than to ever turn down work. Besides, the film was starring Stuart Whitman and I knew it would be a lot of fun as it was a war caper in which I played a British paratrooper, who, with a group of other paras, was dropped into Holland to either bring back, or kill, a Dutch nuclear physicist the Germans were forcing to work on their atomic weapons programme.

I was thrilled to be called up by Walter for the film, but he knew I could deliver. After I had made *633 Squadron*, I asked my agent why I was only on £75 a day for the next British film I made after being paid £100 by Grauman. And my agent said, 'Yeah, but when the Americans say they want an actor, they mean they want one who gets it right first time. They are not interested in someone who will need eight or nine takes to get a line or a scene right. The producers and directors say, "I don't want a £15-a-day actor who makes mistakes and I have to tell him to learn his lines, or instruct him on how to get it right. I want someone who gets it right from the start, because that way I save money." They want results and will pay for them.'

And, not so surprisingly really, I suppose, it was because I was getting the results, along with Roger Moore's success as the Saint, that it finally put paid to my long boozy sessions in the pub.

We had seen less and less of Roger in the pub, and when I ran into him in the street one day and suggested popping into the Salisbury for a drink, he said, 'I am not going to go in the pub any more.'

'Why not?' I asked.

'Well, you never know who you are going to meet,' he said. 'So in future, I am going to go to clubs where every person is known to the manager so you won't get anyone tapping you on the shoulder and saying, "Hey, you're the Saint. How about a fight!" So that's it; I'm not going to the pub any more.'

I thought, 'That's a bit of a shame,' but soon afterwards I took Roger's advice and stopped going to pubs myself. I had played a lot of villains, and then I started playing a policeman in No Hiding Place, and you were quite prone to some guy coming up to you and snarling, 'You think you're tough, do you?'

So I started going more regularly to the Garrick Club with Raymond Francis, my screen boss in No Hiding Place, and then we would move on to Jerry's, an actors' club in Shaftesbury Avenue. We would also still drop in to the Kismet, the Arts and the Pickwick clubs, and sometimes the Mandrake. But they all had the same advantage; everyone who drank there was either a member or was with a member, and there was never any bother.

There were other distinct advantages to using clubs, as I discovered when I joined The Flower Club, which was by the River Thames at Staines. It was in the most beautiful setting and was very exclusive, catering not necessarily for the well-off, but certainly the nicer people around that area. It was a magnet for me as it used to attract some really nice girls down from London for a night out or visiting parents and relatives nearby. It became a regular haunt of mine after my parents moved to Staines, and I was in there one weekend with John Hurt when I met the two girls who rocked Harold Macmillan's Conservative Government in the early Sixties — Christine Keeler and Mandy Rice-Davies.

I hadn't a clue these two gorgeous girls were going to cause the biggest government scandal of the century and eventually dish the Tories, when they strolled into the club. We thought they were just two pretty girls in those relatively

Always the hard man: undercover in *The Last Escape*.

Top: Baby faced as a boy soprano.

Bottom left: On a day out with Mum and Dad.

Bottom right: Early days: High Wycombe Rep.

In one of my butch roles!

Top: Light up the Sky – a great chance to get to know a great man: Benny Hill.

Bottom: Harking back to Forces days in *The Pathfinders*.

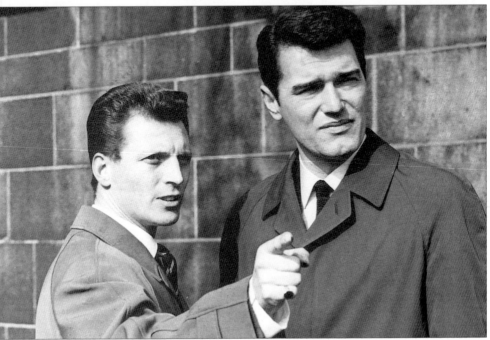

Top: Presenting *Ready Steady Go!*

Bottom: No Hiding Place – note my impressive stature!

Preparing for another steamy encounter! Not that I'm typecast…

Stripped for action: note the medallion. Those where the days!

Top: A great day for me – marrying Christine, my second wife, June 4, 1977.

Bottom left: The family: me, Christine, Jenny and Michael.

Bottom right: Spanish taxis! On holiday in Marbella.

My first appearance on *Coronation Street* – looking calmer than I feel, with
Julie Goodyear.

Top left: Fore! Golf – now there's a good sport!

Top right: Stars old and new.

Bottom: The Queen is dazzled by the famous Briggs charm at the Royal Command Performance.

Mike Baldwin's always out to make a buck or two, but there comes a limit... Panning for gold in Colorado.

Getting the royal seal of approval at a charity golf match at Wentworth,
August 1997.

With my beautiful wife Christine, Christmas 1997.

Yo ho ho! Santa pays a visit to the Rovers Return, Christmas 1997.

One of the most famous faces in showbusiness. And Mickey Mouse, too…

Top: Mike Baldwin gets one in the eye at last!

Bottom: A thorn between two roses! With my daughters Stephanie and Jenny in Disneyland.

innocent days before the Profumo scandal broke. Their names didn't mean anything to us. They were just Christine and a pal, and it was just a case of 'Oh, hello ...' when we were introduced.

The girls knew the man who ran the club, Peter Watson Smythe, who looked like Phileas Fogg, and his wife Virginia. Christine had come down to see her mother, who lived at nearby Wraysbury, and the girls were out on the razzle before heading back to London. But they were such stunners my pal and I swiftly moved in on them and asked them if they would like a drink. They said 'Yes' and we had a couple of drinks before I took Christine on to the dance floor for a couple of dances to the smoochy music of the time. She was certainly very sexy and we had another drink before Christine and her friend left. They used to drop into the club about once a month and we used to have a drink and a nice close-quarters dance, but although I found Christine very attractive, I only saw the girls in the club and never dated either of them.

As far as I was concerned, they were just two super girls who were fun to be with and we always had a dance and a drink. It wasn't until months later, when the scandal hit the papers, that my pal and I realised just who the two charming, very pretty and, seemingly, ordinary girls were. Then, of course, we kept very, very quiet. For Christine, who was accused of being a prostitute, was romantically linked to the then War Minister John Profumo, while also being involved with the Russian attaché Eugene Ivanov. Meanwhile the teenage Mandy had been bed-hopping with the high and mighty of two continents. Spies, sex, scandal, it had them all. But we would never have guessed as we laughed and chatted and danced the evenings away ...

Life seemed to be one long party in those days. There was a boat builder called Bates, who used to throw Sunday lunchtime parties at his place on the Thames, which my mate Ronnie Fraser also used to attend regularly. So I used to go to The Flower Club Saturday night, struggle home in the wee small hours of Sunday morning, get up, have a bath, wash my hair and go round to Bates' parties. Then I would head back to The Flower Club on Sunday night for another evening of revelry. It was great at the club, but in those days there were very strict licensing laws and Peter and Virginia used to make sure we were very careful not to spark a police raid. So when it was finally time to call it a night, all the revellers who were still left would have to leave at different times and exit through different doors in case the police were watching. I got a bit fed up with all that rigmarole and on the odd occasion would suggest to Peter, 'Wouldn't it be better if I stayed the night with Virginia and yourself and left in the morning?' But he would swiftly pour cold water on that idea, telling me, firmly, 'No. Bugger off!' I don't know whether he thought that I had designs on Virginia! But he wasn't having Briggsy staying, and boozing, all night.

By now I was also getting plenty of work. I learned a lot being in television shows with Tony Hancock and Arthur Haynes. Peter Sellers was a huge star then, but while he tended to ham it up a bit, they were the masters — completely and utterly believable comics. I used to stand in the wings, soaking up their acts and marvelling at their timing.

One night, when I was walking from my dressing room to the wings in Arthur's show, he called out, 'Johnny, come and look at this!'

'What?' I asked.

He said, 'They have made me have this pop group on my show. Come and look at them.'

And there was Mick Jagger with his thick lips, waving his bum at the audience and all that.

'Cor blimey, Arthur,' I said, 'what are they called?'

'They are called the Rolling Stones,' he said, adding, 'but they look as if they crawled out from under one!'

Then, warming to his theme, Arthur went on, 'Have you seen what they came in? Come into the car park and have a look!'

So I followed him into the car park and there was a van covered in lipstick messages, such as 'I love you, Mick' and all that business. Arthur couldn't get over it, and insisted that I look in the back of the van, where there was a mattress. Wrinkling his nose in disgust, Arthur said, 'Do you realise that they are kipping in there? Look at it!' And it was covered in beer cans and empty cartons. 'What do you think?' he asked.

'I don't know,' I replied.

'Neither do I, and I don't know why they have made me have them,' he moaned.

Arthur soon found out as the Stones rolled on to megastardom. But that was the joy of the old ITV companies. They were always keen to try something new and with Lew Grade in charge at the old ATV it was a good time to be in television.

It was also a successful time for me in the movies. Apart from *Stitch in Time*, in which I played another Teddy boy, I landed a key role in the 1963 kitchen sink drama *The Leather Boys*, directed by Sidney J Furie. Rita Tushingham, who had made a name for herself in stark black-and-white dramas like Tony Richardson's *A Taste of Honey*, based on the Shelagh Delaney play, was the female lead and I played her macho boyfriend after her character split with her motorcycle-mad screen husband, played by Colin Campbell. And I can truthfully say, making that film was one of my worst acting experiences. I thought Rita Tushingham was a very difficult woman.

It was a very successful black-and-white film about a doomed marriage. It hammered home the message of 'marry in haste, repent at leisure'. There were also strong homosexual undertones with Campbell's character going to live with his friend Pete, played by Dudley Sutton, before beginning to suspect that Pete is gay. As Tushingham's lover, we had a scene in which I played the dominant male, but when I arrived to film it one morning, I discovered that she had rewritten the scene, chucking out most of my lines. I'm not joking, she really had trashed my part. So I stormed off to see Furie and shouted, 'What's all this? You are directing this film.'

Obviously very embarrassed, he started to say, 'Well, Rita thought ...' when I interrupted him.

'What the heck has she got to do with what I say in this film? How dare she alter my part without at least phoning me up or telling me about it?'

So Furie snapped back, 'Well, she's the star of the film.'

'She can twinkle as much as she likes,' I then told Furie, 'but she doesn't alter my dialogue.' Then, boiling with fury, I blasted out, 'Now you either put it back or I'm walking off the film.'

In the end, we compromised, by working out what I wanted to say, and we did the scene. But what we didn't agree — and I should have insisted upon at the time — was a guarantee that my lines wouldn't end up on the cutting-room floor when they edited the film. That, of course is precisely what happened. The scene should have been very good for me as the dominant male lying in bed, bossing her about, while she was doing the cooking.

But in the finished film, the scene ended up with her appearing to have the upper hand, which was not how it was written — or how we played it. I found her very hard to work with.

One day, I had arranged to go to the première of *The VIPs*, a star-studded melodrama about people stranded by fog at a London airport, with Richard Burton. Richard was in the film, with Liz Taylor, and he invited Caroline and myself to the première at the Empire, Leicester Square, and to the party afterwards. I was delighted and told him we would both be there. So that afternoon on the set, I asked the first assistant director, 'What time do we finish tonight, six or half-past?'

'Oh, we're working until eight tonight,' he replied.

'Oh, when was that decided?' I then asked.

'Lunchtime. Rita decided she would like to get these scenes finished and decided to work until eight.'

'Well, she can work on without me,' I said. 'I wasn't informed at lunchtime and, as far as I'm concerned, I'm going at half-past six, because I am going to a première tonight.'

That did it. She became angry and upset. But I stood my ground, telling her, 'You can have your meetings and do what you like, but I wasn't told at lunchtime that we were working later than our usual time tonight, and I'm going to the première.' And off I went.

I felt sorry for Furie because he was a bit awestruck around Rita. I don't know if he was infatuated with her, but *The VIPs* was a big star-studded film and Burton had asked me to the première — and that was where I went.

I knew Burton very well, but I didn't crawl. I wasn't one of the 'yes' men and I think he appreciated that. The première was fun, although I didn't like the film much, but the party was good and made it well worthwhile upsetting Rita Tushingham. I don't know if she took umbrage because she wasn't invited to such a prestigious night out. I don't even know if she eventually went. I wasn't interested in what she did. No one said a word to me about walking out and leaving Tushingham fuming — they knew I had every right to expect to be treated with a modicum of courtesy. As for Tushingham, I just didn't speak to her. Although I played her lover I didn't have to kiss her, thank God.

The Leather Boys involved a motor-cycle race by the guys from London to Edinburgh to post a letter, with the first one back winning all the money the lads had put into the kitty. But Furie refused to spend money going to Edinburgh to shoot key scenes on the city's famous hill, arguing, 'between the trees, a rock is a rock'. So we shot all the scenes that should have been in Edinburgh on Box Hill, in Surrey. I was disappointed to miss out on a nice trip to Edinburgh, but Furie reckoned he had pulled a great money-saving wheeze — until the producer, Raymond Stross, saw the film rushes.

When Stross saw the 'Edinburgh' shots, he exploded. 'That's fucking Box Hill! What are you doing to me? You are supposed to be in Edinburgh, but that mountain is Box Hill!'

'How do you know that?' asked an agitated Furie.

'Because it's a well-known landmark and part of England's heritage,' shouted the furious Stross.

They had to re-shoot the Edinburgh scenes, but I still

didn't get a trip to Scotland. They used doubles because I had run out of my contract time and was on too hefty a daily rate of pay for them to keep me on. I had been contracted for four weeks at £200 a week, but if I continued to film after my contract had finished I was then paid £200 a *day*! So they used doubles. But I wasn't sorry to leave that film set.

The trouble with Rita was that she had had quite a bit of success early on and continued to top the bill with films like *The Girl With Green Eyes*, but I couldn't get on with her at all. I just used to ignore her on the set. I don't like arguments and animosity, so I think the best policy is to ignore someone and don't catch their eye. But, obviously, as a professional, I made sure the scenes I did with her were the best I could do.

I had a lot more fun with *Devil-Ship Pirates*, even if I did suffer my most grisly death on screen. In that swashbuckling romp directed by Don Sharp, I played Pablo, a Spanish pirate, who was backed into a bog in a sword fight, and was swallowed up in quicksand. It looked very spectacular as, fighting for my life, with my arms flailing and my eyes popping, I slowly sank out of sight, with the quicksand finally oozing over my head. But it was just a very wet exit from the film as far as I was concerned. They used cork on water to create the quicksand and, basically, I just held my breath in the final seconds and sank through the cork into the water below. The director then cried 'Cut' and they pulled me out. I then had a shower, dried myself, and that was the end of the film for me. Although it was an adventure yarn, there were no exotic locations. They filmed it at Bray and used British actors to play Spaniards, much to the disgust of one Spanish actor, who couldn't get a part in the film!

The biggest drama in the film, however, occurred when they were changing a camera lens. The film was shot in CinemaScope — and they dropped a CinemaScope lens into the lake. They cost £70,000 — an absolute fortune in those days — and there was a huge panic to try and retrieve it. The producer even got police frogmen to search the lake bottom for it. But they never found the lens and it is probably still lying in the silt at the bottom of the lake.

Roger might have persuaded me that clubs were the best watering holes to avoid trouble, but we still managed to find a jolly pub when we linked up on *The Saint*. That was the series that launched Roger on the road to super-stardom and his performance as the suave, twinkle-eyed, oh-so-cool Simon Templar was the perfect forerunner for his debonair and devilishly charming James Bond.

Roger is a real charmer and it was fantastic working with him. He was wonderful, but he was a terrible 'corpser'. He used to giggle all the time, even when we were going for a take, which, I suppose, was understandable considering some of his more improbable adventures. But the real joke was that every time Roger, playing the smooth, totally self-assured Templar, fired his gun, he blinked his eyes! So when they had shot an action sequence they would have to cut the blinks out. It was ridiculous — the perfect *Boy's Own* hero blinking every time he squeezed the trigger, but Roger just couldn't stop himself. I used to fall around laughing, and Roger, the good sport he was, shared the joke.

I was playing a villain who terrorised Samantha Eggar, who was one of Roger's leading ladies, alongside other Sixties beauties like Dawn Addams, Julie Christie and Gabrielle Drake. As the Saint, Roger, of course, drove his sleek yellow two-seater Volvo P1800, with the personalised number plate ST1. And Samantha caught the car bug and bought a Triumph Spitfire sports car. Like Templar's Volvo, it was a pretty two-seater and Samantha was as pleased as punch with it. One lunchtime I asked her if she was coming to the restaurant and was surprised when she said 'No'.

'What are you doing?' I asked.

'I have just bought this new car — I've had a bank loan — and I'm going to clean it,' she replied.

'Oh, where is it?' I inquired.

'There!' she said, pointing proudly at her car.

'Well, you see that Hillman Minx convertible parked behind it?' I continued. 'Well, when you've finished cleaning yours, you can clean that one,' I said jokingly.

I then went off for lunch and thought no more about it. But when I returned to pick Samantha up on my way back to the set, she said, 'Oh, Johnny, I'm ever so sorry, but I only had time to do the bonnet and two of the wings. I didn't have time to do the whole lot.'

'I was only joking,' I said. 'Oh, I thought you meant it. Never mind. Now you've got a clean bonnet and two front wings!'

Roger is a very talented man, he used to be a newspaper cartoonist and in between scenes he used to relax by doing caricatures of the other actors. He did a wonderful one of me, which, regrettably, was lost or destroyed. But years later, when he was doing the *Bond* films, one of my daughters was desperate to have his autograph. So I wrote to him and asked for a photograph. He sent a big autographed picture to my daughter and a little one to me upon which he had drawn glasses and a moustache, and on the back he wrote, 'Dear Johnny, I hope you get the photograph alright. Excuse the paper, but times are hard! Roger.'

It was while we were making *The Saint* that I got my first real taste of the union power that for years had a throttling grip on television. As the villain who had been hunted down to a television studio, I was supposed to run out on to a gantry in the studio as Roger's Saint walked in, switch on a lamp, blind him with the powerful beam, and then make my escape. But when the director called action we were nearly plunged into darkness by the angry electricians. Although we were using props, the electricians insisted that *they* had to turn on the light — and no one else. So in the end we had to fix up an elaborate switching mechanism with a piece of wire so that when my character was supposed to throw the switch, the light would in reality be turned on by an electrician down on the sound stage.

It was the technicians' greed that killed off the British movie industry in the Sixties. At one time, there were so many studios going full blast — Pinewood, Shepperton, Bray, Elstree, EMI, MGM — but the technicians wanted the same money as the Americans, and they closed MGM, EMI and Elstree, so we all had to move into television. At the time, people said TV would never take over from the cinema, but they couldn't have been more wrong.

Throughout this period, I was particularly chummy with Diana Dors. I had known her for years and we had basically grown up together, bumping into each other around the studios. The film community was very close knit in those days and while I would be making one film in the studios, Diana would be making another somewhere on the lot, and we would meet for lunch. She had a bungalow down by the Thames at Shepperton, before she moved to Sunningdale, and one night when I was working on a film, she and Sid James and some of the boys invited me to a Bonfire Night party being held at a house near hers. Well, that really was the party to end all parties. There was plenty of booze and party spirit, but that soon evaporated when one of the lads threw a jumping jack into the house, where they were storing all the fireworks. There was one hell of a bang as the jumping jack set the other fireworks alight — and the house was burned down.

But that was the sort of explosive lifestyle that Diana revelled in. She really was larger than life and had this magnificent pink Cadillac convertible which perfectly set off her glamorous image. There was only one problem — she couldn't drive it, because she couldn't pass her driving test, She must have taken the test ten times and failed every time. She was keen on me helping her, but I wouldn't get in a car with her — it would have been like driving with a Kamikaze pilot! Diana knew that I had not only been a driving instructor in the Army but had taught Ann Lynn, but that was quite different. Ann was quite a reasonable driver, but Di wasn't. I felt sorry for her and suggested that the only way she would ever get a licence was by going to Ireland and taking a test there, where, in the Sixties, they were more lenient.

A few months later, I was walking down the King's Road with Caroline when Diana screeched to a stop beside us and, leaning out of her gleaming Cadillac, said with a huge smile, 'It worked, Johnny, it worked. Give me a kiss.' I didn't need a second invitation, but Caroline gave me a sharp look and asked suspiciously, 'What worked?' I then explained about Di's long-running driving drama — and we all went off for a drink to celebrate.

Di and I were never any more than the best of friends, but when I was living in Staines and she was in Sunningdale, she looked after me. She was a wonderful friend and if she saw me on my own, she would always say, 'Come and join us.' I was often quite strapped in those days and, feeling embarrassed, I would have to admit, 'I am a bit skint.' But she wouldn't take 'no' for an answer and would insist, 'Don't be silly. Come and join us, we would like your company.' She was lovely, a really wonderful woman. We met in the early Fifties and I was like a little brother to her. She was a delight, like a Pat Phoenix rising, but she was never a girlfriend — she was too expensive for me!

We remained friends for many years, but I didn't like her relationship with Alan Lake, whom she eventually married. I had known for Alan for years, as we had also grown up together with Ollie Reed and the boys. Alan and I had been in films together, but I never liked him.

Incredibly, as we were so often at the studios together, I never acted with Diana. The nearest I got to that was when I jokingly asked her to fix me a part in *Yield to the Night*, in which she scored one of her greatest dramatic triumphs as a condemned killer awaiting execution in the death cell. She said, 'But, darling, it's set in a woman's prison.'

'I can wear a skirt,' I promptly countered.

Surprisingly, I wasn't being as silly as I thought, because the producers did then offer me a small role in the film, but by then, unfortunately, I was already working in a play!

6

I LOVED WORKING WITH ROGER AND SAMANTHA on *The Saint* and found that it really paid to play a bad guy as I started to do more and more television work. It was after I had appeared in the top BBC series *Z Cars*, a hard-hitting police drama highlighting the work of patrol car coppers in a new town near Liverpool, that I got my big break — by being in the pub at the right time.

I was still very friendly with Alec Ross, and I was in the Salisbury one day when he breezed in and said, 'Hello, how are you, mate?' After I had ordered up the drinks, he told me he had just come from an interview at Associated-Rediffusion, one of the major ITV companies in those days, where they were casting two new detective sergeants for their big police drama, *No Hiding Place*.

'How did you get on?' I asked, a touch enviously, and he replied, 'They are a bit too young for me, actually, but I think you would be dead right.'

I didn't need telling twice. I went straight to the pub's phone and rang my agent, telling him to get me an interview for the show. I had already appeared in it playing a villain and my agent thought I wanted him to put me up for another gangster part. So when he suggested that, I swiftly cut him short, saying, 'I know I play villains, but I would hate to this time. I want you to get me in there for an interview as one of the new detective sergeants — or I will be looking for another agent next week.'

It was tough talking; Johnny Briggs slipping into 'hard man' mode, but I recalled some advice Dirk Bogarde had given me when we were filming *HMS Defiant*. Dirk told me, 'An agent can't get you the job; all you ask the agent to do is get you the interview.' Well, I wanted that interview and I expected my agent to get it for me. For, as I had told Dirk, 'If I can get to the producer I will get the job.' And Dirk had agreed that getting the interview was everything, as he, too, had had problems getting to see producers when he started.

What I hate about casting directors in Britain is that they put actors into categories and then you are trapped in that little box. All the American actors I have met — Paul Newman, Steve McQueen, Robert Mitchum, Stuart Whitman — can't understand how in England an actor is categorised into a class. They don't understand how an actor as good as I'm told I am would never be cast as an army officer, a dentist or a solicitor, because casting directors see me as a Cockney villain. James Villiers, an old drinking pal, once told me, 'Johnny, my darling, I would love to play a villain, but because of my bloody accent I will never get the chance.' In America, actors can be a company director, a villain, a schoolteacher, a Congressman, anything. But I would never be cast as an MP, although some of the MPs in Parliament speak so badly I can't understand what they are saying. In the same way, I would never be cast as an army officer. I would always be the sergeant. So I knew I had to get that interview come what may.

And, my agent, appreciating the note of urgency and determination in my voice, said, 'Hang on, stay where you are and I will phone you right back.' He then got on to the bosses at Rediffusion and persuaded them that I was the man they just had to see. And, as good as his word, he was soon ringing me back to tell me that I had got an audition. That was marvellous news, and I duly went up to see the programme's bosses.

No Hiding Place, with Raymond Francis as the genial, snuff-taking sleuth Detective Chief Superintendent Tom Lockhart, was already a major hit, but Eric Lander, as Detective Sergeant Harry Baxter, had decided to move on and they wanted two replacements; a tall, dark-haired sergeant, and a short, fair-headed one, which fitted me perfectly.

They told me it initially meant six months' work and I went down to Wembley to do a screen test.

Before I did the test, I bumped into Raymond Francis. Apart from Roger Moore, Raymond was one of the most charming men I have ever met, but he gasped when he saw how short I was to play a hard-nosed detective. But, gentleman that he was, he gave me a piece of invaluable advice. 'Johnny, wear some lifts in your shoes, dear boy,' he said. 'Give yourself an extra inch because, you're a bit small.'

He wasn't kidding about my size — I am just 5ft 7in tall, but I can act big! So I put a pair of lifts — wedges shaped like your heel which give you some height — into my shoes. They are great for boosting short people, but they have a major drawback. While they increase your height they tend to thrust your body forward, and the more you put in the more you lean like the Tower of Pisa. But they gave me what I thought was sufficient height to play a copper, although I was conscious, as I tottered on to the set, that if I put in any more I would end up on my nose.

As I went into action, however, the director, Ian Fordyce, came up to me and said, 'Johnny, why don't you put a pair of lifts in your shoes to give yourself a couple of inches?'

I thought, 'Oh Lord, I'm in trouble here,' but I could see why he felt I needed the boost the minute I met Michael McStay, who was lined up to play the tall, dark Detective Sergeant Perryman. Michael, standing well over 6ft in his socks, towered over me. Talk about Little and Large! But we clicked immediately. I knew instinctively that we would make a perfect team and we would have a lot of fun together. And we did. We were to become great pals, but neither of us knew we had got the jobs when we finished the film tests and went into the studio bar for a much-needed drink.

I knew that the bosses used the bar, so I said to McStay, 'Let's go around the corner by the dart board so that if anyone comes in they won't see us, but we will be able to get an idea of how things are going.' Well, we were knocking back a couple of pints, when in walked Peter Willes, the executive producer, with the director and Raymond Francis, who was saying, 'I like Johnny Briggs.'

Raymond carried a phenomenal amount of clout on that programme. He was the darling of the viewers, was paid an astronomical salary and had a crucial say in everything that happened. With Raymond urging that I should be given the part, Willes swiftly agreed, saying, 'Yes, Johnny and Michael make a good couple.'

'They do, but Michael is 6ft 1in tall and Johnny is much shorter,' cautioned Fordyce.

With Raymond backing me, Fordyce's objection didn't cut any ice with Peter Willes, who replied, 'Well that's not a problem, we can give him some lifts.'

'Yeah, that's a bloody good idea,' added Francis!

I was overjoyed, but I almost dropped my pint laughing at the way they were all trying to make me forever taller. I feared they would have me on stilts before they were satisfied!

So a deal was done, I signed a contract to play Detective Sergeant Russell, and the TV company sent me round to specialist boot makers, who crafted a superb pair of shoes for me that were built up three inches inside.

McStay, the swine, used to tease me by calling them my orthopaedic boots, but they were fantastic. They gave me a good three inches for jumping around in all the action scenes and were simply superb.

I kept them well after the series finished. But after that, I found I didn't need them. My characters have all been so powerful I haven't needed any extra inches to command respect. Baldwin, for instance, is such a big character height doesn't come into it.

No Hiding Place was a joy to do and Francis and McStay were simply wonderful to work — and play — with.

Raymond was incredible. He was so relaxed I put him on a par with Roger Moore. He never lost his temper and was never flustered. Which is more than can be said for me when he invited me for a get-to-know-each-other lunch at Simpsons on the first day of rehearsals.

'Let's make it just after 12 noon and we will have time for a beer and lunch,' he said, adding, 'and don't be late because we have to be in rehearsal at two.'

In those days, the series was transmitted live, with only the big action punch-ups and car chases filmed in advance. We also shot them extremely fast with just a 10-day turn-around between each hour-long episode.

We did three days of action filming, then completed the rest in just three days, including two days' rehearsal. To speed everything up, we used stand-ins who worked out all the moves in advance so that when we arrived they had already rehearsed the action and told us where to move. So it was vital that we weren't late.

On the day of the lunch, butterflies were dancing around in my stomach as I realised just how important it was for me to make a good impression with Raymond. So instead of driving and having to find somewhere to park, I thought I would go by train to Waterloo and then catch a taxi to Simpsons.

So I duly arrived outside the main doors of Simpsons, where a splendidly uniformed gentleman sprang forward, opened the taxi door, saluted, and asked me where I would like to go.

I said the restaurant and he asked, 'Are you meeting a member of staff for lunch?' When I said, 'I'm meeting Raymond Francis,' he said, 'I think you mean Simpsons in the Strand, sir.'

I had arrived at the famous clothes shop on Piccadilly!

With my face flushed a deeper shade of red than a beetroot, I hailed another taxi and finally arrived at the restaurant at 12.10pm.

'Where have you been?' asked Raymond, agitatedly waving his silver beer tankard in my direction. I was mortally embarrassed and made some elaborate excuse, never daring to tell him what a clanger I had dropped.

Raymond was in his element in the Victorian grandeur of Simpsons, with their great roasts carved at your table, discreet service and clubby atmosphere. Over the years I worked with him, I also became such a regular visitor to the restaurant that I also graduated to a special silver tankard for my beer. But my lips always remained firmly closed on the real reason for late arrival on our first lunch date.

I was only in my twenties when I joined *No Hiding Place*, so I didn't find the show particularly physically demanding, but it was for Raymond, especially night shoots. It explains why he never seemed to do many of them.

But, as I explained, Raymond wielded an enormous amount of power and was the only actor I know who had script approval. He used to get the scripts, first in green and then in pink and anything he didn't like he crossed out, before we finally got the finished white scripts. In the pink, for instance, it would have Raymond, Michael and myself on a night shoot, but by the time it got to the white, it would only have Michael and myself — with me having been given most of Raymond's lines!

It wasn't just the hours, however, that could make a night shoot particularly stressful. On one occasion, I was supposed to go into a cave where a robber, armed with a shotgun, was holed up. In the original script, Raymond was supposed to have gone into the cave and tackled the thug, but in the final script it was, as usual, down to me — for the robber had an Alsatian dog, which was to attack me!

'Oh, great,' I thought. But it was all part of the high adrenalin feel of the show and I have always enjoyed action scenes. The production crew were confident that the stunt would work perfectly. They had worked it out so that as the dog leaped at my throat, a stuntman would swing into action off camera, and grab the dog. But, like every actor, I knew that you can't rely on animals. And this stunt went spectacularly wrong. As we did the take, the dog ran right round the stuntman and flew straight at me. Fortunately, I had my arm up, as I was supposed to, for the dog, its jaws menacingly wide open, hurled itself at me — and sank its teeth into my arm.

The scene looked fantastic and the director was thrilled, but I finished the night being taken to hospital to have the bite dressed and be given an anti-tetanus injection. I took it as all part of a day's, or rather, night's work and reckoned we could use the accident to boost the show even further. I told the director that the dog attacking me would make great publicity along the lines of DOG SAVAGES JOHNNY BRIGGS. I was really keen but the front office bosses wouldn't have it. And instead of using the incident as a publicity boost, they insisted that we had to it keep it quiet.

But I thought I'd get one advantage out of the dog saga, and the next day I said to Raymond, 'After that, you can do the night shoots.'

He took it in good part and chuckled away as I waved my bandaged arm at him. But I had my own back on one of the rare occasions we had Raymond on a night shoot.

We were out filming in mucky fields until 2.00am and it was so wet we wore Wellingtons. When we finally wrapped for the night, Raymond said, 'Let's get back to the hotel for a couple of drinks.' Well, I was all for that after freezing for hours on end.

When we returned to the hotel, however, we found, to our horror, that we had been locked out. We had keys to get in, but someone had put the security chain on and we couldn't raise the night porter.

Raymond was furious. It was the only occasion I can recall him ever losing his cool and, momentarily, the urbane, courteous mask slipped as, without a moment's hesitation, he put his boot into the door. And Raymond kept kicking it until the door finally crashed open, and was left hanging drunkenly on its side, held up only by the chain.

'Oh God,' I thought, 'this is the end of me, they will sack me.' But Raymond didn't turn a hair and simply said, 'We had better find the night porter.' How the porter, or any of the other guests, had slept through the clatter is a complete mystery to me, but with Raymond, at his most magisterial, we marched through the downstairs rooms and eventually ran the porter to earth. When the porter saw the front door hanging by its chain, he moaned, 'Look what you have done to my door!' But Raymond, fixing the man with his most commanding and imperious look, barked, 'Never mind the door, you'd better fetch us two large whiskies first.'

The porter, completely overawed, scuttled away to return with the whiskies, which were the first of many on that long night. I felt a lot better with the whisky coursing through my veins, but I was still worried about the way we had wrecked the door. And while I realised that Raymond was above reproach as far as Rediffusion were concerned, I was convinced I would definitely get the sack.

But Raymond remained as cool as a cucumber. He was only irritated that he had had to waste so much time getting his whisky and, telling me not to fret, got the production manager to get the unit carpenter to come and fix the door when they returned from the shoot. The damage was finally repaired by 4.00am and, as a lot of scotch had been sunk and we had to be up at 7.00am, I said to Raymond, 'I am off to bed.'

He simply nodded, clutching his glass, as I weaved my way up the stairs.

The next morning I was woken by the phone ringing and, in panic, I thought, 'It's the producer telling me I've got the sack, or else I've badly overslept.'

But it was Raymond, turning on the charm and saying, 'Do you want to rehearse this morning's scene?' And before I could utter a word, he continued, 'Come to my room.' This was most unusual, for Raymond never normally bothered to do unscheduled rehearsals. So, quickly dressing, I went round to his room and knocked.

The moment he heard me, Raymond threw the door open, and ushered me inside, 'Ah, Johnny, come in , come in,' he greeted me warmly. He was already fully dressed in trousers, shirt, Wellington boots, the lot. I was impressed and said so, declaring, 'My, you're really keen.'

'Don't be a berk, ' he replied, with just a hint of a blush colouring his features. 'I haven't been to bed. I couldn't get these blasted Wellingtons off and have had to sleep in the chair,' he confessed. 'It's so embarrassing, I don't want anyone to know, so be a good chap and help me out of them.'

I thought it was hilarious. Here was the urbane and sophisticated Raymond Francis, who had been so firmly in control bossing everyone around the night before, worried that someone would know he couldn't get his wellies off. Suppressing the giggles I could feel welling up inside, I duly got down on the floor and eased his boots off.

'Oh, thank God for that!' Raymond said with a great sigh of relief as his boots hit the floor.

But then he started to worry in case I told Michael and everyone had a good chuckle at his expense. No-one, he told me, was ever to find out — and he insisted that I help him rumple up his bed so that it looked as though it had been used. Then, drawing himself up to his most imposing height, he warned me, 'I don't want anyone to know about this. If you tell anyone I will see you get the sack,' he said, with a twinkle in his eye.

I thought that was a bit heavy handed, but still seeing the funny side of Raymond's discomforture, I said, 'Why didn't you come and knock me up last night?'

'I did, three times,' he said.

'Well, I didn't hear you,' I told him.

'You didn't because you were pissed!' he retorted.

I resented that and told him so, arguing, 'I couldn't have been, because I haven't got a headache!'

It was a marvellously funny story at Raymond's expense, but I was still worried about the damaged door, so I dutifully kept my mouth shut. Whether Raymond could have had me fired if I had talked is debatable, but he could certainly have made life pretty hot for me. And, besides, I didn't want to make a fool of him. He was much too nice a gentleman.

That was the only time I ever saw Raymond flustered. Nothing bothered him when he was working, although we were doing the Number One show and it went out live, just before the main news. And that really put the pressure on us. If there was the tiniest slip up in the timing, the consequences were enormous. You were literally heading for a disaster — and eventually we had one — and ended up as a key item on the main news bulletin.

Raymond had been doing it for so long that he made it look easy, but we all had to keep an eye on the floor manager, who timed the live broadcasts on a stop watch.

Stop watch timing was essential because then, just as they are now, the advertisers were the kings, and we had to ensure that we came up to the commercial breaks at the exact moment they began. Otherwise, we would be chopped in mid-action as a jingle for washing powder or coffee filled the screen in our place.

If we were running too fast the floor manager would signal us to slow down, or else there would be a blank screen before the commercials began. In the same way he would signal us to speed up if we were running a fraction late.

Normally, it worked like a dream. Associated-Redifussion was such a professional organisation they had everything taped and we were all used to working on live shows. But one night, disaster struck.

In this particular episode, they were giving Raymond, as Lockhart, a break and in the storyline he had to go away on a course after we had started on a new case. But before he left, he told McStay and myself, as Perryman and Russell, that he was convinced one of three people was guilty of some particular crime. Michael and I duly solved the case, but the viewers didn't know who the real villain was because we had arrested all three key suspects.

At the end of the episode, in the lead up to revealing just who was guilty, I, as Russell, came into the office and said to

McStay's Perryman, 'I told you so.'

He said, 'How did you know?'

'I had this gut feeling.'

'Are you going to tell the Guvnor?'

'Yeah.' I answered.

'Who did he think it was?' Perryman said.

'He didn't think it was him,' I told him, just as Raymond, as Lockhart, walked in having finished his course.

Putting down his case, Raymond asked, 'Now I have got to know, was it who I said it was?'

Then, just as I began, 'No. It was ...' CUT.

The commercials cut in just as I was in mid-sentence, leaving millions of viewers totally mystified as to who the guilty man was.

There was uproar and the switchboard was swamped with complaints from angry viewers desperate to know the outcome.

No Hiding Place had such huge ratings and there was such a fuss that the show had been chopped off the air at such a crucial moment because it over-ran by seconds, that the ITV bosses put out a special bulletin on the main news, which followed the show.

So, along with all the politics and national and world news, the newscaster announced, 'We have had so many people jamming the phone lines to find out who was the guilty man in tonight's No Hiding Place, that I have to tell you that it was so and so ...'

But, surprisingly, even when things went as monumentally wrong as on that occasion, we didn't find working under those conditions particularly stressful. Nowadays people think it must have been a nightmare working on live shows like No Hiding Place, but Raymond took it in his stride and Michael and I were so young we didn't even think about it. And it was quite normal for those days. Z Cars started live and they had real problems — with technicians walking across the back of the action scenes! But the Rediffusion crew were really clued up, with second units and third units — and they were all equally good.

We also had some very good directors like John Franco, whose father Ronald was a comedian, and Ian Fordyce and Peter Croft, the brother of David Croft, who has created some of our greatest comedy classics, such as *Dad's Army*, *It Ain't Half Hot, Mum*, *Hi-De-Hi!* and *'Allo 'Allo*.

I was in *No Hiding Place* from 1963 until my final episode, *Bottle Full of Sixpences*, in May 1966 and it was such an enormous hit that Mike and I were mobbed by girls wherever we went. The adulation we received was just incredible, and, in many ways, was far more intrusive than anything I have ever received from fans since I joined *Coronation Street*. There were only three of us then, whereas in the *Street* there are a lot more stars. So the pressure on Raymond, whose suave charm delighted the mums, Michael and myself was far more intense. Not that I ever complained. It was wonderful, but I was married and Caroline must have found it difficult to deal with. Michael, however, was single, so it was much easier for him to deal with screaming girls trying to kiss him.

But, let's be honest, what fella wouldn't enjoy being chased by girls all the time? It was great and we took it in our stride. Besides, Mike and I were great flirts. Mike eventually married one of the most beautiful girls of the time, Jennifer Culow, who used to look a little like Grace Kelly.

Mike was one of the nicest guys I have worked with. He had a great sense of humour and, with Raymond, we worked as a superb trio. It was three of the happiest years of my acting career.

As the two young stars of the show, Mike and I used to be invited to everything and we had some tremendous fun. On one occasion, we were asked to be guests of honour at the opening of Britain's first bowling alley at Heathrow. Hugh Hefner had just opened his first Playboy Club in Britain and some of his stunning Bunny girls were there too, so it was a really glitzy event.

We were expected to say a few words at the opening ceremony and I tried to dump that boring task on Michael. But when I asked him, 'Will you do the speech?' he refused outright, saying, 'No, you do it. I am not so good at making these speeches.' He then got stuck into the vodka and started really to enjoy himself. In fact, he had such a good time that, half a bottle later, he had sufficiently mellowed to suddenly volunteer to make the speech. One look at him should have told me this spelt trouble, but I was delighted to be let off the hook and thought, 'Now I can really have a good time.'

So I said fine, relaxed and had another drink. But I wasn't relaxed for long. Mike swaggered on to the stage with the directors of the company opening the alley, and within moments of him starting his speech I was desperately trying to hide under the table.

'It's very nice of you to ask Johnny and myself to open this bowling alley along with all these Bunny girls,' said Mike, beaming broadly at the Playboy babes. 'They are very beautiful, and I think my sister must be a Bunny girl, because Johnny says she goes like a rabbit!'

You could have heard a pin drop in the deathly two-second silence that greeted Mike's joke. I was praying the earth would open and swallow me up, when, suddenly, the silence was broken by a great roar as the hundreds of guests started to cheer and stamp their feet. Mike was the hero of the hour — and I vowed that from that night on he would always make the speeches in future.

But while Mike had pulled off a great coup, I really put my foot in it one New Year's Eve. Because of the popularity of No Hiding Place, we were frequently asked to do guest appearances on other television shows and on this occasion I had to sit in a chair on the hit pop programme Ready Steady Go while Sandie Shaw sang to me to usher in the New Year — live!

In those days, they used to transmit the show live from the Lyceum in London between 11.00pm and 12.30am, which would normally have given me plenty of time to travel from the set of No Hiding Place in Wembley to Ready Steady Go in the West End. But that particular night we were running late on No Hiding Place and I was starting to get into a mild panic as the clock ticked away.

Finally, they called a wrap for the evening and I dashed off the set and into my dressing room to change into my dinner suit. I then raced to the lift, just as a vicar came out of make-up.

At the time, Ian Hendry was doing a show called *The Informer*, in which he played a struck-off barrister who worked as a police informer and, assuming the 'vicar' was in it, I started effing and blinding, moaning that this was the one fucking day I didn't want to be late. Then, turning to the 'vicar' I said, 'Oh, what are you in? Are you doing Ian Hendry's show?'

'No,' he replied, 'actually, I'm reading the epilogue.'

'Oh, Father,' I mumbled, blushing with embarrassment. 'I'm sorry.'

'I'm not a Father,' he admonished.

I blurted out, 'Oh well, I'm terribly sorry anyhow,' and made a very fast exit from the lift.

By then, I had had plenty of experience of moving fast on my feet — and it saved me on more than one occasion when we were filming the action scenes. But Mike wasn't always so lucky and one day he came a real cropper when a passer-by thought he was in the middle of a real-life police chase.

We were filming in Villiers Street, next to London's Charing Cross railway station, and, as was usual in those days, we hadn't cleared the whole street while we shot the scene. We had a camera set up on a roof to zoom in on the action when a police car, carrying Michael and myself, roared around the corner and screamed to a halt. We were supposed to be chasing a villain and Michael said to me, 'Can you see him?'

I said 'No, I can't.'

At that moment, the villain stepped out of a doorway and I yelled, 'Yes, there he is.'

In the plot, the villain, having spotted the police car, started to run. At which point, Michael and I leapt out of the car and, followed by the driver and another policeman, both of whom were in uniform, raced after him.

We all started running down the street, with me in the

lead, after the actor playing the villain. At the end of the chase I was supposed to rugby tackle the fleeing villain and when Michael caught up with us, he was to put the man in an arm lock before we marched him away under arrest. But it didn't work out like that at all.

As we were running down the street towards Embankment underground station, an old boy with a walking stick, who had nothing to do with the filming but was out walking his dog, looked up and saw the 'villain' running towards him. Then he saw me pounding along behind, followed by Michael. Then he spotted the two uniformed 'policemen' chasing after us.

He assumed we were three villains fleeing from the uniformed coppers, and decided to do something about it. But he was elderly and a bit slow in his reactions. So the villain in the plot succeeded in racing passed him, swiftly followed by myself. Michael wasn't so lucky. As he tore alongside, the old man, swinging his walking stick like a baseball bat, went WALLOP! smashing Michael straight on the head with it.

It was a terrific blow and Michael span in a complete pirouette, before collapsing to the ground.

I heard the crack, but, not realising what had happened, I carried on running. When, however, I couldn't see Michael out of the corner of my eye, I turned round to see what had happened to him. To my surprise, Michael was lying prostrate on the ground with a group of people bending over him.

'Oh,' I thought, 'something has gone wrong. We will have to do another take.'

So I and the 'villain', not realising just how badly it had gone wrong, started to amble back up the street towards Michael lying on the ground. As we got closer, we saw Michael had blood pouring from his head.

Meanwhile, the old guy with the walking stick, realising that we were only shooting a film, had vanished into the crowd.

Michael was taken to hospital, where they stitched up his

wound and kept him in for observation. Filming was cancelled for the day and we were all worried about Michael. But he was as tough in real life as on television. He came out of hospital the next morning — and we shot it all over again.

Normally, however, everything was so beautifully rehearsed, we had very few accidents, and the only injury I ever suffered was the dog bite!

The only problem with being in the show was that people believed Michael and I were real life policemen — and that could have a sobering effect on your social life — as we discovered when we went in search of a late-night drink after a long day's filming.

In the Sixties, pub licensing hours were strictly enforced and you could only get a drink after hours if you were friendly with a landlord and he would throw a private 'party.' So the last person late-night revellers wanted to see was a copper. The very sight of one was guaranteed to clear a pub — and that's just what we did.

That particular night we finished filming in Hammersmith at 11.15pm and I said to Mike, 'Shall we have one before we go back?' He reckoned it was too late and said, 'Where will we get one now?' But I was confident I could get one at a pub where I was friendly with the landlord and said, 'We will get one at the Catherine Wheel.'

'Are you sure?' said Mike, but I told him not to worry and told our driver to take us to the pub. When we arrived, as the lights were still on, I got out of the car and peered in over the top of the pub's half-frosted windows.

As I had hoped, there were still a dozen people in the bar, and I knocked on the window so that the landlord could let Mike and me in. As I knocked, the drinkers turned in my direction — and panicked. The moment they saw me, convinced I was a real copper, they started diving for cover. You have never seen drinkers abandon a bar so fast; as they fled out the back to hide in the toilets! The landlord, who knew me, fell around laughing, and let Mike and myself in for a drink. Sheepishly, the drinkers who hadn't dived out of the pub through the lavatory windows, came back and joined us and it was shaping up for a good night, when our driver told us he was on overtime, and so Mike and I sadly had to leave.

7

No Hiding Place changed my life. I settled into a family routine at home and my two eldest children, Mark and Karen, were born. After living in a succession of bed-sits, in 1965 I also bought my first house, a brand new town house in Percy Avenue, in Ashford, Middlesex, for £3,500. We were the Number One show and I also appeared for the first time on the front cover of the *TV Times*, along with Raymond and Michael. Life was good, but clouds were gathering ...

In an attempt to get over the shock of Barbara's death, my mother used to run a mobile hairdressing service for invalids and old-age pensioners from my parents' bungalow by the River Thames at Staines. For years, she had ridden to each appointment on a bicycle, but had long coveted a moped to speed up her travelling. It was during my last year with *No Hiding Place* that I decided I should do something about it, and bought her a moped.

She was thrilled as it made her life so much easier. I didn't think much more about it. I was either busy filming, playing the family man or getting in a round of golf.

Then, one day, my mother told me that the scooter needed a service.

'So what!' I said.

'I don't think I can afford it,' she replied, so I told her to get it serviced, adding that I would pay. She duly took the scooter into the garage, with my father following her in his car so he could drive her home. When the scooter was ready, my father drove her to the garage to pick it up and said he would follow her home.

It was one of those everyday journeys we don't even think about. But this trip was to have another shattering effect on my family. As with Barbara's death, it all seemed so ordinary and routine. One moment my mother was serenely riding through the streets of Staines, the next she was in a horrific crash when a lorry came out of a side street and smashed into her, knocking her under a Rover car.

My horrified father jumped out of his car and raced to where my mother lay with appalling head injuries. Realising immediately that she was far too badly injured for him to make any attempt to move her until medical help arrived, he carefully placed a coat over my mother to keep her warm, and then gave vent to his grief and fury. My father was by then so distraught that he tried to murder the lorry driver. He hurled himself at the man and was attempting to strangle him when he was pulled off by passers-by.

When the police and ambulance men arrived, my father was still so consumed with anger at the the lorry driver's reckless driving, that the police told the driver to get into his cab and keep it locked for his own safety. My mother was then rushed by ambulance to Atkinson Morley Hospital, in Wimbledon, the same brain specialist hospital to which Barbara had eventually been taken, and where my sister had died.

This made the accident even more difficult for my father to cope with as it brought all the old memories flooding back. Fortunately, my mother didn't die, but she lost an eye and ended up paralysed down her left-hand side. She had to have a caliper on her leg and, as with my sister, I again blamed myself for the accident.

When I heard the awful news, I went into shock and thought, 'Oh, Christ, if only I hadn't given her that bike this wouldn't have happened.' I was mortified. The fact that a few years before I had begged my mother to buy me a motorcycle, but she had refused, fearing I might have an accident, made me feel even worse.

I was terribly distressed by it. I started to fear I was jinxed as far as my family were concerned. It was terrible. I found it very hard to come to terms with, but I finally threw off the worst feelings of guilt when a pal pointed out that the accident could have happened if she had been on her ordinary bicycle and told me I shouldn't hold myself responsible.

My mother took a similar line when one day I blurted out my feelings of guilt to her. 'Don't be silly,' she told me. But the guilt still haunts me. And at the time, I decided that at least I could make the lorry driver pay for wrecking my parents' life.

On *No Hiding Place*, we had a technical adviser, George Davis, who was a former detective inspector, and I felt he was just the man to help me on my quest for vengeance. So I phoned him and asked him to get me the address of the lorry driver.

'What for?' he immediately asked.

'Because, between you and me,' I replied 'I am going to have a word with the boys and I am going to have him either done over or killed — and if they kill him, that's fine by me.'

He came straight round to see me, calmed me down and told me not to be so stupid. But I was still bent on revenge and said, 'I tell you this, George, if I find out where he lives, I am phoning the boys, and, to make sure I am not implicated, I will be miles away at the time.'

George eventually talked me out of it, but I was quite prepared to have the guy either severely beaten or killed. And I wouldn't have had any conscience about it whatsoever.

The lorry driver was later convicted for dangerous driving, but I was absolutely shattered by that accident. It was dreadful, and revived all the bitter memories of

Barbara's death from a simple fall.

Despite all the pain and her injuries, my mother lived for another ten years, eventually dying in 1976 from leukaemia. But she had been severely injured and had difficulty getting around.

So I came up with another present, which was to prove an absolute boon to my mother and gave her a reason to clamber painfully out of bed in the mornings.

I won £25 on the Premium Bonds, which were the big national flutter in those days, and bought her a little white poodle. That dog became a real companion to her and wherever she went, the dog went, too. It gave her a new lease of life, because it meant she couldn't vegetate and had to get up to feed the dog and to let it out when my father was at work. Just as I had hoped, the dog was an incentive that gave her back the will to live.

Despite my mother's disability, my parents managed to cope and when my mother finally died, my father seemed OK, until he fell under the spell of a woman, called Ivy, who had found out where he lived from a magazine.

Ivy was a widow and she telephoned my father out of the blue, telling him that she had known my mother when they were young. She went on to say that they had been good friends and, together with Ivy's husband, they had gone out in a threesome. Having established her credentials, she went down to the bungalow to see my father, and the next thing I knew they were going to be married. I was absolutely amazed, but if she made my father happy that was OK by me.

I wasn't so pleased, however, when my father died from cancer. He hadn't made a will so Ivy inherited everything. She picked up the lot; I didn't get the watch I bought him, the car I bought him, or the money he owed me. I was so angry and upset that, initially, I put a stop to all his assets. But my solicitor advised me against it, pointing out that she was my father's widow and that as my father hadn't left a will she was entitled to inherit it all.

I was very bitter about the whole business because my mother had expected Dad to leave everything to me. When I went to see my mother in hospital just before she died — and she must have known that she was dying — she told me, 'Look, I have not made a will, because there is only you and your father and when he goes, you will, naturally, get everything.'

What made it even more painful was that after his funeral, Ivy came up to me saying, 'That's the name of the undertaker. Pick up your father's ashes. I don't know what to do with them!'

At the time of my mother's accident, I was moving towards the end of my run with *No Hiding Place*, although I didn't realise it at the time.

We were still at Number One, and we were all still enjoying making the series. But, paradoxically, our very success was to lead to Michael and myself quitting — and the show finally crumbling.

We were being paid £250 per episode, which was big money in the Sixties and we were certainly quite well paid for what we did in *No Hiding Place*, compared to the variety artists. But we wanted more, and considering the huge success of the show and the fortune it was pulling in for Rediffusion from the advertisers, we didn't think we were being unreasonable. And I still don't think we were.

Raymond was paid a lot, lot more than Michael and myself, and we were only asking for an extra £25 per episode, to take our money to £275. Those really were the golden years of ITV, when it was once famously remarked that owning an ITV franchise was a licence to print money. We argued that as we were only working for six months of the year we should get a pay rise. Under the system that Rediffusion operated, we worked in three-month blocks — three months on and three off, and that prevented us from taking on much other work. And the company wouldn't let us do commercials, for fear that an advertiser might try and slide a slot into *No Hiding Place*.

Because we were the nation's top show, the pressure was always on us to keep the standard up. So when you had a three-month break, you didn't tend to do much, other than the odd guest appearance in a Rep that was struggling and wanted to revive its fortunes with a big TV name. That would take a month — two weeks' rehearsal and then the two weeks of the show — and when you finished you just wanted to rest to clear the air.

So I don't feel our demands were unreasonable, but, looking back, we should have stayed in the show. It was the best series of its time and was really too good to walk away from. Now I know better and always advise actors to stay with winning formulas unless they have something very solid lined up. Otherwise, you end up full of regrets — and that's never healthy. I regret leaving now. It was fun to do, we were a superb team, and we were surrounded by people who liked the show. But it wasn't *No Hiding Place* that Michael and I were annoyed with, but Rediffusion.

I thought we were entitled to a little bit more and didn't think that asking for an additional £25 an episode was greedy. If I had demanded, 'Double our fee,' or even asked for another £100, an episode I could have understood the bosses' reluctance to pay up, but they dug their toes in and wouldn't budge. Neither would Michael and I. I suppose it came down to the accountants, who worked out that if they got rid of Michael and myself and replaced us with just one actor — which is what they did — they would save a lot of money, and make even more profit.

Finally, it came to the crunch. We couldn't reach an agreement so Michael and I gave them a final ultimatum: either they paid up or we would quit. They wouldn't pay, so I said, 'Right, that's it.' I said to Michael, 'I'm off, but you can stay if you want to, mate.'

'No,' he said. 'If you are going, I am going.'

I urged him to think twice, saying, 'Don't be silly, If you want to stay and do it, stay.'

But Mike was adamant. Like me, he felt they were giving us the runaround. What really annoyed me was that they wouldn't even offer a token rise, of £15 or £12.50. Even my agent thought they would have given me £10 — and I would have settled for that. But they just said 'No.' They wanted a complete victory and I thought that was wrong. Raymond was on an extortionate rate of pay, apart from script approval and all his other perks.

But although they wouldn't give us anything, they wanted our help to smooth over such a huge blow to the series. The Rediffusion bosses were well aware of the damage that could be caused to the show by having two of the three stars walk out in a row over money. So they then asked us not to tell the papers before they had signed a replacement, to which we agreed. But somehow the story leaked and one night I was awoken at midnight by the telephone and a reporter asked, 'Would you like to give your side?' I denied the whole story, saying, 'No, it is completely untrue.'

The press, however, eventually tracked down Michael, who was holidaying in Spain, at 3.30am — and the story hit the papers, causing panic at Rediffusion. I then received a frantic phone call from Muriel Cole, the casting director, in which she claimed I had betrayed them. I told her that I had done no such thing, but that led to a lot of bad blood between Muriel and Michael and myself over our decision to quit.

What made our departure even more annoying, was that I discovered that our replacement, Sean Caffrey, as Detective Sergeant Gregg, was paid less than we were. They just couldn't resist saving a few bob wherever they possibly could.

Strangely, I didn't think it was a gamble at the time because Michael and I were confident that we would be going on to another series.

Raymond stayed on and Sean was signed up to do 13 episodes. But they only made the first six. When they were screened, the ratings plummeted to rock bottom and the show was taken off.

The Rediffusion bosses were furious and Muriel Cole said it was all my fault, blaming the collapse in the ratings on our departure.

By the time I quit *No Hiding Place*, I had quite a bit of money in the bank and so at first I sat back while I decided what I would do next.

Fortunately, I had already done quite a bit in the theatre, films and television so I didn't think I'd have any problem with being typecast, but I found that I had been. Once again, I found myself being pigeonholed by casting directors and I had a terrible time trying to find work. People were keen enough to cash in on my name and the *No Hiding Place* fame, but I turned down all the tatty tours I was offered. I was only getting £25 a week when I was playing a lead at the Royal Court and that was still the salary for the West End. I used to say, 'It's not art for art's sake. I can't pay the bills with my name on the letterhead. I need hard cash.' It is all right when you have your millions in the bank to work at the Royal Court for theatrical prestige, but I couldn't afford it.

That is when my life started to go to pieces — the lean period when I just couldn't get work. It is a period every actor and actress goes through; I don't think there is an actor who has not been through it, and it lasted for 18 very long months. It was awful, absolutely dreadful, especially with two young children who looked to their father to support them.

They were growing kids and they needed new clothes, apart from the most basic essentials like food and warmth, let alone the odd treat. I used to wake up in the middle of the night fretting and wondering where the next month's mortgage was coming from.

That is when you start selling your watch and various bits and pieces to get some money for groceries and the kids' shoes. That was the start of my first marriage dissolving because Caroline probably thought, 'Well, you can't be any good at acting, or you would be working.'

I tried to explain that acting is one of the few professions where people don't want to be unemployed — they genuinely want to work. It was not through lack of trying that I wasn't working, it was just one of those things. I had to get a part and I had to be right for it. And it is the old Catch 22 situation, where you can't take a job outside the profession because if you do, and you then get an interview for a part, you can't go to the audition because you can't get the day off!

So it eventually led to the collapse of my marriage. And goodness knows I didn't want the marriage to end, as it inevitably did some years later. It was horrendous. I didn't want to leave my children. I loved them and adored them. Who would want to leave the 11-year-old boy and 9-year-old daughter you adored? You are put on earth to provide for them and love them.

Fortunately, other people did have faith in me, like my old pal Captain Brian Wallace, who was a pilot with British Airways. It was during this dreadful period that he rang me up one day and said, 'How about a game of golf?'

'Sorry,' I said, 'but I can't.'

'Why?' he asked.

'I am having a bit of a problem with the bank,' I replied.

'What's that?' he then inquired.

'Well, I have a gas bill, and then there's the phone bill and the electricity bill, and I can't actually pay them.'

So he said, 'Go and see your bank manager and I will meet you at the golf club at 11.00am. And bring the bills with you.' But I still protested, saying it would be embarrassing for me to be in the club because I couldn't afford to buy a drink. Brian, however, was insistent and said, 'There will be a time when you can afford to buy me a drink, let me pay for it.' So I took the bills along — the gas bill was about £8, the phone bill about £12 and the electricity bill was about the same.

Brian said, 'Leave those with me.' And he paid them, and never asked for the money back.

It wasn't just the gas and electric I couldn't pay. At times I couldn't even pay the milkman. I was on the dole, but it didn't cover all my costs with a young family and I was desperate. But, in the end, I pulled through and started to get work again.

I have known Brian for 30 years, since we first met at a children's playgroup that both our daughters attended. I used to drive Karen there and back in my pride and joy — a splendid Rolls-Royce Bentley — and one day in 1967, while I was waiting for Karen to come out, he came up to me and asked if he knew me from the airline business. In those days, he was a First Officer and whenever he wasn't flying he used to collect his daughter Linda. I told him he probably recognised me from *No Hiding Place* and we started chatting. He was keen to take up golf again and when I told him I was a member of Ashford Manor golf club he asked if he could phone me for a game. We played soon afterwards and hit it off from the start. Then, when Engelbert Humperdinck joined the club, we all played together regularly, often with guests Engelbert would bring along. Freddie Starr used to join us and we had a lot of fun.

When Brian finally retired three years ago, Engelbert and I promised we would go on his last flight, which was to Johannesburg. Unfortunately, Engelbert couldn't make it because he was on a concert tour in America, but I did. I kept my promise, and wouldn't have missed it for the world. It was a five-day trip during which we played golf in Sun City, on a course where you have to drive over a pool full of crocodiles!

When we landed at Heathrow on our return from South Africa, there was a kilted Scottish piper waiting on the tarmac. He boarded the plane as they broke open the champagne and, to the skirl of the pipes, we toasted Brian. There was a huge cake and we had a magnificent party. A great occasion.

Brian bought the home of Bobby Davro's father, Bill Nankerville — a gold medal winner in the 1936 Olympics — at Ashford, in Middlesex. And every time Brian and I now see Bobby he tries to buy the house back. It isn't surprising because it is a lovely place with its own swimming pool, but Brian won't sell. Whenever I stay with Brian I always sleep in Bobby's old room, and tease him about it, saying, 'Kept your room warm last week!'

I certainly needed pals like Brian in my lean period. After the giddy success I had enjoyed it was a bitter lesson in how your luck can change overnight. But I was still confident that I could get the next break that would put me back at the top. I knew it was all about getting the right job. If I landed that I would be on my way again. But the real offers didn't come. I wasn't prepared to compromise and do a load of rubbish as I realised, tough though those times were, that if I lost credibility I was finished.

Sadly, Caroline couldn't understand that. She thought I was lazy and wasn't trying. Trying! I would have given my right arm for the right role. You are not 'resting' because you want to, or you haven't tried, it is because there is no part available.

But Caroline couldn't understand. I was confident in my ability, but she wasn't — and that is what ruined our marriage. If she had had a bit more faith in me and realised I wanted to be an actor more than anything else in the world, I think we would probably, and I emphasise the word 'probably,' still have been together. It was her lack of faith that finished us.

She couldn't understand that you can't get an acting role unless you are asked. You can't demand; you have to wait to be asked. She loved it when I was in *No Hiding Place* and I was flavour of the month. But she couldn't cope with me not working and having to borrow money from friends. But that is what friends are for — as long as you pay them back. I think she is regretting it now.

Muriel Cole had threatened vengeance over my departure from *No Hiding Place* and after a time I thought she was getting it — in spades. In fact, it was just the way things can go when you come out of a top show and producers are wary of using you because they feel you may still be too closely associated with your last hit production.

I am not lazy and I was desperate for work. But when your luck is out it is out. Period. Life was tough at home as I fretted about getting a job and I jumped every time the phone rang. So I finally decided to take Caroline on holiday to Spain. She protested that I was just being lazy and should be getting a new starring role, but I insisted that the break would do us both good. And, eventually, off we went. We hadn't been there five minutes when I thought the Spanish break had done the trick and pulled me round the corner. My agent phoned me from England saying that I was wanted for a major television advertising campaign for Aspro. 'Brilliant', I thought. Some prime-time advertising slots were just what I needed to get the Briggs face back in front of the viewers. And, even more importantly, the money was very good.

The advertisers were so keen to have me that they flew me back to London, where a limousine was waiting to whisk me from Heathrow Airport to the London studios. This was the sort of treatment I liked, especially as when I got to the office I was jumped to the head of the queue and taken in to see the bigwigs organising the advertising campaign. Then my luck ran out. They took one look at me and said, 'You don't look like the sort of person who has a headache.' And that was it. Cancelled without even speaking a line. I was, for once, dumbstruck. I couldn't believe it. But they had made up their minds that I wasn't the headache sort with a single glance. They drove me straight back to the airport and I was back in Spain that evening.

Caroline just couldn't cope with that — and blamed me!

In a bid to raise some cash I took my first non-acting job when I joined Abbey Life. They liked the fact that I played golf and encouraged me to play with clients. But they didn't pay the green fees, which was an expense I could ill afford, and I soon realised the only people making any money out of it were the ones for whom I was working! I also realised that if I was to ever break back in acting I had to be available for work, so, after a couple of months, I packed it in.

After 18 months without any acting work — and they were the longest months of my life — I was really desperate. I had sold everything I cherished to raise a few bob and was at my wits end, when there appeared light at the end of a very dark tunnel. Ray Cooney was putting on *Doctor at Sea* in Blackpool, and I was offered the role of the cockney steward. I was so delighted to be working again that I went into the Green Room Club with my old pal Alec Ross to celebrate. While we were having a drink there, we bumped into Bill Fraser, who was moaning and groaning that he hadn't worked since *Bootsie and Snudge*, and they weren't doing the follow-up series until the following February.

I was in such a good mood that, foolishly as it worked out, I said to Bill, 'I have been offered this role in *Doctor at Sea*, why don't you get in touch with Cooney, because you could play the irascible surgeon Lancelot Spratt?'

The next day, I realised how badly I had shot myself in the foot when my agent rang up and said, 'Why don't you keep your mouth shut until the contract is signed!' Then he dropped the bombshell. 'Fraser has talked Cooney into having Alfie Bass (Fraser's co-star in *Bootsie and Snudge*) for your part, while Fraser is doing Lancelot Spratt.'

I was beside myself with fury and frustration. And I gave vent to my anger when Cooney asked to see me. He apologised profusely, and gave me a bottle of vodka. I told him where he could stick his vodka — and as far as I know it's still there!

It was a terrible blow because the job would have paid £200 a week for three weeks. I was absolutely crushed, and I thought my luck would never turn.

During the long months of unemployment, the mortgage on my new home at Ashford may have felt like a millstone at times, but the move soon proved a winner socially. I had earlier joined Ashford Manor Golf Club and found that I could temporarily escape from my worries on the golf course as I strove to improve my game. Then, as now, golf played a large part in my life and I made some life-long friends. Ashford was also near the the film studios, particularly Shepperton, and I used to have a regular meet with a group of stars in the oak-panelled, fifteenth-century Anchor on Shepperton's Church Square.

I had long been a pal of Ian Hendry, who had scored a big hit in the film *Live Now Pay Later* and the television series *Police Surgeon*, which quickly evolved into *The Avengers*. In his time, Ian played a lot of hard drinkers, which took no acting effort on Ian's part. He could drink for Britain, and his wife, Janet Monro, liked a drop, too.

In a bid to curb his boozing, Ian bought a house on an

island in the River Thames near Shepperton. He reckoned that living on an island would make it more difficult for him to just pop out of the house and nip down to the pub for a quick one. Well, the theory was right, but it wasn't a very effective deterrent. Ian was by then extremely successful and drove a magnificent Bentley, which he used to keep parked beside his mooring on the banks of the Thames opposite the island. So when he went off to work, or wanted to go for a drink, Ian would row across to it from the island in a little dinghy, and then drive down to the Anchor to join John Gregson, the much admired film actor then playing Commander George Gideon in the TV series *Gideon's Way*, and myself.

We used to have the most marvellous sessions in which we would sink a fair drop, which didn't exactly improve Ian's driving skills. He would roar off down the road towards his mooring at the end of a splendid evening — and, frequently misjudging his braking distance, wouldn't stop soon enough. It would then be a case of 'Oh, fucking hell!' as, with an almighty splash, the Bentley's front wheels shot into the drink!

On other occasions, when Ian managed to stop the car safely and totter into his boat, he still wouldn't make it back home under his own steam. He would cast off, and, rowing in an unsteady crab, would miss the island completely, drifting off down stream in the current.

It happened so frequently that it was almost routine for him to be picked up eventually by the river police, who would tow him back to his island home..

But Ian was in good company in the unsteady Bentley drivers' stakes.

There was a retired naval captain who used to drive his sit-up-and-beg Bentley to the Anchor for a bracer or three. He was splendid company and could have drunk the Thames dry, but he was an even more lethal driver than Ian.

Inevitably, he was banned for drink driving, but a little detail like that wasn't going to stop him from driving to the pub for a morning tipple. He bought a horse and trap for his expeditions to the pub — and was then banned for being drunk in charge of a horse and carriage! So he resorted to using a bicycle, and was eventually even banned from riding a bike, because he was still a total menace to every motorist, weaving all over the road, causing cars to crash! Finally, his wife made him get a taxi.

It was a marvellous drinking school in the Anchor: John Gregson, who had a house opposite the pub; Ian; a choreographer with the Royal Ballet called David, who used to throw fantastic parties to which he would bring all the ballerinas; and a very good friend of mine, John Dark, who was assistant producer of the spoof James Bond film *Casino Royale*, which starred Peter Sellers, David Niven, Ursula Andress, Orson Welles, Woody Allen and just about everyone else.

We were in there as usual one Monday, when this Welshman came in chattering away and splashing his money around ordering bottles of champagne. We couldn't understand a bloody word he said and didn't take a lot of notice until one of the locals said, 'Do you know who that is?' We all looked blank, and then he added, 'That's the singer who was on *Sunday Night at the London Palladium*.'

'Oh, yes,' we said, totally unimpressed, and carried on drinking. But we eventually invited him to join us and discovered that he was called Tom Jones. Tom had just made it big with 'It's Not Unusual', which was a hit both in Britain and in America, where they thought he was black. He had bought singer Dicky Valentine's house, which was just around the corner from the pub, and he was soon one of the regulars.

Tom swiftly became very, very rich and famous, but he kept that little house for quite a while. We used to call it the The Goldfish Bowl, because one side of the house was a wall of glass and anyone could look in as they walked past. But it didn't seem to bother Tom. He was always going away on tours, particularly to America, and he would bring back trophies from all over the world — African masks, Indian artworks — and hang them on the wall opposite this huge window. It was like an Aladdin's cave with spears from Africa, goat pipes from Turkey and so on.

So Tom became a member of our drinking club, but he was not one of the most generous. He had deep pockets and short arms. When we were drinking halves of bitter he would always be on champagne. You would say to him, 'What would you like to drink?' and he would say, 'Ooh, I can only drink champagne because of my voice.' We took a pretty dim view of that and would say, 'Oh, well, you'd better buy your own drink then!'

He used to laugh it off, but we really caught him out when he had nodules on his throat and couldn't talk for ten days.

Tom had bought himself a little pad on which he would write down everything, so that he could carry on conversations, and we were waiting for him when he walked into the pub one night after dinner.

'Oh, hello, Tom, how are you? Alright?' we chorused, adding, 'Buying us a drink?'

Tom nodded, reaching for his notepad, but his smile vanished when we added, 'Right, we'll have four bottles of champagne. Sign here!'

Tom's face was a picture as, desperately searching for his pad, and growing redder and redder, with perspiration beading his forehead, he anguishly croaked, 'No. No. NO.'

We didn't want the champagne, of course, but Tom fell for the wind-up hook, line and sinker, and we fell about laughing at his discomfiture.

We used to drink in the Anchor on Monday and Wednesday evenings, and on a Wednesday we would usually stay until midnight because Derek, the landlord, would throw a private party once the non-regulars had left. Derek was very good to us and would spend the evenings keeping people away from us so we didn't have to sign autographs.

It was all very matey, but one night this little bloke came in and shuffled up to the bar with one of those curious gaits much favoured by car park attendants who always look as though they need a hip replacement. Looking every inch the nightmare pub bore, with his flat cap jammed over his eyes and his little nicotine-stained moustache twitching under his nose, he sidled up to Derek and grumbled belligerently, ''Ere, over the road there, bitter is penny a pint cheaper than over here. Why is that?'

To which, the landlord, affecting his grandest tone, and dramatically sweeping his arm in our direction, replied, 'Because, my dear boy, over there you don't have the likes of Mr Johnny Briggs, Mr Ian Hendry, Mr Tom Jones, Mr Fergis Cashin (a Fleet Street critic) and Mr John Gregson, the celebrated actor!'

Game, set and match to the landlord, or so he thought.

But the little bloke coolly looked us up and down, pondered a moment, and then, turning back to the landlord, declared, 'Well, throw the fuckers out — and reduce the price of your beer!'

Derek was the sort of landlord who, when you went in would say, 'What are you going to have?' I only drank halves of bitter, but the boys would be on whatever — there would be a brandy and John would be on scotch, and so on — but I never saw Derek put any money into the till. So when there was a stock-take coming up he would say, 'Oh Christ, I'm short. I want a crate of scotch, two crates of gin ...' So he used to go across to Archie, who was the owner of the pub opposite, The Kings Head, and say, 'Can you lend me so and so ...' Archie would oblige, and when the brewery came round for the check, everything would be fine. Derek would then take the booze back.

Eventually, however, a couple of days before Christmas, an agitated Derek rang me up and said, 'Are you coming round on Monday?'

'Yeah. Sure,' I replied. 'I'll be coming round with the boys.'

'Well, I won't be there,' he said.

'But it's just before Christmas, Are you going away?'

'No. The brewery people came around this morning and we were asked to leave — immediately.' He then explained that, as he opened the pub doors at 10.30am, the brewery guys walked in, closed the doors and did a spot stock check. He was then thrown out.

As I commiserated, he said, 'Can you lend me £250?'

That was a lot of money in 1970 and I said, 'No, but I know Ian's working.'

'Oh, right, I'll phone Ian,' he replied.

Half-an-hour later, Ian phoned on the warpath. 'You rotten bastard!' he exploded.

'Well, I haven't got £250,' I replied.

'I haven't either,' stormed Ian — and he had been in the drink in his Bentley about four times that week!

In the days he was a drinking mate, Tom used to throw wonderful parties and we had some good times. As his house was only round the corner, we would go back there quite a lot until his career really took off and he bought a house on the St George's Hill private estate at Weybridge. And then he moved to the States.

But I did Tom a favour, too, by helping him land one of his early hits. I was in the Anchor when John Dark, who was then assistant producer on the 1965 film *What's New Pussycat?*, came in. The film, starring Peter Sellers, Peter O'Toole, Woody Allen, Ursula Andress and Richard Burton, was to become a classic comedy of the swinging Sixties, but I had heard, whether it was right or not, that they had offered the title song to Shirley Bassey, and that she had turned them down. Anyhow, as we had a quiet drink, John asked, 'Who should we get to do the song?' I suggested Tom, and eventually a deal was done. Tom recorded it, scoring a Number 11 hit in Britain . He did even better in America, with the recording making Number 3.

The Anchor was our holy grail, with Sunday lunchtime our biggest time for a drink. We would meet in the Anchor and say, 'Where are we going this afternoon?' And something always came up.

We would be drinking and the phone would ring with someone's wife or girlfriend saying, 'Are you coming home for lunch?' He would say, 'I am with so and so,' and she would reply, 'Well bring them along, too.' So we would troop round and pay for our lunch with bottles of champagne and wine. Then we would all pile back into the Anchor at seven for another session. David, the choreographer, always kept open house for young starving actors, which was a welcome haven.

So was the Ashford Manor golf course, which is where I met Engelbert Humperdinck, who was to become a very close pal — and still is, although for years he has spent most of his time in America. After Engelbert hit the big time following his huge Number One hit, 'Release Me', in March 1967, he bought a sumptuous house, Glenbrook, on St George's Hill, near Tom and their manager Gordon Mills. Enge had deliberately moved out of London so that he could join the élite Sunningdale Golf Club. But being a pop star cut no ice with the golf club committee. They turned him down flat, saying that they had already turned down Frankie Vaughan as they then had a policy of frowning on entertainers.

Engelbert was furious but, determined to join a club near his new home, he came along to Ashford Manor seeking membership, and I introduced him to the club officers. They asked me if I would propose him for membership, to which I happily agreed, and the secretary sent me a letter asking me to accompany Engelbert when he appeared before the captain, the president and the membership secretary on a particular night. I was fully aware that we were expected to wear suits and ties on such an occasion, and duly put on my best suit. But my heart sank when I arrived at the club and saw Engelbert's gear. He had turned up in cowboy boots, black trousers, a leather jacket trimmed with tassles, and was smoking a huge cigar. Fortunately, the officers weren't too stuffy and they accepted him for membership after I spun them a yarn that Enge hadn't settled into his new home and still had to sort out his clothes. Otherwise, I assured them, he would have worn a Saville Row suit!

I took to Engelbert from the start. He is a smashing guy, the sort of bloke you like instantly. We were big mates and I saw a lot of him, until the early Seventies when, as his fame grew, he went to live in America. There was a lot of rivalry between him and Tom Jones, but it was good natured. Tom had given Enge a helping hand at the start, when Enge was still known as Gerry Dorsey. Enge's career really hit the high notes, however, when he changed his name to Engelbert Humperdinck, with a little assistance from *Hansel and Gretel*.

Tom was great, too, but he didn't play golf, so we had less in common. Enge, though, not only loved golf, he was also superb at other sports. He could be world class at darts — and proved it when the British World Championship darts team went out to Las Vegas and met Enge. He took them back to his place for a drink and then proceeded to beat the lot of them, every single player.

He is so good I wouldn't dream of playing him. You might as well give him the money, because you don't stand a chance. But then Enge has had a lot of practice. He uses darts as a method of relaxation before every concert date, and if you go into his dressing room before a show you will always find him playing darts.

He could have been totally corrupted by his fame and the adoring girls who swoon around him. But he hasn't. He's still a great family man and although his idol is Elvis, Enge has always kept his feet on the ground. Well, almost. He was totally besotted with the image of the late Jayne Mansfield and bought her house in Los Angeles, which he has christened the Pink Palace. It is a quite incredible pile just off Sunset Boulevard in Beverly Hills with heart-shaped motifs, including a heart-shaped marble swimming pool. It would drive me mad, but I suppose it has a certain over-the-top Hollywood charm — if you like that sort of thing. Even Enge eventually got fed up with the hearts that adorned the bottom of the pool with the legend 'I love Jayne' all over them. He had them ripped out and replaced with plain tiles, and put the house on the market.

When I was visiting him in Los Angeles, Enge said, 'Do you fancy a game of golf? I know somewhere really good and very exclusive.' I was all up for that and said I would be delighted, swiftly bundling my clubs into the back of his Rolls-Royce convertible. It was a fabulous, smog-free, sunny morning as we glided through elegant Beverly Hills before turning into the super-rich private estate of Bel Air, with its restrained, monied grandeur, perched on the hills above Tinseltown. Finally, we swept up to the gates of the Bel Air Golf and Country Club to be greeted by the security guard, who asked, 'Good morning, gentlemen, who have you come to see?'

'No-one,' said Enge, flashing a 1,000-watt smile. 'We've come for a game.'

'Sorry folks, no can do. It's members only,' drawled the guard. Enge, now getting visibly cross, started to explain who he was and, gesturing towards me, added that he had brought a 'very important British actor' for a game — and we wanted that game.

But the guard wouldn't budge. The rule was members only and that was it, no matter who we were. Enge had said the club was exclusive and it was precisely that. I have played in the most prestigious golf clubs in the world, but I didn't even get past the gates of the Bel Air club. Enge took it very badly and I feared he was going to burst a blood vessel with rage. It probably reminded him of the snub he had received from a golf club years before! But there was nothing we could do about it, so, feeling rather foolish, we turned round and headed back the way we had come.

Enge steamed all the way home, and when we finally walked into his house he was still so annoyed that he immediately rang up his manager and, thirsting for vengeance, told him to buy the Bel Air club. 'Buy it — and sack that bloody man on the gates,' he stormed. 'He humiliated me in front of my friend.'

His manager tried to calm him down, pointing out that it would cost countless millions to buy such a prestigious club. But Enge wouldn't listen. 'I don't care,' he roared. 'Buy it, and sack that guy!'

Nowadays, Enge is a member, and promises me that I am on his guest list, but that incident had the same unreal quality as the day years before when Enge invited me back to his house for a drink after a round of golf at Ashford Manor to show me a solid gold putter he had been given by a fan in Texas. We jumped into Engelbert's brand-new Rolls-Royce Corniche and zoomed off down the road towards his house on St George's Hill, eventually turning into his drive and down the slope towards his garage. His garage had electronic doors which he operated from a remote control in the Rolls. If you pressed the switch once, the doors came up, but if you touched the switch again after pressing it, the doors stopped, locking them in whatever position they were then in. Then, if you pressed it again, the doors reversed. Well, as we soared down the slope towards his house, I started to get a bit alarmed. 'Aren't we going a bit fast?' I cautioned Enge.

'No,' he said. 'Just watch this,' flicking the remote control. 'By the time we get to the garage, the doors will be wide open and I've just got time to stop inside.'

So the garage doors started to lift up as we sped towards them … and then they stopped, with the bottom edge pointing straight at the magnificent Rolls bonnet. Enge must have touched the remote again after his initial flick, and as he frantically slammed on the brakes, while trying to reverse the doors, his gleaming new motor went CRASH! It was a nasty bump and cost Enge £440 to repair, which was a lot of money then.

But I was used to the unexpected whenever I had a round of golf with Enge. There was the time he introduced Brian Wallace (a London pub owner we called Whiplash because of the way he whipped his club through the air) and myself to a new drink at Ashford Manor — and nearly did for the lot of us! We had gone into the bar after a game and Enge said, 'I have found this new drink — brandy and Benedictine. Do you want to try it?'

Well, none of us had tried that combination before, so Enge bought a round of doubles. They went down very smoothly, so I put my hand in my pocket and we had another round. Then Brian bought a third round. Finally, as we grew louder and more glassy-eyed by the minute, Whiplash got in yet another round. By then we could hardly stand up. We were absolutely pie-eyed. Enge was the most sober and, somehow, tottered off to do a radio interview, but I was not at my best when I rolled home. I fell over, smashing a lot of expensive crystal. Caroline was incandescent with fury and we had a blazing row, which didn't do a lot for my marriage.

But I behaved impeccably compared with Whiplash. He had a violent row when he staggered home — and ended up strangling the pet cat!

I never discovered quite what Brian got up to, but he was as sky high as the rest of us and neither he or I have drunk brandy and Benedictine since then. I value my skin too much.

But while Brian and I have cut out the Benedictine, we have worked brandy into a golfing ritual. And the 15th hole at Ashford Manor became known to Enge, Brian and myself as The Brandy Hole. It all began when Enge, Brian and I were playing with Glen Campbell, whom Enge had brought along when Glen was on one of his European tours. Enge would often turn up with a big star like Glen or Johnny Mathis, and this day Brian had decided to mark the occasion. So at the 15th hole he produced a half-bottle of brandy from his bag and said, 'Why don't we all have a sip. we've earned it.' Well, there is nothing quite like a little nip of brandy after playing for three hours and it tasted absolutely fabulous.

Enge was so impressed that a few weeks later, again at the 15th, he said, 'Hang on a minute,' and brought out of his bag a collapsible silver stool. He then produced a silver tray and four tiny silver goblets. Finally, he pulled out a bottle of Delamain brandy, which is absolutely superb, and we all had a magnificent pick-me-up. Since then, we have always created a brandy hole, wherever we play in the world, and have a tiny sip of brandy.

It's always tremendous fun playing with Enge — totally relaxed, and we only play for tiny sums of money, like 20p, with the winner getting in the first round. We all play off a 16 handicap so it's pretty even, except for the time Enge and I decided to fix Brian and wrote in to the secretary saying that he had graduated to a 12 handicap. The secretary wrote to Brain congratulating him, and he was horror-struck. It took him weeks to insist there had been some mistake — and it took him as long to find out that Enge and I were behind his increased standing in the club!!

But he had his revenge on me when he and Engelbert fooled me into believing I was hearing voices in the middle of a golf course — with golf instructions from heaven!

Enge had brought a walkie-talkie — which were virtually unknown in Britain at the time — back from one of his trips to the States — and slipped it into my golf bag when the three of us were having our normal game at Ashford Manor. We had played about eight holes and I was in the middle of the fairway and they were about 30 yards away. Enge was beside a clump of trees and Brian was off on the other side of the fairway.

'Are you going to take your shot?' they called to me.

'No,' I said, 'after you.'

So they hit their shots and I then prepared to take mine. I brought my club slowly back, and just as I reached the top of my backswing I heard a deep voice from alongside me saying, 'You are swinging too quickly. Slowly, Johnny, slowly …'

I spun round. Nobody … I thought, 'What the bloody hell is that? I must be hearing things.' The lads were a good 30 yards away and there was no-one else in sight on the course. Enge was scratching around for his ball in the woods and Brian was leaning on his trolley.

So I went to swing again. And again the calm voice said, 'You are swinging too quickly … Slowly, Johnny …'

I looked up into the sky. Was it *Him*?

Then Enge called out, 'Are you going to hit the ball or what?'

'Yeah… yeah,' I said, obviously looking perplexed.

'What's the matter?' called Enge.

'Nothing ... nothing ...' I said, preparing to play the stroke again. As I went to swing again, I again heard the voice — and stopped in mid-stroke.

Once more, Enge and Brian called out, 'What's the matter?'

'I am hearing things,' I called back. 'I am hearing voices ...'

By this time, Enge was so creased up with laughter that he forgot to switch off the walkie-talkie and I heard him chortle. I thought, 'This is ridiculous, it's coming from my bag.' But I still didn't cotton on, although my bag was laughing.

Finally, Enge came out of the trees exploding with laughter, while Brian was curled up over his trolley. Mystified, I asked, 'What's going on?' Unable to keep the joke going any longer, they put me out of my misery and told me. I felt an absolute idiot, but I had to admit it was a very good gag.

It was also a laugh a minute the day we played with Glen Campbell. He could match Ken Dodd for joke cracking. He never stopped in the four hours we were on the course, and there were some very good ones. We had a very good golfing school in those days. Gordon Mills, the song writer Barry Mason, and Tom Jones's musical director Johnny Spence would all turn out and we had some wonderful times, which helped a lot because those were not the happiest days of my life. Although I was in quite a few films and television shows, work was hard to find and didn't really pick up until 1971, which seemed a very long time out in the cold.

But Enge was always very kind to me. One day, when I was not having it so good and was pretty broke, we were sitting in the living room of his house on St George's Hill and he said, 'Fancy a brandy?'

'Wonderful,' I replied.

Enge went on, 'I'll get you one you've never tasted before.' It was like nectar and it cost £30 a bottle — and I'm going back to 1970, so it was very expensive – but it was superb.

'Did you really enjoy that, Johnny?' Enge asked.

'Yeah.'

'Did you really enjoy it? Then have another.'

So I had another tot.

Smiling, Enge then asked a third time, 'Did you really, really enjoy it?'

'Yeah, it is magnificent.'

'Then take this home with you when you go,' said Enge handing me an unopened bottle.

'I can't do that. It must have cost a fortune,' I protested.

'If you have enjoyed it, you take it home,' said Enge, pressing the bottle into my hands. 'And enjoy it. And give some to your wife.' It was such a kind gesture, it brought tears to my eyes.

He also brought tears to my eyes when we were in his house in Los Angeles and he was showing me some self-defence moves. Enge is not only world class at darts, he is also extremely good at karate, kung-fu, ju-jitsu and the martial arts discipline Steven Segal uses to such devastating effect in the movies. Engelbert certainly devastated me. He got carried away and knocked his elbow on my jaw almost knocking me out.

He was distraught and as I lay on the floor with my head spinning and lights flashing in my eyes, he cuddled me and kept saying 'Sorry, I'm so sorry, Johnny.'

'Don't worry,' I eventually told him, 'I'll sue.'

'Yes, you sue,' his wife Pat agreed, smiling.

Enge adores his family, another reason why I like him so much. We were in Las Vegas and he turned up at the hotel with Sarah and Scott, two of his four children and, smiling proudly and embracing them, said, 'This is what it's all about.'

It was while I was in Las Vegas with Enge that I saw another side to the glittering big money scene. Enge was topping the bill in one of the main casinos and was billed to do a 50-minute slot. Well, Enge went out there and gave it his all. The crowd went wild and kept calling for encore after encore. And Enge, bless him, lapping it up, gave them what they wanted — and performed for one hour and ten minutes.

When he joined me later for a drink, I naïvely remarked that I thought he was fantastic. But Enge said the bosses hadn't been too pleased with his barnstorming performance — he had kept the punters off the tables for an extra 20 minutes!

Golf has always played a major part of my life since I switched to the sport from weight training in the late Fifties, but my interest really took off when I was on holiday in Majorca and ran into the guy who had just started the Variety Club of Great Britain's golf society. He asked me if I wanted to join and explained they organised matches to raise money for children's charities. I thought it was a smashing idea and since then I have played charity golf all over the world — the United States, Hawaii, New Zealand, Spain, Germany, Italy and France.

But the most memorable was at Turnberry, where I partnered Arnold Palmer against Gary Player and Ronnie Corbett, and we won five up. They were fantastic to play with, but then I have played with quite a few of the world's greatest golfers, such as Bernard Langer, Nick Faldo and Ian Woosnam. And it was just fun, because it was for charity and there was no need to get nervous or feel over-awed.

Some people do take it all a trifle too seriously. I was playing at Wentworth once with a car dealer called Geoff Doe and at the eighth or ninth he hit three balls straight into the nearby lake. He was so angry, he snatched his golf bag off his caddie's back, shoved the club he was using back into the bag, and hurled the lot into the lake. Then, still in a blazing temper, he stomped off back to the clubhouse — only to realise that he had put his car keys in the golf bag. So, in an even greater rage, he got his caddie to rake the lake. The caddie succeeded in retrieving the golf bag and gave it to Geoff, who got his keys out, and threw the bag, clubs and all, back in!

Other guys know how to weight the odds in their favour and, on this occasion, mine. I was again playing with Johnny Matthis at a country club in Los Angeles and there were about nine of us in the party. I was playing with a huge guy called Bill, who used to supply parts to Boeing, the plane makers, and he decided to play for $20 … $40 … $60. I told him that I didn't want to play for that much money and he said, 'Don't worry, you'll be alright.'

Well, after three holes we were three down and I said, 'Bill, what are we going to do?'

'Johnny, don't worry,' he replied. 'Wait.'

At about the fifth or sixth hole we came to a cliff face, on which there was a sign: 'Beware of the Rattlesnakes'.

I soon realised why Bill had been so confident. As we strolled up to the sign one of the guys we were playing against prepared to take his shot. Then, as he went into his back swing, Bill slipped a rattlesnake's tail out of his pocket, and shook it. The guy jumped, skewing his shot completely off line. Startled and rather rattled himself, he said, 'Did you hear that, Bill?'

'What? What?' replied Bill, pretending he wasn't quite sure what the other man was on about.

'That noise,' the man continued agitatedly. 'I heard that bloody rattle.'

Then, when the guy's partner went to take his stroke, Bill rattled the tail again, very, very gently …

Our two opponents were scared of rattlesnakes and Bill knew how to capitalise on that.

Every time they came to a crucial shot, Bill rattled his rattlesnake's tail and, of course, we won.

So we got back to the clubhouse and I said, 'Bill, I've got to spend some of this $100.'

'Oh no,' he said, 'you can't do that. We work a system of chits here under which we have to spend so much — or it is wiped off our cards. So we have to get rid of this money.' So we started to drink and had a very good time.

Eventually, I said, 'Fellas, I've got to go,' left the clubhouse and got into my hire car.

I then drove out of the golf club heading for the nearby dual carriageway. But instead of driving over the dual carriageway and then turning left, I turned left immediately, and suddenly I saw all these car headlights bearing down on me. 'Oh Christ …

bloody hell,' I thought and, in the nick of time, managed to turn into the first drive I came to, and escape the on-rushing traffic. But the moment I turned in, my blood again ran cold. I was flooded in light and Doberman Pinscher attack dogs appeared from nowhere, surrounding the car.

I felt as if I was in a nightmare when next a security guard loomed out of the dark, complete with gun and night stick. He ordered me to wind down my window, but I refused. I wasn't budging with all those dogs barking and snarling all around me. Eventually the guard called off the dogs and then came over to ask, 'What's your problem?'

I told him that I had just left the golf club and turned down the wrong road.

'Are you English?' he then asked.

'Yeah,' I said. 'It happens to you guys a lot,' he smiled. He then told me to back up and watched me back out on to the dual carriageway, facing in the right direction.

So there was only one thing to do — I went back to the club.

'What the hell are you doing here?' they asked as I entered the bar.

'I have just had a very nasty shock ...' I began — and had one for the road.

But I didn't feel as foolish as a woman I encountered while playing in the Henry Cooper in Spain. Her husband had his ball down in a scrub-filled valley and she called down, 'You'll never find your ball down there.'

'Oh yes I will,' he called back, disappearing from sight. He then called up, 'I've found it. Throw me my sand-wedge ...'

So she disappeared and when she returned she called down, 'I've got a cheese one and and ham one — which one do you want?'

'My *sand-wedge*, you silly cow,' he roared back, 'not a sandwich!'

I have had exceptionally good days, and quite a few bad ones. But one of the best was when I went to New Zealand for a charity telethon with a gang of celebrities, including Ernie Wise and Frank Bruno, in the late Eighties. They asked me to play the professional, which was quite an honour as no one had beaten the pro on that course since he had arrived at the club.

But I did. I beat him on the last hole and the club not only gave a massive donation to the telethon, they gave me a gold putter!

We were only in New Zealand for a few days, but it was tremendous trip. We were relaxing by the hotel pool when the receptionist came out calling, 'Phone call for Mr Bruno. Phone call for Mr Bruno. Is he here?'

'Yes,' calls Ernie, 'that's me,' much to the amusement of Frank.

But there is one person I will never play for again in any tournament he organises and that is Jimmy Tarbuck, because once, not in so many words, he accused me of cheating.

I was playing in a tournament in Spain for the Variety Club with the guy who set the Americans' handicap over there. We were the last in and when we got to the green, Tarbuck, who was standing there with his wife, asked, 'What did you get?'

'I don't know,' I told him.

'What do you mean, you don't know?' snapped Tarbuck.

'I'm not keeping the score ... he is,' I said, indicating the handicapper.

So Tarbuck then asked him how many points we'd got.

'We got 79,' he replied.

I didn't say a word, but Tarbuck's wife turned to me and said, 'Thank you very much, you have just beaten me into second place.'

So we went into the bar and were having a drink while waiting for the prizes when Tarbuck came up to me and said, 'Why did you have a drop on that last hole?'

'I was in a tyre track,' I said.

'Oh, yes,' said Tarbuck, adding, 'Did he say you could have a drop [move the ball from an unplayable lie if it is not stuck in a natural hazard].'

'I asked him,' I said, in turn adding, 'You know he is a handicapper!'

'Mm, yes,' said Tarbuck. Then he said, 'What tyre track?'

'That tyre track over there,' I said pointing out of the window, 'that one of the machines made.'

At that, Tarbuck disappeared and went and collected a golf kart to have a look.

That did it for me. When he returned I said, 'Look, A, I don't cheat at golf, and B, if your wife wants a prize I will be happy to let her have it. The chances of me getting a glass bowl home are nil. As far as I'm concerned I'll smash it — and I'll never play in another competition you organise again.'

In the end, I went up to Kevin Keegan, who had a house there called Seventh Heaven, and gave it to him, saying, 'I don't want this bloody thing. Here, you have it.' And I have never played in any tournament Tarbuck has organised since. I was furious at the suggestion that I had had a drop to get a better shot. Needless to say, Tarbuck didn't apologise. I don't think he has ever apologised in his life. Now if I see Tarbuck I just ignore him. He is not worthy of my conversation.

The great bonus for me these days, however, is that wherever I am in the world I can get a game of golf. My great ambition is to play Augusta, but whether I achieve that or not, I am now guaranteed a game at the top Spanish course whenever I like. And that came about because of a drink I had one night at Skeibo Castle, Inverness, with Peter de Savary, who owns it, when I told him I didn't play in Spain any more.

Peter then did me a very big favour. He said, 'I would like you to meet Jamie, who is a very good friend of mine.

So I met this charming man, who said, 'Peter tells me you don't play golf so much in Spain any more. Why is that?'

'Well, Jamie, it is very expensive and there is only one course worth playing and that is the Ryder Cup course Valderama, and you can never get on it.'

'Well, the next time you want to, just phone me,' he said with a smile, passing me his card. And he was Jamie Patino, the owner!

You could have knocked me down with a feather, but, seizing my advantage, I said, 'Suppose I get there and tell them this story and you are not there?' And he said, 'Give them my card. Just give them my card.'

I find that you get more in life by not asking. People have been very generous towards me and I am very grateful. People say, 'How did you do that, Johnny, you jammy blighter?' And I don't know. But apart from my lean period, I have been very lucky ...

Which is more than could be said for Frank Carson when Frank and I went to the Isle of Man for a charity golf tournament. On our way to the course from the airport we passed over Fairy Bridge, and Frank decided to cash in on the legend that the fairies will grant any wish you make while crossing the bridge.

'This is your Uncle Frank, here in the Isle of Man, let me win this tournament,' boomed Frank, adding for good measure as we reached the end of the bridge, 'Frank Carson, Isle of Man, signing off.'

Sadly, the fairies weren't listening to Frank that day, for when he swung into action in the tournament he played like an idiot. To make matters worse, Frank didn't even have time for a consolation booze-up as he had to fly back to Blackpool for a show that evening. So, when he was re-crossing the bridge, Frank vented his fury on the fairies with a four-letter broadside telling them just what he thought of them and their magic. Then, as he unleashed his final verbal onslaught of, 'So, bollocks to the lot of you,' his front tyre got a puncture — and he missed his plane.

I may not have spooked any fairies but I certainly once spooked the American Secret Service, when I chatted too intimately with former President Gerald Ford when we met at a lavish dinner after I had played in the Bob Hope British Classic in the early Eighties.

We were all standing around having a drink when I got into conversation with President Ford. I found him a smashing guy to talk to and remarkably open as we chatted away, far too open for his minders who finally muscled up to me and said, 'Move on'. I didn't like their tone and I asked them why, because I wasn't drunk or anything and Ford was perfectly relaxed. So they took a different tack and said, 'You have had Mr Ford's attention for 15 minutes. Can you give someone else a chance!' It seemed perfectly reasonable and as the guys were built like brick outhouses, I thought, 'Oh, OK.'

But I think the real reason was that they didn't like the way the conversation was going. I had asked Ford why he had such a huge protection squad — six Americans and six British Special Branch officers — as he was no longer President.

'Well,' he said, 'mine were disarmed at the airport when I flew into Britain and the others are armed to stop people shooting me. But the American Government isn't frightened of me being assassinated, in fact they would be very happy if I was assassinated as it would save them a fortune. Because they wouldn't have to protect me, my wife and my family any more. What they are worried about is me being kidnapped and brainwashed. It is what I know that they have to protect. If someone bumps me off the problem is gone ...' and that was when the heavies moved in.

One person I will never see near a golf course is my wife Christine. I once talked her into coming to watch me play with Max Bygraves in Spain and, as luck would have it, we had one of those freak weeks during which it was very cold and windy, and Christine sat in bed all day in her fur coat reading a book. Finally, we had one good day and Christine came out by the pool, where they were barbecuing. But it still wasn't quite the success I had hoped for. As the barbecue sizzled away, I got Christine a drink and a sandwich, but she was still far from happy. Instead of relaxing on a lounger with her food and drink, she stood, still wearing her fur coat, with her eyes hidden behind her sunglasses, moaning that there were flies everywhere — and especially around *her*. So Max looked up quizzically and asked, 'What's the matter, Christine?'

'What's the matter!' she snorted. 'I come to Spain with him,' she continued, waving her fur-clad arm towards me, 'and look at it! Just look at it!'

'Christine,' purred Max, 'you are with two of the best-looking men in the world. One is the most fantastic comedian, and the other is one of the best, well known and very good actors in the world. And here you are in Spain with the sun out and you are standing there with us and, let's face it, 40 million flies can't be wrong, can they?'

Christine was very browned off — and that's why she doesn't come golfing with me any more. But then I have a very unfair reputation for not liking women near any golf course.

I freely admit that I do find some women golfers a pain and I certainly set the cat among the pigeons in 1997 when I was quoted as saying women golfers were a bunch of bossy cockroaches with no idea of etiquette. Well, I have been an amateur golfer for 33 years now and, playing off a handicap of 16, I have a very good appreciation of just how the game should be played. After all, unlike most women, I have been lucky enough to play with the greatest golfers in the world, and I am a quick learner when it comes to knowing how to behave.

The 'cockroaches' quote caused a huge storm, but I never said anything about cockroaches and I haven't got anything against lady golfers, although I did say that on ladies' days it's best to keep away because they are all over the course like ants. In the article, I was quoted as saying that women golfers are 'an abomination on the course and shouldn't be allowed except in women-only clubs', and, let's face it, there's a lot of truth in that. I have had women run in front of me on a course to get to the tee first and it is frustrating. If you are more than a hole behind you're supposed to let the players behind pass in front of you, but women don't do that. They do not seem to understand the etiquette. I don't disapprove of women as long as they play by the rules and stick to their day. Many men think the same way, but wouldn't dare say so. And I am afraid that some women in golf clubs and on the course can be treacherous. I have always fought shy of club politics because golf club committees tend to be wife-orientated. The wives exert an influence on decisions and generally have a lot to do with the running of a club.

I don't have a vendetta against women golfers, but I really feel they should have their own courses. They pay reduced green fees, reduced subscriptions, play off a different tee, and they stand everywhere. I would say that 80 per cent of women don't know the etiquette of the course. They are oblivious to what's going on around them. They chat between themselves, take their time and just couldn't care less. All those blue rinses — you can forget it!

A lot of women golfers sounded off furiously against me at the time. Some members of the Essex Golf and Country Club ladies' team booed and hissed at me as I teed off in a match there, while the Lady Taverners withdrew their invitation for a celebrity tournament, with the organiser and former England women's cricketer Rachel Heyhoe Flint suggesting other charities should do the same. But I was offered honorary membership of two clubs because of my stand. And I am offered a game in 200–300 golf tournaments a year, because by playing I can up the gate a little and so bring in more money for charity.

Even my ex-wife Caroline joined in the row. She claimed that she was a golf widow during our marriage and after criticising my remarks as chauvinist, said I thought 'women should be in the kitchen cooking my dinner and then get ready in bed wearing a long nightie'. But that's way off the mark. Christine has always said, 'When I go to bed, the only thing I will wear is a little Cartier' — and I don't mean a watch!

Top: Mike propping up the bar with Bet and Dawn Perks.
Bottom: Elsie Tanner and Mike Baldwin.

Top: Len Fairclough, Mike Baldwin and a couple of bottles of his favourite tipple.

Bottom: Gotcha! Mike gets his revenge on his hated enemy Ken Barlow.

Top: Mike and Deirdre in mid-fling.

Bottom: One of many confrontations between Mike and Ken, with Deirdre stuck in the middle as usual.

Mike and Susan's happy day – but it was not to last.

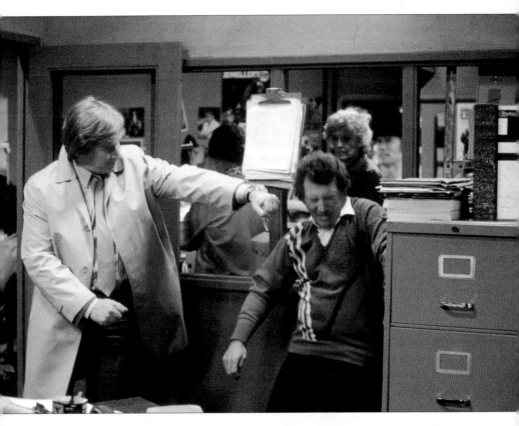

Top: Fists fly on the factory floor.

Bottom: With old flame Bet, as husband Alec looks on.

The start of another doomed marriage: wife number 2, Jackie Ingram.

Top: Third time lucky? With present screen wife Alma.

Bottom: A tense moment outside Alf's shop.

Mike lays down the law in the Rovers Return.

8

WHAT WAS SO DEPRESSING ABOUT MY LEAN PERIOD was that it followed such a magnificent run of luck. When I was up I was really up and, I suppose, that is why I was so confident I could walk out of *No Hiding Place* and still scale the heights. For, even when I was doing the hit police show, I was also getting offers of major films, like *The Intelligence Men* in 1965. This was the movie début for Eric Morecambe and Ernie Wise and, paradoxically, the fact that they were already the darlings of British television by the time they shot it, made their leap into films all the more difficult for them.

It was fascinating to watch them in action because they were used to working with live audiences, either in the television studio or on stage, and they visibly warmed to the audience. So when they were rehearsing a scene and the camera crew fell about laughing at their antics, they were superb. They would improvise in the blink of an eye and it all worked magnificently. But when the first assistant director called, 'Right, we are going for a take. Hush, everybody,' and the cameras started rolling, it was a different story. Eric and Ernie would once again go straight into the routine but it just didn't work. This time there wouldn't be a sound, let alone laughter, and that used to throw them completely. The boys were waiting for the laughs that never came, and it took them quite a while to adapt to working in a world where everyone wasn't collapsing with mirth at their zany antics. But once they had cottoned on to what was required and became used to the absence of laughter, they were fine, and they were fantastic to work with. Eric, in particular, could be a dreadful tease and used to revel in mercilessly winding people up.

One of his pet gags involved a very expensive and elaborate watch which was meant to be one of his magic Secret Service gadgets. The film company had borrowed it from one of the top jewellers and it was treated as if it was one of Liz Taylor's diamonds. The producer was so concerned about the watch that he had given the prop boy specific orders that he had to collect it from Eric at the end of each day's filming and lock it in the company safe. The prop boy was then tasked with collecting it from the safe the following morning and giving it to Eric.

It didn't take Eric long to realise that he could have some real mischief with this watch. So every evening when they called, 'Cut. That's a wrap, everyone, see you in the morning,' his ploy was to nip out of the studio as fast as he could, still wearing the watch.

This had a devastating effect on the poor props boy who would then start running around looking for the watch, desperately asking the cast and crew, 'Has anyone seen Mr Morecambe?'

They would say, 'Oh, he's gone.'

'Gone?' the props boy would shriek in a panic. 'Gone? No, he can't have gone, he's still got the watch on.' Then, looking totally miserable, he would forlornly ask, 'What am I going to do?'

Eric, of course, would simply be hiding in a toilet somewhere, or sitting in his car, waiting for this demented prop guy to come running up. Oh, it was very well done, and we all had a good laugh at the prop guy's misfortune.

I enjoyed doing comedy films and in 1968 had my first peek inside the totally crazy world of the *Carry On* films when I joined up as a sporran soldier in *Carry On Up The Khyber*. That was a rather draughty experience as I was one of the kilted Third Foot and Mouth Regiment. It was a complete madhouse and in one spectacular scene we had to lift up our kilts on parade to prove to our commanding officer that unmanly practices, like the wearing of underwear, had not become commonplace!

That was my first of three *Carry Ons* — and they really were a carry on. Kenneth Williams, who played the Khazi of Kalabar in *Up the Khyber*, was hysterical and working with the regular gang — Sid James, Charles Hawtrey and Bernard Breslaw — was a barrel of fun. It really was a case of laugh, laugh, laugh. It was one of those jobs where you thought, 'Christ — and I'm getting paid for this!' Not that it was very much. The films, produced by Peter Rogers and directed by Gerald Thomas, were wonderful, but they undercut you something rotten if they could get away with it. You got the worst money possible and there were no stand-ins. But what fun.

We used to play poker in between takes and Sid James would almost explode with frustration he got so exasperated with Charles Hawtrey. Charles had a purse and used to count out his money, coin by coin, ever … so … slowly. Sid would say, 'What's the bet?' and Charles would say, 'Sixpence.' Sid would then say, 'Right, your sixpence and up half-a-crown [12.5p].' Someone else would then say, 'Half-a-crown and up another sixpence.' And so it would go round until it got back to Charles, who would say, 'Right! How much is that?' and Sid would explode, 'Oh, for God's sake Charles, look …' and as he tried to explain he became so irritated that his blood pressure used to soar right up. 'Oh, for God's sake, come on, keep counting,' he would shout at Charles, who'd be counting the coins very deliberately. Then he would say, 'How much is that? Let me see, that should be …'

By this time, Sid would be almost incandescent with fury, shouting, 'OH, FOR GOD'S SAKE, CHARLES!' And if Charles won, you could almost see Sid's blood vessels burst. He just couldn't stand it, because he was a great gambler and I think it hurt his pride... He played the horses, everything.

He was a lovely man and why Tony Hancock was so foolish as to split with him I shall never know. They were so close.

We used to pop down to the pub near Pinewood for a quick one at lunchtimes, but it would only be the one, or at the most two, when we were working. If you have one drink while you are working and you mess a scene up, you can bet your bottom dollar that they are going to say, 'Oh, did you just smell his breath, he's been drinking.' I have seen it happen to so many of my mates, I am very wary of it.

I worked down at Beconsfield a lot during my film career and, if you were lucky, as one film was coming to an end, you could get picked up for another. If a director hadn't fully cast his film, he would see you in the bar and say, 'What are you doing Monday?' If you said, 'Oh, nothing much,' he would say, 'Do you want a part in my film?'

'Oh, yes please,' I would hastily reply and, in all, I did 50 films.

I was at the studios one day when it seems that the Briggs charm was even more powerful than I had anticipated in my wildest dreams. Jane Seymour, looking an absolute vision of loveliness, walked into the bar and asked me for a date.

Well, to be precise, she asked me if I was going to the Hammer Horror picture party that night. I said I had been invited and she then asked if I would like to take her.

I was a bit taken aback as she looked fabulous with her lovely long hair, so giving her a slightly old fashioned look, I asked straight out, 'Why?'

Her reply wasn't as flattering as I had hoped, as she explained that she would love to go but hadn't been invited. So, always one to help a lady, I naturally agreed.

But she wasn't with me for long. As we walked into the party I saw one of the Hammer Films bosses, who said, 'Hello, Johnny, how are you?' Then turning to Jane, his eyes lit up and he asked, 'And who is this young lady?' I told him that she was Jane Seymour, and before I could blink, he had coolly whisked my 'date' away, smoothly murmuring to her, 'How are you, my dear, come and have a drink.' That was the last I saw of her — and I thought I might as well go home.

But I did get lucky in 1968 when Walter Grauman finally evened the score for killing me off so early in 633 *Squadron*, and I went to Germany to join Stuart Whitman in *The Last Escape*, in which I played a British parachutist dropped into Holland on a secret mission in the Second World War.

They filmed it near Munich and we had tremendous fun one lunchtime when I moaned to Whitman that I was fed up with always having to eat sauerkraut. He agreed and said, 'You're right, let's go down the pub.' And we did, although at the time we were dressed in SS uniforms for some scenes in which we were supposed to be posing as Nazis.

So there we were, dressed in the forbidden black SS uniforms, complete with hats, driving through the Bavarian countryside until we came to a pub we fancied. Then, without a second thought, we marched in. The pub could have come straight out of a tourist guide with one wall completely covered in stags' head hunting trophies, upon which we neatly hung our hats.

The atmosphere was electric as we walked up to the bar. The pub was full of men, but they had fallen so silent you really could have heard a pin drop.

Stuart didn't turn a hair. He knew that I spoke German and, running his eye casually over the room, he waited for me to order.

In my best German from National Service days, I asked, 'Two beers, please.' The guy behind the bar then asked whether I wanted large or small ones. When I replied large ones, I realised everyone in the room was watching me with baited breath. So I paid, and Stuart and I started chatting about the film in English — and that broke the atmosphere. Gradually, the locals started talking again, and eventually one came up to us and asked, 'What are you doing here?'

I explained that we were actors doing a film. As he had a

little broken English, he said, 'Ah, this uniform,''and pointing at our outfits, went on, 'This is the SS — I was in the SS.' Then, touching one of the medals on my uniform, he said proudly, 'I had one of those.'

Then they all started to gather around and out came this bloody book — and it was full of pictures of these guys in their SS uniforms over the years. By chance, we had stumbled on the pub where they held their reunions every year. Each year, they would once again struggle to get into the uniforms they had worn when they were young men. As the pictures progressed, their ranks grew thinner while the buttons on their jackets strained a little more. In the early pictures, there were twenty of them, but at the last reunion they were down to just five. But they were still standing there proudly in their uniforms with their medals. They were so pleased to see us wearing their old uniform that they made the inn keeper give us our money back and we had our beer on them. Stuart thought it was a great hoot and couldn't get over the fact that, out of all the pubs in Bavaria, we should have chosen that one for a beer.

He was great fun. He was also completely unpretentious, although he was a big Hollywood name in those days. Mark you, that did help when we were out on the town.

One night, we went on the razzle in Munich's equivalent of Chelsea and Stuart was well known in every bar and café we entered, whereas no one knew me in Germany, although I was well known back home. The girls were all over Stuart but I, and the other actor who was with us, had our noses put firmly out of joint. After years of not having to chat birds up, I found it distinctly off-putting trying to charm a German bird. To be honest, I would have found it difficult enough in English, but with a German girl I found it a complete waste of time. Not that I was that bothered, anyhow. So I and the other guy left Stuart to it, and we headed home to bed.

The next morning, Stuart arrived on the set with the jaunty step of a man who has had a very good time. So, with a tinge of envy in my voice, I called across to him, 'Hi, Stuart, what happened last night?' I didn't really need telling as he looked at me with a wicked grin, and drawled, 'Johnny, I was a baaaad boy ...'

He had evidently been enjoying himself all night and, smiling, I said, 'You rotten blighter, you could have let me have one.'

'Johnny,' he protested with an emphatic shrug, 'you had gone. What was I supposed to do?'

He was a wonderful character, like John Wayne — a man's man whom all the women loved.

But life generally was still very tough for me. In the Seventies, my movie career picked up again and somehow I managed to jog along doing various films and bits and pieces in television, including *Yus My Dear*, with Arthur Mullard and Mike Reid.

That finally put a bit of money into my pocket and in the early Seventies I decided Caroline and I had earned a holiday after all the bad times and sleepless nights when I couldn't get work. Our marriage was by then very rocky and I thought a complete break might help us to sort it out.

So I said to Caroline, 'Pack your bags, we are off to Spain.' She was reluctant to leave the children, but I thought we needed time on our own, and told her, 'We will find someone to look after them. We are going away on our own for a week.' And off we went.

The holiday didn't help to save our marriage, but I still got lucky while relaxing in the sun. I returned to the hotel one day to find the phone ringing. It was my agent who told me that I had been offered a stint on *Crossroads*. I hadn't a clue what he was talking about and asked, 'What's that?'

He explained that it was a television soap opera that was made in the Midlands and that the storyline revolved around the lives and loves of the guests and staff of the Crossroads Motel. Apparently, I had been offered an initial three-month contract to play garage owner Clifford Leyton. It sounded fine to me — anything would have sounded fine in those days — so I said, 'Yes, fine. I'll do it.'

But then my agent really shook me by urging me to give it a wide berth, declaring, 'My advice is not to take it.'

I couldn't believe my ears and said so, adding, 'Why not, what's the problem?'

'Have you seen it?' he then asked.

I admitted I hadn't, adding, 'I've never heard of it.'

He then once again warned me against taking it, saying, 'Well, if I was you, I would give it a miss.'

That really took me aback and after thinking about it for a few moments, I then asked him how much money I would earn in *Crossroads* if I did the three-month stint.

He told me, and I said, 'If I don't do it, will you guarantee that I will earn that amount of money over the next three months?'

He swiftly said 'No,' and, as far as I was concerned, that clinched it. Work was work and I couldn't afford to turn down a good paying job, so I told him, 'I have got a couple of kids to feed so I am going to have to take it.' When I returned from Spain, I raced home and rushed into the sitting room to turn on the television to see just what *Crossroads* was all about. Talk about the moment of truth.

I just couldn't believe it. I sat on the sofa, completely and utterly aghast, thinking, 'My God, I am not going to do this, it is terrible!'

I knew Noele Gordon, who, as Meg Richardson was the queen bee of the soap as owner of the Crossroads Motel, around which all the action revolved, but I thought, 'Never mind the money, I can't do this!'

I immediately rang my agent and said, 'You were right. Can you get me out of it?' But I was right out of luck, and he left me feeling completely shattered when he replied, 'No. You have agreed, and you have got to do it.'

So I went up to Birmingham, where they made the series, and that was my first real introduction into the world of television soap operas. And it wasn't anything like as bad as I had expected. In fact, it was to prove my biggest single break since *No Hiding Place*, for *Crossroads* helped me turn the corner and after I had stepped into that mythical Midlands motel I never had a bad break again.

The critics used to slaughter the show and it had become

a standing national joke. And I soon saw why. The sets were taken down after every show so that the studio could be used for other programmes. Unlike *Coronation Street*, they were not permanent buildings, and the walls really did move if you touched them. And you often couldn't avoid doing that. We made four episodes a week and they rattled through them without any of the care you now get with our top soaps. The scripts were pretty dreadful, too, and there was no time to rehearse properly.

There were, however, major bonuses for me. Despite our holiday and the fact that I was in regular work, things were not going particularly well with Caroline, and I realised that my marriage was falling to pieces. So I was happy to spend three months in a hotel in Birmingham, because, basically, I only went home to see the children.

Noele had taken a bit of a fancy to me and liked having me in the show and, even better, it was while I was making *Crossroads* that I first met Christine.

My friendship with Noele was very important because she was a very powerful lady at ATV. She had been left a lot of shares in the studios and she could make life very difficult for people because, in effect, she hired and fired. She was supposed to be autocratic and hard-nosed, but I thought she was all right.

So when they offered me another three-month contract, I thought, 'Well, the critics can say what they like about the show, but the fans like it and it's pulling in big audiences. And staying here is a lot better than going back to London with no work lined up.'

By then, when I did go back down south, I was basically living with my parents in Staines. Caroline and I just weren't getting along any more and it was a very difficult situation because of the children.

Divorce is awful at any time, but when children are involved it is particularly difficult. I just didn't know what to do. But eventually I decided it would be best if I carried on working, and stayed away in Birmingham.

Noele had her little quirks, though, and would always try

it on. No one ever contradicted her and, to a large degree, what she said went. Once, when I caught her out trying to come the *grande dame*, she had the brass neck to claim that I was the only actor in the world she had ever dried on, after she fluffed a line in the middle of a scene we were doing in the motel.

To mess up a scene was quite a crime in those days of recording as live. You couldn't go back on just a part of a scene if something went wrong, you had to go right back to the beginning of the take and do it all over again. In this particular scene she had paused, mistakenly thinking that I should say the next line. When I didn't speak, she imperiously called to the director, 'We can't go on because Johnny hasn't given me his line.' Furious at the arrogant way she was trying to shift the blame on to me, I swiftly put her in her place saying, 'It's not my line, Noele, it's yours.'

'Nonsense,' she snapped.

'You're not getting away with this,' I thought and said out loud, 'Go and call the prompt girl over.'

Everyone knew it was Noele's fault, but they were too frightened to say so. But I wasn't scared of her, or even leaving the show, come to that, so I insisted that the prompt girl came over and join Noele and myself. When she arrived I said, 'Who should have said the line?'

'Er, um, um,' she mumbled.

Exasperated, I said, 'It was Miss Gordon, wasn't it?'

When she again just mumbled something inaudible, I grabbed the prompt script and, showing it to Noele, pointed at the line, saying, 'There, look for yourself!' She was shaken to the core. No one had ever had the nerve to face her down before.

'Oh,' she said all contrite for once, 'I am so terribly sorry.' Then, regaining her usual haughtiness, she fixed me with a winning smile and said, 'You know, Johnny, you are the only actor in the world I have ever dried on ...' So, beaming the Briggs smile at mega-wattage, I riposted, 'Well, that's going to cost you a drink at lunchtime!'

She didn't buy it, of course, but I said it just for devilment as I knew it would annoy Reg Watson, who was then producing the show.

Reg had very strict rules about drinking and had issued a strict edict that artists were not to drink alcohol on taping days. Watson also had a rule that you didn't go to the pub at lunchtime when you were rehearsing. But I soon changed all that — within hours of arriving at *Crossroads*.

We were in the rehearsal room when it came to lunch time on my very first day and, rubbing my hands together, I said, 'Right, where's the nearest pub?'

There was a deathly silence, broken only when Roger Tonge, who played the wheelchair-bound Sandy Richardson, said, 'We're not allowed to go.'

'Who says so?' I asked.

'The producer,' Sandy replied.

'Well, I have been going to the pub at lunchtime for the past 20 years, and I am not changing the habit of a lifetime now,' I declared. I then marched out through the door and, after a momentary pause, the others called after me, 'Oh well, if you're going, we're coming, too.' And we all trooped around the corner to the pub.

We only had the one because we were working, but when Reg found out he collared me and said, 'Look, Johnny, will you please not encourage them to go to the pub.'

'It's nothing to do with me,' I told him. 'If they want to go, they go.'

That really had him worried, so, changing tack, he then said, 'Well, will you make sure they just have the one.'

But I told him, 'Sorry, Reg, but I can't control them ...' And we continued going to the pub — and it was a much more cheery atmosphere all round.

I had put my marker down on how I would behave from the moment I walked through the studio doors. I was so aghast at what I had let myself in for, that I was determined that no one was going to push me around, including Noele, whom I already knew. Noele had her own special chair in the rehearsal rooms and it was absolutely forbidden for anyone else to go near it. So when I ambled into the rehearsal room I, unknowingly, plonked myself down in Noele's special chair. The rest of the cast immediately began sniggering and laughing, and I wondered what on earth was going on. I soon found out when Noele regally swept in and saw where I was sitting.

'Johnny, darling,' she gushed flashing me an enormous smile, 'lovely to see you.' But then, her eyes hardening, she continued, 'But I don't like seeing you sitting in my chair.'

'Oh, is this your chair, Noele?' I replied , having already twigged something was afoot, but feigning total surprise.'

'It is,' she said in a voice like chipped ice.

'Well, nobody told me,' I said, acting the complete innocent.

'I always sit there,' Noele continued, determined to put me in my place.

'Well, perhaps you would like to sit on my lap,' I said with a roguish chuckle.

'Oh, you are naughty,' said Noele, with the faintest glimmer of a smile. 'You really are a naughty boy.'

Game, set and match to me. But what made it even more pleasurable was that Ronald Allen, who, as suave David Hunter was one of the big stars, and the rest of the cast were standing there open-mouthed, expecting me to get a right rollicking, which never happened. But it showed me just how much power Noele wielded, although we got on famously. And the longer I stayed, the more I enjoyed myself.

The rest of the cast were completely under Noele's thumb, but there wasn't really time for rows and backstage squabbling. And although we spent a lot of time together, taping four shows a week meant we just didn't have time to socialise. It was a very short rehearsal time and you just got there and did it.

We would go for a drink at lunchtime on rehearsal days, but you really only had the one because you knew if you messed something up and you had been to the pub the first thing the producer would do was smell your breath. I stayed at the Holiday Inn, bang next to the studios in Birmingham's Bull Ring, during the week, but most of the cast scuttled off home the minute we finished in the evenings. Ronnie was quite pleasant, a nice guy, but I found him quite wooden. Jane Rossington was all right, too. Jane, as Jill Richardson/Harvey/Chance, was rather special in the life of Crossroads as she had the unique distinction of saying the first ever words on the series: 'Crossroads Motel. Can I help you?' — and the very last as, in the closing episode, she drove off with the new man in her screen life.

But, as a single guy, the girl I fancied rotten was Susan Hanson, the blonde bombshell in the show. Susan, who as Diane Lawton/Parker/Hunter, the waitress who steadily worked her way up the motel ladder and became the idol of woolly-hatted Benny Hawkins (Paul Henry), really was a very pretty blonde. In fact, I thought 'Miss Diane' was absolutely gorgeous and I was very fond of her, but I had no chance as she was married to the singer Carl Wayne.

The show may have been regularly drubbed by the critics but it lasted for so long because there were some great characters in it, and there was a huge outcry when it was axed by Central Television in 1988 after more than 4,500 programmes. Characters like the gossipy Amy Turtle, played by Ann George, had become very dear to people's hearts.

Ann was a real one-off who was completely interchangeable with her character on screen and off, apart from a forest of diamond rings on her fingers. Ann was so determined to show the world how well she had got on, that she ended up in the ridiculous situation where she was playing a Birmingham charwoman with her fingers covered in genuine diamonds.

'You can't play Amy with all those rings — take them off,' barked the producer. But Ann was as tough as Amy and refused to remove them. 'It has taken me years to earn enough money to buy these, and I'm not taking them off now,' she declared defiantly. And she wouldn't budge. So in the end they had to put Elastoplast over her fingers to hide them!

But then a lot of the cast were just like the characters they played, apart from Roger, who wasn't wheelchair-bound in my days.

In *Crossroads*, Sandy was confined to a wheelchair and, sadly Roger himself was later confined to a wheelchair, before dying prematurely in 1981.

In all, I stayed at *Crossroads* for well over two years — on and off — because they kept asking me to renew my three-month contract. The first producer I met on the show, Reg Watson, an Australian, seemed to like my character and I felt that the show was getting better. The ratings also started creeping up and the bosses were so pleased that Watson went to Australia with 13 episodes to try and sell the show to Australian TV. When he returned, he resigned, went back to Australia as head of drama at ABC, and ended up originating *Neighbours* and *Prisoner: Cell Block H*, the cult soap set in a women's prison.

Fortunately, the new producer, Jack Barton, who was a smashing bloke, also liked me. That was very fortunate for me because one day I said to him, 'I don't mind staying in the show if my part gets better, you know, not so wishy-washy.' And Jack, bless him, dreamed up great storylines for me.

The biggest bonus for me, however, was that *Crossroads* led directly to my joining *Coronation Street*. When Bill Podmore, the then producer of the *Street* wanted to bring in a Londoner to boost ratings in the south, he phoned Jack, and asked, 'Who's the Londoner you had in your show?'

Jack said, 'Johnny Briggs.'

Podmore then asked 'Is he alright?'

Jack said, 'Yes.'

And that was it.

By now, my marriage had completely collapsed, but I was about to meet the girl of my dreams — Christine.

9

I HAD ALWAYS BELIEVED THAT CINDERELLA WAS STRICTLY FOR PANTO, Walt Disney and very young children — until the day I discovered that fairy tales really can come true, much to the delight of a cynic like myself. And the magic began from the moment I first set eyes on this vision of loveliness in April 1974.

She was a slim, blonde, very good looking 25-year-old girl with everything a guy could want. She was well spoken with a great sense of humour, and I was absolutely captivated.

There was only one problem — she was going out with a fella called Derek Hobson, who compered a talent show, and was known as 'Swoop' throughout the studios because of the way he always swooped down on her the moment he saw her chatting to a man. But I was determined that he wasn't going to stop me.

I first met her at a party in the bar of the ATV studios in the Birmingham Bull Ring and I couldn't take my eyes off her. She was sitting by herself on a bar stool as I casually sauntered over and said, 'Hello,' flashing the famous Briggs smile. I was pretty well known and if I said 'hello' to someone I expected them to say 'Hello' back.

But she just looked at me over her shoulder as if to say, 'Who is this idiot?' and, dismissively, looked away again.

That knocked me right off my stride and I thought, 'You stuck-up little snob.' But I was already under her spell, and just had to talk to her. And, always prepared, I had already worked out a pretty neat chat-up line.

She was wearing a hat with wax cherries on it, so, turning on the charm, I said, 'If you don't say hello, I will have a bite of your cherries!'

That worked. She gave me a smile — and a cherry. But at that moment, bang on cue, Hobson swooped in and swept her away. So much for the Briggs charm!

I thought, 'That's the end of that.' But I couldn't get her out of my mind. The fact that she appeared so inaccessible only made her the more attractive and, to be frank, I was haunted by her face. I couldn't go to sleep at night without her flashing into my mind. I was determined to date this aloof beauty, and eventually I did, following an incredible incident that could have come straight out of a modern version of *Cinderella*.

At the time, I was staying in the Holiday Inn, which was right by the ATV studios in the Bull Ring, and one morning, as I was walking into the foyer, I saw the girl standing there looking extremely agitated.

'Hello,' I said, strolling over. 'What are you doing here?'

'Oh, I'm looking for a shoe,' she replied.

'A shoe!' I thought, as a look of obvious astonishment swept across my face.

She hurriedly went on to explain that she had somehow managed to lose one of her shoes the night before, while dropping off a couple of friends at the hotel after they had been to a party. Still looking bemused, I said that I didn't understand how she could have lost a shoe without noticing it.

'Ah, well, you see, I wasn't actually wearing them at the time.' This was sounding weirder by the minute, until she explained, 'I was wearing a pair of my mother's, and she had told me not to wear them while I was driving, as she didn't want the heels scuffed. So I had taken them off and driven the car in my stockinged feet. But one of my friends must have inadvertently kicked the shoe out when they got out of the car. But I can't find it.'

This was too good a chance to miss, so I asked her for a date. 'What about going out for a meal or a drink some time?' I said.

'Oh, I don't think so,' she coolly replied, trying to give me the brush off. But I wasn't giving up that easily and, persevering to the bitter end, I then asked, 'Well, give us your number.'

She then gave me a killer reply, saying that she hadn't got a phone. But I refused to be fobbed off and, reluctantly, she gave me her parents' phone number. Even then, she continued to play hard to get, telling me, 'Don't bother ringing me for a few weeks because I am going away on holiday to Spain.'

Normally, if anyone had been so reluctant, I would have knocked it on the head and decided it wasn't worth the candle. But this girl was. And, to be fair, she explained that she was going to see a friend who was looking after the industrialist Sir Bernard Docker, a semi-invalid, who was living on a big boat there.

The Briggs ego had by now taken a real bruising, but I still couldn't get her out of my mind. Weeks went by and I didn't ring because I thought I would simply be asking for another brush off. But then my luck changed — and I reckon bookies would give better odds on me winning the National Lottery than what happened next.

I was driving to Birmingham when my car started to overheat. I pulled to the side of the road, opened the bonnet and found that the radiator was leaking. So, when I got to Birmingham, I took it into a garage just around the corner from the Holiday Inn, where I was staying. And it was then, as I was idly glancing around the garage while they were fixing my car, that I spotted a woman's shoe, delicately hanging from a nail, next to a nude calendar!

'How did that shoe get there?' I asked the garage manager, who told me that one of his mechanics had found it lying in the gutter outside the Holiday Inn when he had gone to the hotel to fix a broken-down car a few weeks earlier.

The mechanic had brought it back, and they had hung it on the nail in case some one called looking for it.

Instantly, I realised that this was the opportunity of a lifetime finally to clinch a date with Christine. She would never be able to refuse, I reasoned, as, with a broad grin spreading across my face, I said, 'I think I know who's shoe that is.'

The day I found that shoe was, without doubt, the luckiest moment in my life. Now, four kids and a mortgage later, it's the full catastrophe!

The moment I left the garage, I raced back to my hotel and rang Christine. After she had hesitantly returned my greeting, I played my ace, casually remarking, 'Oh, by the way, your missing shoe is a size 6 and the colour's dark blue, right?'

Christine was absolutely knocked out and there was a stunned silence down the line before she finally gasped, 'Yes, but how do you know?'

'I have found it,' I replied triumphantly. She just couldn't believe it but, quickly pressing my advantage, I asked her for a date.

This time she finally agreed. But she still appeared to be playing hard to get as she said she had only one day off, which was the coming Sunday, and she was already committed to a attending a choir practice at the Oratory in the Hagley Road. That, however, was fine by me, because I also had a prior commitment — as a celebrity guest on Bob Monkhouse's top game show, *The Golden Shot*, in which contestants fired a crossbow at cartoon targets in a bid to win cash prizes.

So, five months after she had first given me the brush off, we agreed to meet at 7.30pm that August Sunday in the foyer of the Strathallan Hotel, in Birmingham. I was still a little uncertain whether she would actually keep the date and, rather than once more end up looking a complete chump, I said to her, 'If you are not coming tell me now, because I don't want to be messed around.' To my delight, however, she assured me she would be there, and so, with butterflies fluttering in my tummy, I spent the week feeling as excited as any love-sick teenager. And I prided myself on being a love 'em and leave 'em man of the world!

But even then, it nearly ended in tears, and they would have been mine. For, incredibly, on the night I nearly blew it.

I drove up from London to do *The Golden Shot* and, naturally, joined Bob for the party afterwards. It was good fun as the contestants relaxed and Bob was on top form. But I deliberately left early so that I had time to head back to the Holiday Inn, where I was staying, to change before my big date. When I got to my room I had a shower and thought, 'I'll just have five minutes on the bed.'

That, of course, was fatal. I fell sound asleep — and woke up at five minutes to eight. As I glanced at the clock, a wave of overwhelming panic swept over me. 'Oh my God, ' I gasped out loud. Realising that I should have met Christine at 7.30pm, I fought to calm my nerves and, dressing in record speed, raced down to the car park and roared to the hotel as fast as I dared. And I got there in the nick of time.

I was half an hour late — and we met in the revolving doors as she was furiously sweeping through on her way out. As we spun round in circles in those wretched doors, I tried to apologise and calm her down. But she was in no mood for a load of Briggs' best soft soap, after I had initially made the bad mistake of trying to carry off my late arrival by breezily greeting her with, 'Hello, how are you?'

She had already left me a note saying, 'Thank you — goodbye!' and, with eyes flashing, she blasted straight into me, telling me that not only was I late but that she was off. And she meant it. That really knocked the bounce out of me. I could see the date I had been dreaming about vanishing before my eyes, and desperately tried to make up the lost ground.

I told her I was terribly sorry, and she must have sensed

just how contrite I felt for I eventually persuaded her to stay for a drink after making some excuse about problems in the studio, which I don't think she found very convincing.

The evening didn't improve and our first date was a disaster.

I thought she was a stuck-up snob and she thought I was a bit of a spiv. She had her own Triumph Spitfire car and we drove in that to a club I knew. I thought it was a fun place, but Christine hated everything about it, dismissing it as a 'gin palace full of motorbikers in leather jackets'. Christine was convinced I had taken her there to try to put her down on that first date, so she went out of her way to show me she was having a good time — by chatting to all the other blokes!

How I persuaded her to see me again I shall never know, but somehow I did, and then I nearly blew it again on our first dinner date. Christine has never forgiven me for that either.

I was staying at the Holiday Inn, so when I invited her out for dinner, she naturally thought that, at the very least, I would wine and dine her at my hotel. But that was the last place on earth I wanted to take her. It was always full of television types and I wanted a bit of privacy, not to become the centre of studio gossip. So instead I got her a special treat; fish and chips — in the paper, of course — washed down with champagne. I shall never forget her face when I sprang that little surprise on her. She was not impressed, although I think I won brownie points for the sheer cheek of it. But , despite our disastrous first date, I was confident I could get away with that, and I did, although Christine later told me that she didn't find me particularly attractive when we were first dating.

It certainly wasn't love at first sight as far as she was concerned. We were such incredible opposites. She had led a very sheltered, Catholic upbringing and I was so much older than her and very street-wise.

But I knew how to have fun, and could make her laugh. And, fortunately, I still can. Laughter made our marriage, and has kept our marriage going. We laugh a lot, and find each other incredibly funny.

But it wasn't the Briggs charm, or the laughter, or even the excitement that finally won over Christine. It was another girl, who persuaded Christine to take me seriously.

Christine was still undecided about me as a long-term prospect when one of her girlfriends — who was so stunningly good-looking that all the boys wanted to date her — spoke up in my defence. Christine admits that she had always felt second best when she was out with this girl, yet this beauty told her, 'If Johnny asked me out, I would go with him like a shot!' That did it. Christine started seeing my better points and we've been together ever since.

I was now very keen on staying in *Crossroads* for as long as I could, especially as I had been able to fit in a string of film and other television roles while still playing garage boss Clifford Leyton.

In the early Seventies, my movie career started to boom again and from the 1970 comedy thriller *Perfect Friday*, starring Stanley Baker and Ursula Andress, in which I teamed up again with Roger Moore, I found I was once again in demand. The Seventies were very good years for me in movie terms. In 1971 I did *Quest for Love*, which wasn't, as the title suggested, a love story, but an off-beat science-fiction movie about a physicist who finds himself in a parallel world after an accident in his laboratory. Once again it saw me linking up with Joan Collins and Tom Bell, along with Denholm Elliott.

The following year I was in a string of films including Val Guest's raunchy sex comedy *The Au Pair Girls*, which followed the erotic adventures of a string of foreign beauties in English households. I played a gambler, who lost his stunner to an Arab, played by Ferdy Mayne. There really were some great girls in the cast, including Gabrielle Drake and the improbably named Me Me Lay! I was also in the Rank comedy *Bless This House*, with Terry Scott and Sid James, based on the popular Thames TV series of the time, and in which I played a truck driver. Other films included

Mission to Monte Carlo and *The Best Pair of Legs in the Business*, with Reg Varney, of *On the Buses* fame. This was a rather unusual comedy as it was about a female impersonator who made great sacrifices to send his son to a top public school, only for the boy to reject his father. Reg could raise a laugh anywhere and Lew Grade particularly liked it. I got on well with Reg and made another comedy with him, *Go for a Take*.

In 1973, I was in another erotic British romp, *Secrets of a Door to Door Salesman*, playing a guy called Loman, in which the secrets, surprise, surprise, were wholly sexual, as it revolved around the adventures of an innocent from the West Country who comes to London and finds the sexual side of the city too much for him! That year also saw me in *Naughty Wives*, and it was while I was filming at Pinewood that I ran into Paul Newman, who was making John Huston's stylish espionage thriller *The Mackintosh Man*.

I was a bit late and was hurrying along the corridor to my dressing room, where I could see my dresser hovering in the doorway waiting for me, when, as I speeded up, I noticed a guy about my size walking towards me. As he drew nearer, I thought, 'I know that face from somewhere,' and as we passed we both said 'Good morning'.

When I reached my dressing room, my dresser was all over me, exclaiming, 'Oh Mr Briggs, I didn't know you knew him!'

'I don't,' I said with a shrug. 'Who is he? He looks very familiar.'

'Oh, that's Paul Newman,' he said, his face lighting up with pleasure.

'What's he doing here?' I asked, and he told me he was making the Huston film. That lunchtime I wandered into the bar and ran into James Villiers, who told me he was making *The Mackintosh Man*. So I related the story to him and he said, 'Well, he'll be here in a minute.' When Newman walked in, James introduced me and I said, 'You know this morning, I could have sworn I knew you.'

'I felt the same.' he replied, 'Didn't you do the police

series *No Hiding Place?'*

I said 'Yes,' and he recalled that he had seen the programme, adding 'I sort of remembered your face.'

The following year, I made *Bedtime with Rosie* and *Man about the House*, based on the hugely successful TV series. This light-hearted comedy was about the battle that goes on in and around Myddleton Terrace, when developers need only two more houses to complete their take-over and get on with their plans to tear down the whole street and rebuild it in their money-making image. It had an incredible cast peppered with the best known faces on British screens. Everyone appeared to be in it with me, including Richard O'Sullivan, Paula Wilcox, Sally Thomsett, Brian Murphy, Yootha Joyce, Spike Milligan, Bill Pertwee, Arthur Lowe, Bill Maynard and even telly pundit Bill Grundy.

In 1974, I also got another huge television break apart from *Crossroads* when I once again teamed up with John Thaw in the situation comedy *Thick as Thieves* for London Weekend Television. I thought this would prove I was right back at the top as it was an eight-parter by top writers Dick Clement and Ian La Frenais and starred Bob Hoskins as a petty criminal who on release from prison, found his best pal (Thaw) shacked up with his missus. But rather than punch each other's lights out they agreed to share the house. I played a character called Spiggy and we thought we were lined up for a long run as it was an immediate success. But once again, my luck turned. Clement and La Frenais wanted to develop the series and the producers were keen, but Thaw was offered the pilot for a new police series called *The Sweeney*, and he said, 'Sorry, chaps, but I am going to do that instead.'

It was certainly the right move for Thaw. *The Sweeney* became a massive hit with its ground-breaking, no-holds-barred approach to hard living, fist-swinging Flying Squad coppers, while Thaw became a household name through his gutsy portrayal of the hard-nosed Detective Inspector Jack Regan, who was forever snarling 'shut it' at friend and foe alike. But it put he kibosh on the comedy and Clement and

La Frenais returned to the BBC to develop their Ronnie Barker pilot *Prisoner and Escort* into another old lag comedy, *Porridge*.

There was always something just around the corner, however, and in 1975 I was back in the wonderfully wacky world of *Carry On* humour when I played a plasterer in the outrageous *Carry On Behind*, which featured Kenneth Williams and the sexy Elke Sommer as two crackpot archaeologists, and a revealing Sherrie Hewson, with whom I was later to link up with on *Coronation Street*, as a bikini-clad camper.

But although I was head over heels in love with Christine, I eventually became restless being in *Crossroads*. I liked to have more freedom to do more films and I went back to the theatre, playing the Scotsman in *The Hasty Heart* at Windsor. I got absolutely rave notices and they were talking about taking the show on tour, but I didn't fancy touring, and ducked out. To be truthful, I have always found the theatre a bit tedious. The luvvies witter on about it being the only true dramatic art form, but, basically, you do the same thing night after night and can never really relax. You spend all day waiting to go to the theatre, and when you finally finish all you want to do is pop around to the nearest pub for a quick one. But, as often as not, you can't even do that as the luvvies come backstage, declaring, 'Wonderful, darling, wonderful,' and you have to smile sweetly when all you really want to do is go and have a drink. No, I have had my fill of the theatre.

In 1976, I made two more films, which, as events turned out, were to prove my last. I made my final *Carry On*, playing the major's put-upon driver in the army send-up, *Carry On England*. Proving there's no gag like an old gag, producer Peter Rogers and director Gerald Thomas had decided with *Carry On England* to once again to return to Army barracks to raise a laugh 18 years and 27 films after the series began with *Carry On Sergeant*. But this time, although *Carry On England* had the same insolent 'up yours' attitude to officers, it took a far raunchier approach to sex, with the shambling shower of men and women manning an experimental mixed anti-aircraft battery in the dark days of 1940 rather more keen on making love rather than war! Sadly, it was the year that Sid James died, and even Kenneth Williams gave this one a miss, but we still had a lot of fun with Kenneth Connor, Windsor Davies, Judy Geeson and Patrick Mower falling in for laughs.

I certainly needed a few laughs after my previous movie experience of the year in the raunchy, soft porn sex film *The Office Party*, in which I teamed up with Alan Lake and Julia Bond. The film was set against the background of a permissive party held in the office of a firm of sex movie makers — and I ended up having a blazing row with the director, David Grant, when I refused to strip off for the cameras.

They wanted me to peel off completely for a scene where I was supposed to have had sex with Julia as we rolled around the office, but I told them I would only strip to the waist. Grant got very angry — and so did I. I'm not shy and my body was in superb shape in those days. I still think it's pretty good with the golf keeping me in trim, but from the waist down it's private.

Grant argued that everyone had to strip off in the kinky party he was filming, with my character scoring with Julia, with whom I was to make love behind a filing cabinet. But I told Grant that I was not stripping beyond my waist because it was not in my contract. My agent confirmed that this was the case, insisting, 'If it's not in your contract, you don't have to do anything that could prejudice your career.' I certainly didn't want to do anything that would embarrass my children, so once again, I told the director that I wasn't doing it.

Grant was furious and threatened, 'If you don't do it, I will fire you.'

By now, I was equally angry and told him, 'Fire me, and I will go this minute.'

In the end, we came to a compromise, in which I did the scene, but kept my pants on. They still managed to make it look raunchy though, by re-writing the scene so that Julia's character got me stand on a pile of telephone directories in some drunken foreplay. Then, at the crucial moment, she kicked them away and the last the audience saw was our bodies disappearing out of sight ... I never worked for that director again.

In the end, it wasn't so much a case of my not wanting to do a graphic sex scene, as my anger at the way I felt I had been treated. When I went to see the director about the film he never mentioned anything about my having to strip naked. I don't mind people thinking I am a bit of a berk, but I get a bit annoyed when they take me for one.

I was travelling to the Midlands to see Christine as much as possible and jogged along doing the films and various TV roles, until I landed a key part at the Royal Court, playing the white detective in the otherwise all-black play, *Parcel Post*. I found that exhilarating and relished being in such a prestigious theatre again after the dire threats I had received when I had walked out of the same theatre more than a decade before. When *Parcel Post* ended its run in the summer of 1976, I deliberately stayed out of work for three months because Ingrid Pitt had told me that she wanted me for a spy series she and her husband Tony were planning to make with Ian Hendry in the Argentinian capital of Buenos Aires. It was to be a co-Argentinian production in which Ian and I were to play Secret Service guys, with Ingrid as our boss. I was particularly keen as Ian and I had been great pals for years and he always treated me like a naughty younger brother. We were completely in tune with each other and could almost read one another's thoughts. Both Ian and I thought we would make a fantastic screen team, but until Ingrid and Tony teamed us together for the spy series, producers had always fought shy of putting us in the same show. They feared *I* would lead Ian astray!

Ingrid and Tony headed for South America to set it up, and I received a string of telegrams and messages from them reporting their progress. At first, they were brim full of confidence, saying, 'Everything is fine, should start in July.' Then it was, 'Everything fine, starting August. Slight hiccup.'

Finally, I received a desperate telegram stating, 'Everything scrapped. So sorry. Returning home.' When Ingrid got back to Britain and I asked her what had happened. She explained that the film had been scrapped after a political crisis in which the ministers with whom they had been dealing had been tumbled from office.

'There was a coup,' she said, 'and the new régime scrapped everything that had been planned by the old régime!'

That was another body blow and I thought, 'Oh, Christ, I am going to take a holiday to forget it all.' So that August I scraped together my last few bob and took Christine to the island of Gozo, near Malta. '

And, just as I had landed my part in *Crossroads* while on holiday in Spain, once again a foreign holiday proved to be a major turning point in my life.

I was relaxing in the bar when Marina Martin, who by then had become my agent, rang me from London. And I nearly spilt my drink, when, after the usual pleasantries, she said, 'Johnny, you have been asked to do *Coronation Street*.'

Coronation Street! I stood there in stunned silence for a few moments trying to take it in, but instead of shouting to Christine to order up the champagne to celebrate such stupendous news, I said cautiously, 'But I'm not a North Country actor.' That was the whole point, Marina explained, adding, '*Coronation Street* isn't in the ratings in London and they want to see if they can boost their figures by bringing in a Londoner.'

Incredibly, when I think about it now, I still wasn't convinced, and said, 'Oh no, I have done *Crossroads* and I don't want to do another soap.'

'This is a bit different to *Crossroads*,' Marina persisted.

But I was still not very keen and murmured, 'Oh, I don't know ...'

Marina, however, realised that this really was an excellent opportunity and, as I continued to hesitate, she said, 'I'll tell you what. I will put it on the long finger. When you come back from holiday have a look, and then you can decide. By the way, have you seen it?'

Well, I hadn't seen the *Street* since it started in 1960, when I had been working in Manchester, and I told her, 'I have seen it once, but I'm not sure ...'

But I respected Marina's judgement. We had become very good friends, and I have found that if you can have a mature, purely platonic relationship with women they make much better friends than men. They don't want anything from you; there is no rivalry, and they are just terrific pals.

So when I returned home, I flicked on *Coronation Street* and, staring at me out of the television set was my old friend Pat Phoenix. The sight of Pat in all her glory was all the convincing I needed and I thought, 'Oh, yes, I wouldn't mind having a go at that.'

I later discovered that when *Coronation Street*'s famous producer Bill Podmore first decided to bring in a Londoner to try to boost ratings, he had rung up my old *Crossroads* pal Jack Barton and said, 'What's the name of that London bloke who had the garage in your show?'

Jack had told him, 'That's Johnny Briggs,' and Podmore then asked him if I was any good. Jack then gave my CV to Podmore, who explained that he was looking for a Londoner for the *Street*, adding, 'What do you reckon?'

Jack, I know, had a high regard for me and told Podmore, 'Oh yes, have him.' And that is how I got the deal to join Britain's favourite soap. Bill Podmore told me it was a three-month contract , which suited me perfectly at the time, and I told him so, adding, 'That's fabulous.' So in September 1976, I headed for Weatherfield.

Christine and I had become very close by this time and I didn't relish leaving her while I went away to Manchester for three months, especially as she had just lost her father. But it was quality work on a top show and, reasoning that it was only a 90 minutes' drive up the motorway from the West Midlands where we were living, I thought, 'Oh great, wonderful.'

The death of Christine's father was particularly tragic as he died while we were on our holiday in Gozo and it cast a dark cloud over what should have been one of the best holidays of my life.

Apart from landing the role in the *Street*, the whole holiday seemed jinxed from the very start. I had booked the holiday through Philip Dudley, a director at the BBC, who had a house in Gozo and had said that Christine and I could have it for a month. But when we arrived at Philip's house it was already occupied by his ex-girlfriend and her family.

I told her, 'We are supposed to be here.'

She just shrugged her shoulders and retorted, 'Tough, we are here!'

And that, as far as she was concerned, was that. I couldn't believe it and was steaming with anger. But Christine wasn't going to allow the fact that we no longer had anywhere to stay spoil the holiday. Christine is only slightly built and weighed just 7st 12lb, but, shrugging her shoulders, she picked up her huge suitcase and said, 'Right! Come on, we are going to my brother's.'

By an incredible coincidence, Christine's brother, Christopher, and his wife had also booked a holiday on the same island at the same time. Unfortunately, we were once again out of luck. They didn't have any room for us either because they were already sharing with another couple.

Now I really was getting worried as we were strapped for cash and I didn't know how I could meet a hotel bill from the spending money I had brought with me. Christine, however, remained undaunted — and we finally got lucky. We went to the Duke of Edinburgh Hotel, where we told the manager our plight, and he came up trumps. 'You can stay here for the whole of your holiday — just send me a cheque when you get home,' he told us cheerfully.

That was an incredibly kind gesture, but towards the end of our stay Christine's father, who had been terribly ill with cancer of the throat, died. Her mother, naturally, desperately wanted us to return home, but the ferry between Gozo and Malta, from where we could catch a plane, wasn't running. The only person who would help us was a Roman Catholic priest, and he wanted the astronomical sum of £25 to take us across the water. We decided, however, that it wasn't worth it, and so we stayed until the end of our holiday and caught our normal flight home, which, unfortunately, was on the day of Christine's father's funeral.

Christine was very upset by her father's death. He was a great man, founding the biggest estate agents in the Midlands, and it took some of the shine off my landing the role of Mike Baldwin.

But I still had a spectacular start to what has become the most successful and best period of my life. On the first day I had to kiss Julie Goodyear in a car and I thought, 'My God, what has happened to me?' It was, however, a great scene and set the seal for my *Coronation Street* years.

Joining the *Street* also enabled me to get to know Bill Podmore, who was one of the most wonderful men I have ever met in my life. He was like an older brother to me, in the same way Alec Ross had been all those years before. Sadly, Alec had died of cancer during the worst period of my life when money was short and everything was collapsing around me, but Sheila had found happiness with John Thaw.

Cancer is such a terrible scourge. My father died of it, my mother died of it and my best friend died of it, as did Christine's father, which is why I do as much as I can for cancer charities, To lose a loved one is bad enough, but to see them waste away with cancer is heartbreaking.

At *Coronation Street*, I was extremely lucky from the very beginning. I became very great mates with one of the writers, John Stevenson, who liked the character of Mike Baldwin, and started writing for me as if he knew me intimately, although we had only just met. He would write stuff for me that was so acute I didn't have to learn it, I knew it the moment I read the lines. It was as if he had read my mind and had written down a script of what I would say in similar circumstances! It was quite remarkable.

I also had the most wonderful time with Bill Podmore and had a terrific three months playing street-wise Mike Baldwin, who had moved to Weatherfield to open a factory. In the plot, Baldwin then had an affair with Bet Lynch, lived with her and finally threw her out, before moving back to London.

The introduction of Baldwin, and the affair, did wonders for the London ratings and took *Coronation Street* to Number One in the capital, but I had only been on a three-month contract and shortly before Christmas I met Bill in the bar for a farewell drink.

It was then, as we were crying on one another's shoulders, he dropped his bombshell. As we downed our drinks he casually remarked, 'I'm sorry to see you go, Briggsy. Now we are doing so well in London, it's a pity we are losing the Baldwin character. The writers like him, too, so it is a shame you can't do any more.'

'Who says I can't do any more?' I swiftly countered, a tingle of excitement starting to course through me.

'Your agent said you didn't like soaps, but would do this for three months,' Bill replied.

'Yes, that is normally true,' I said, 'but I've had such a good time, Bill, I wouldn't mind doing some more.'

'Well, you are a berk, why didn't you say this before?' said Bill, with an edge of exasperation in his voice.'As you know, the scripts are written three months in advance and we have now done them to the end of March. But if you want to start again in April, I will have you written back in.'

'That would be fantastic,' I said, beaming with delight, and ordered up another round of top-quality claret to celebrate.

Bill told me to keep myself available, and I was only too happy to oblige. I had realised from the very first day that *Coronation Street* really was different and I wasn't going to miss out again.

From the moment I first saw Christine I realised that she was the girl I had been waiting all my life to meet. I don't think I was ever really in love with anyone until I met her. I had adored blondes since I was a young man, and always had this vision that one day I would marry a very good looking blonde, with a superb figure and a nice personality — but I gave up waiting. It was not until my very late thirties, when I was 38 or 39, and I met Christine, that I thought to myself, 'This is what you have been looking for all your life.' And I do believe it was fate. In the early days of our courtship, and long before Christine was really serious about me, one of the directors of *Crossroads* suggested that Christine and I should visit a clairvoyant he knew, and the clairvoyant told Christine she was going to marry and have four children. And that is exactly what happened. So, with my future looking rosy at *Coronation Street*, I decided to take the plunge and make my happiness complete by marrying Christine.

As it was a leap year, I decided, in true Baldwin style, to ask her to ask me!

That wasn't Christine's idea of a proposal, but she was prepared to go along with it, under one very strict condition. She said, 'OK, I will ask you on the firm understanding that as soon as I do that, you will ask me.' I was only too happy to comply — and that December we became engaged.

The following March, I signed a six-month contract with *Coronation Street* and, as life was now looking very fruitful, we decided to get married — twice.

We were officially married in a register office on 14 May 1977, and then did it in style, with a church blessing on 4 June, when a big crowd of *Coronation Street* stars, including Julie Goodyear, Jack Howarth, who played Albert Tatlock and Geoffrey Hughes (bin man Eddie Yeats) came along to cheer us on.

It wasn't all hugs and kisses, however. Christine's mother put a real frost on the actual wedding day. She didn't want me to marry her young daughter one little bit, and let both of us know exactly how she felt. As a staunch Roman Catholic, she was absolutely horrified that her pretty 26-year-old daughter was taking me as a husband. She regarded me as a 40-year-old roué, who, to make matters worse, was divorced from his first wife. As far as she was concerned, I was a complete disaster, and she made her feelings abundantly clear to the whole wide world when she turned up at the register office dressed from head to foot in black, like a giant black widow spider.

Even at that late stage, she made one final effort to persuade Christine to jilt me. As she, Christine, Christopher and their younger brother David were riding in the lift to the floor where the ceremony was to be held, she pleaded with Christine, 'Look, you don't have to go through with this!' Fortunately, despite wedding day nerves, Christine didn't have any last-minute doubts and told her mother, 'No, mummy, I'm fine.'

Christopher then weighed in on our side, declaring, 'Look, Mummy, leave Christine alone.' In a bid to clinch matters, he then added, 'She knows what she is doing.'

My mother-in-law tartly retorted, 'I hope to God she does.'

So the ceremony went ahead and we were married very quietly. And, afterwards, much to my surprise, when she realised there was nothing she could do about it, my mother-in-law became very pro-Johnny Briggs. She is now one of my greatest friends. She won't hear a word against me and has done everything in her power to keep Christine and me together because, naturally, you have little hiccups in a marriage — and we had one big one. But she has been a fantastic woman; a staunch matriarch and absolutely wonderful.

In contrast to her black widow protest at the register office ceremony, she gave us the most fantastic wedding party after the church blessing. It was the best wedding I have been to in my life. Thousands of people flocked to the church and it was a really wonderful, happy day. Christine's brothers, Christopher and David, were there, as were my children from my first marriage, Mark and Karen. There was a big marquee that must have cost thousands of pounds, and I had the time of my life.

I just hope I will be able to do as well for my daughters when they get married.

Then Christine and I experienced all the joys of setting up home together. Christine had bought this house, Whitton Cottage, in Whitton Street, Stourbridge, and we were soon hard at work renovating it and extending it. We started preparing children's bedrooms because we were keen on having a baby as soon as possible — and, to our joy, we did!

The transformation of the cottage was amazing — and we won the award for the best converted cottage in the West Midlands, of which I was very proud. And it was all down to Christine. She did one heck of a job, because it was her ideas that made the transformation so perfect, and she supervised everything, because I was always away in Manchester working. It was a lovely little house and even now I sometimes drive past and take a look. You never know, one day they may put a blue plaque on the wall: JOHNNY BRIGGS LIVED HERE ... ha,ha!

10

MIKE BALDWIN IS A WOMANISER with a list of conquests that would send any man green with envy. In the 22 years I have been playing him, Baldwin has built an incredible reputation for loving 'em and then leaving 'em. But while Baldwin may be the flashest Romeo on television, I have always been more of a man's man.

There is a world of difference between Baldwin and Briggs. Johnny Briggs is a family man — and that is something Mike Baldwin will never be. Johnny Briggs has a lovely, beautiful wife and four fabulous children by her, and he realises just how lucky he is. Sometimes I feel a little bit sorry for Mike Baldwin, because he has none of that.

In 50 years in showbusiness, I have never really been what is called a ladies' man. I have always spent more time with the guys than the girls. I certainly haven't made that choice because I couldn't land a date. I have been lucky enough to have spent my entire working life surrounded by girls, many of them great beauties, and over the years I have had endless chances to whisk pretty girls off their feet. As I have recounted, when I was a young man I had as many opportunities as Peter Stringfellow to score with topless beauties.

But even in my wild partying days, I used to weight train or play golf, rather than chase after an endless succession of girls. In the early Sixties, I used to lift weights every Sunday with two mates in Richmond, Surrey, and, strangely enough, that led to me becoming such a fanatically keen golfer. When the the guys lost interest in weights and started playing golf on the local municipal course, I decided to join them.

Because money was always tight, we could only afford to go to municipal courses, and would take it in turns to make sure we could always get a game. So when we left a party at one or two in the morning, one of us would drive to a course and wait in the queue so we could guarantee getting a round in. The rest of the guys would then totter off to bed for a few hours kip, before rolling up at the designated course at 7.30am. It was a great system. And, more than thirty years later, I will still get up at crack of dawn for a game of golf. When I am working in *Coronation Street*, I will happily tee off at 6.30am with a gang of mates, before going into the studios for a full day's work. Right now I am working on my new pal in the *Street*, Bruce Jones, who plays the sponging, skiving Les Battersby, to get him out on the course at 6.30am. He tells me he hasn't had time to keep his golf up in recent years, but I tell him, 'You have got to make the time!'

Christine knows where my heart lies. She always teases me that while I like the ladies, I would run a mile if they chased me. And there is a lot of truth in that. I would rather play golf with the boys.

You get too much aggravation from the girls and women want to tie you down. I have always found women very possessive — and I don't like that one bit.

That is why I have never gone in for for dating actresses. I have socialised with some of the most beautiful women in the world, but never felt the need to pursue them. When I was an up-and-coming actor, I didn't want to get involved with actresses, although I had a mad fancy for Susannah York when she was making the romantic drama *The Greengage Summer* in 1961. I was doing another film in the same studios and I used to meet her after we finished filming.

I thought she was lovely and we would have a drink together, but nothing came of it. I didn't want to get involved, so I let that slip away. It seems strange thinking about it now, but in those days I was a one-night stand man — wham, bam, thank you, ma'am!

But there was a far deeper reason for my reticence than just not wanting to get involved. I had a different agenda, and there just wasn't time for serious relationships in it. I wanted to make it as an actor at any price and was resolute that nothing — including girls — was going to divert me. All my young life, no one, apart from my mother, had ever had any faith in me. I was constantly knocked by the rest of my family, who jeered at the very thought that Ernie Briggs' little boy could become an actor, let alone famous, and I was determined to prove them wrong. So, to that end, I would take any job that came along, so long as it wasn't total rubbish, firmly believing that a bird in the hand is worth more that a dozen promises flying just out of reach. You are always in a stronger position if you are working and, for as long as I can remember, I was working, trying to prove to the doubters that I could make it. Which, sadly, meant that girls had to take a back seat in my affections.

I was driven, without a doubt, which is probably why I now don't have many friends. I have lots of acquaintances, but friends are harder to come by. The people I could rely on and who stood by me in my hours of need are still my friends, and are welcome wherever I am in the world. But I can't be bothered with the doubters. If I am in a good frame of mind, I might just say 'Hello'. But I would rather just keep walking ...

And some of those doubters carried a lot of clout. When I was called up for the Army after spending all those years with the Italia Conti, Ruth Conti told me, 'I think you should find yourself another career when you come out of the Forces, because the chances of you still being an actor are very remote.' Her brutal assessment really floored me, especially as I had had a fair measure of success in my years at the school. So, feeling more angry than upset, I asked her, 'Why not?'

She replied, 'You wouldn't lose your accent, you wouldn't conform — and I just don't think you will ever have a career as an actor again!'

As if that wasn't a bad enough assault on my hopes and dreams, she was equally uncompromising and obnoxious a few years later, when I met her again at an Italia Conti reunion in the mid-Sixties to celebrate an auspicious anniversary of the school. I was standing with a group of my old colleagues — Millicent Martin, Joan Collins and Anthony Newley — when Ruth came swanning over and said, 'Joan darling, how lovely. You have made such a success of your career, haven't you!' Turning to Anthony, she continued to gush, praising him for all the films he had been in. Then she spoke with equal enthusiasm to Millicent, declaring, 'Milly, we just can't turn on the television without seeing you, can we?' Finally, she spoke to me. 'Now, Johnny,' she said, 'what did you make of yourself? Are you still acting?'

I was in *No Hiding Place* at the time, so Millicent said, 'What do you mean, is Johnny still acting? Of course he is. He is in *No Hiding Place*, the Number One rated show in England!'

And Ruth, at her sneeringly, dismissive best, simply said, 'Oh, I don't watch that sort of thing on TV. But it is nice to know that he is acting, anyway.' And with that, she walked away ...

So Ruth Conti was one of the few people in the world I honestly didn't want to see when Thames made my edition of *This Is Your Life*. I thought, 'What a bloody hypocrite.' Not only that, but she spent the rest of the evening annoying my mother-in-my-law!

As a result of that sort of sniping, the last thing I felt I needed was a girl clinging around my neck, although, like any red-blooded male, I had my fair share of dates and some very nice romantic nights. But as I never even seemed to get to first base with the girls at the Italia Conti, my first real girlfriend was a local girl called Pat, who also lived in Colliers Wood. I had seen her around, but we first became very pally after she saw me filming in *Cosh Boy*, part of which was shot just down the road at Wimbledon Palais.

That certainly made me appear very glamorous and that romance was a big number at the time — and it was then that I lost my virginity. But it didn't last. She was very keen — too keen for my liking. She wanted to get married before I went into the Army, using the popular excuse of the time that I would get more money if I was married when I was called up. This was perfectly true, as the married guys were paid considerably more than the single soldiers, but it was still only a measly few quid. Besides, I wasn't faintly interested in getting hitched. She was upset and there were scenes, but I was adamant. When she realised that she wasn't going to get me up the aisle she lost interest, and I breathed a huge sigh of relief.

Quite honestly, until I met Christine, women didn't really interest me. Oh yes, I would date them and go to bed with them, but it wasn't the most important thing in the world as far as I was concerned.

I would take them out and if some bloke came along and took them away from me I couldn't have cared less. My attitude was simply, 'So what?' Even when I was going out with a beauty from the Windmill Theatre, if a guy whipped her away, it didn't bother me, because I rightly thought, 'There are always other girls just around the corner.' The last thing I wanted was any sort of commitment.

But when I met Christine I knew instantly that I had found the girl I had been waiting for all my life. The incredible thing is that Christine gives me room. She understands me, and I think she's glad to be rid of me sometimes!

Baldwin may be an out-and-out rogue, but my marriage to Christine is so solid it even survived an ill-fated trip I took to Barbados with a beautiful air stewardess half my age. That really put our love — and marriage — to the ultimate test.

They say there's no fool like an old one ... well, there is.

There's the man who has everything and risks it all for a pretty face. There I was, successful, married to a beautiful woman I adored, three fabulous children … and I completely lost my head the moment I clapped eyes on brunette air hostess Hilary.

She looked stunning when we met at a charity dinner in the summer of 1986 and I was captivated. Now I realise that it was the male menopause that made me fall so completely for a girl less than half my age. But that's what I did after we met again in a Manchester club, where she worked as a part-time barmaid. I popped in for a drink but found myself besotted. I realised that I was playing with fire, but I couldn't resist the temptation to stray and to behave like womanising Baldwin. At 50, I became a smooth, single-minded Romeo who couldn't resist the charms of a young lady. For the first time in my life, I found myself acting like one of the characters I played.

In the past, I had always been able to shrug a character off effortlessly the moment I left the set or came off stage. But somehow Baldwin had really got into my skin, and I was playing the part for real.

It was madness. I took her on a romantic holiday to Barbados, after telling Christine I was heading to the Caribbean sunshine alone to organise a celebrity golf tournament. I was so confident and full of Baldwin-style bravado that I foolishly booked on to a flight with Hilary as Mr and Mrs Briggs. We even checked into the same hotel — the Southern Palms Beach Club — where I had previously stayed with Christine! But our sunshine idyll didn't last very long and it all ended in the most bitter tears as the story broke in the newspapers, and I had to come back home to face the music. We were to have stayed for two weeks, but after our romance hit the headlines, Hilary was so embarrassed that she returned five days early. Then it was my turn to take the flak, face the reporters waiting for me on the tarmac at the airport — and, more importantly, face the woman and family I loved so dearly.

I have known plenty of bad times in my life; my sister's

death, my mother's accident, being down on my luck and not having a penny, the collapse of my first marriage — but this foolish escapade was the most distressing because of the pain I caused with that heady fling.

It is inconceivable to me now how I could have been so selfish and stupid. Christine suffered great anguish and and was terribly upset that I had gone abroad with another woman. It was deeply wounding and I bitterly regret it now — not only the distress I caused to Christine, but also to my children and to my wife's side of the family.

Yet Christine, despite the pain, stood by me and wouldn't let me go, and I thank God every day for her strength in doing that. And looking back now, I think what a very, very wise woman she was to realise that my affair was something unique, an aberration because I had reached a critical time in my life when this type of behaviour can happen. They talk about the male menopause and people laugh, as if it is some urban myth, but I don't because I have been through it. This was the time — and my affair with Hilary was the result.

The only thing I pray for now is that my wife doesn't go through it, because I couldn't be as strong as she was. My trip to Barbados was my slip, and now I realise it was just a silly hiccup. But there was nothing silly about the pain it caused all round. If Christine did somthing like that, I just couldn't cope. I wouldn't have her strength and determination to put up with it, like she did.

It took me a long time to woo Christine back and heal the wounds and I can never forgive myself for what I did. Even now, I find it difficult to believe that I was capable of causing so much hurt to my family. I vowed then that I would do everything in my power to make it up to them, but that's easier said than done when you have been responsible for such a cruel act.

I changed to make that possible and devoted myself to my family. Now I couldn't be happier. I have the best children in the world and a truly wonderful wife. I have not been tempted since and never will be again. I've been down that path once and will never stray again. Whenever I think about that episode in my life, I shudder. It was as if I were another person in a different life.

When I flew back to England after the story broke in the newspapers, I just kept praying that Christine would be able to forgive me, but deep down, I didn't honestly think that was possible.

I was convinced that our marriage would be over, and that Christine would swiftly show me the door and demand a divorce, taking the children with her. But instead of considering a divorce, Christine did the opposite — and refused even to contemplate taking such action. When we met as I shamefacedly slunk back home, Christine simply looked me straight in the eyes and told me that I had been the biggest fool of all time. She then went on to say that if I wanted a divorce then I would have to file for one myself, because she wouldn't.

I can't describe the sense of relief that swept through me when she said that. I had been so self-centred and cruel and yet, here she was, giving me a second chance. I grabbed it with both hands. I will be eternally grateful to Christine for that. Most women would have told their husbands where to go. But, thank God, she didn't.

She was dead right, however, about my having been incredibly foolish. I had been, in spades. But, more than anything, I was heartbroken that I could have been so bloody selfish and hurt so many people. I hated myself.

Christine was devastated by the whole messy business and the children, regrettably, were hit even harder — as they were taunted at school by other children, who had read about my affair.

Getting things back to normal was a slow and difficult process, but I was back with my family; I had once again discovered where my true happiness lay, and I felt we were embarking on a whole new beginning to our lives that could only get better with every passing day.

My mother-in-law was a tower of strength throughout those difficult first few weeks. The woman who had once been so against me marrying Christine, now did everything in her power to put our marriage back together. When Christine and the family had got over the initial shock and troubles, my mother-in-law offered to look after the children while Christine and I went away to have some time together.

We went on a skiing holiday, and everything took off between us all over again. That didn't mean Christine forgave me just like that. The damage I had done took ages to repair and I had to court my wife all over again to get back the magic we had enjoyed before my affair. But that was great and I must confess I enjoyed the courtship. It made me realise how close I had come to losing what is most precious to me in life.

I had to win back Christine's trust, for trust is the basis of all relationships and I had destroyed ours. Happily, we managed to rebuild that trust and I never stop realising just how lucky I am.

I realise the true value of my family and appreciate what a marvellous wife Christine is. She is thoughtful, kind and tolerant, among many other qualities. I am very proud of her and the thought of losing her is too awful to contemplate. I know I would never be able to replace her.

Christine has proved her love and loyalty to me beyond my wildest expectations. Ever since then, it has been my turn to prove that I, too, can give her the same love and support.

People who have affairs would stop immediately if they really thought about just what they are risking. Some men think it's fine being Jack the Lad when they are getting away with it, but that's not good enough. I realise what a fool I was and my advice to anyone having an affair is to stop and take a good look at what you stand to lose, and how much pain you will create.

I learned my lesson the hard way — that nothing is worth the loss of my family. I had kicked Christine in the face once, and that is enough for any lifetime.

The cast of Coronation Street were very good to me at the time, but some friends weren't so understanding. I found that I lost respect, especially from the wives. Yet, ironically, some of those friends who became self-righteous were actually having affairs themselves. That really hurt.

But the important thing for me was that I got my family back . It took a while to make it solid again, but that is the most precious thing in the world for me. I was happy to change my ways. I have mellowed a tremendous amount since then and got my priorities right.

At the time, I am sure there were cynics who thought I hadn't really changed. But I did. It was a hard way to learn, but we all came through it. I love my family so much and get more joy out of my wife and family than anything else in the world — and I am never going to lose them.

Christine and I sealed our love in the best possible way — by having another child, Anthony, who is now nine. And after all the traumas there was almost a touch of magic about his arrival. He came as a complete and wonderful surprise after our son Michael wrote to Father Christmas asking for some chocolate pennies — and a baby brother.

It was incredible and totally unexpected, for within a matter of days, Christine became pregnant. Santa was really working overtime!

With her blonde hair, Christine has kept her beauty, but she is resolutely down to earth and has become more tolerant over the years. She's been very good for me. She's very straightforward and honest and doesn't lie. She's very protective of me, but she's also a great critic of mine. She doesn't make a point of criticising me, but she's not frightened of saying, 'I don't think you did that scene very well.'

Apart from Mark, 34, and Karen, 32, from my first marriage, I have four wonderful children whom I absolutely adore: Jenny, 20, who is studying graphic design at High Wycombe University College, Michael who is 18 this year and has finished his A-levels in business studies and psychology; Stephanie, who at 16 is such a good gymnast she is qualified to teach younger children, but is very keen on going to drama school; and young Anthony, who is already a better speller than me! He's also going to a be a lot richer. He has a marvellous trick with money — he never spends a penny but always gets exactly what he wants. He will say, 'I think I will buy so-and-so,' and start to hunt around for his purse. When he finally finds it, he then proceeds to count out his money ever so slowly, just like Charles Hawtrey. And I find myself getting as exasperated with Anthony as Sid James used to with Charles, only in Anthony's case I always seem to end up paying — just to get him out of the shop!

That probably explains why Anthony wants to stay with Dad for ever. 'I will drive you around when you are an old man,' he cheerfully tells me. So with a bit of luck I'll always have one fan, unless he gets swept away with football fever and ends up fulfilling his ambition to play for Aston Villa! Having a young child helps to keep me young. It's magic. The children are wonderful. You can't get stuffy and old-fashioned when you are surrounded by youngsters bursting with vitality.

If I hadn't had four children by my second marriage, I might have considered retiring in a couple of years' time, but there's no chance of that with school fees to pay. I adore having a child as young as Anthony and my only worry is that by the time he's 20, I'll be 70-something! I'll just have to keep on taking the vitamin pills, and hope they are working.

The four children Christine and I now have are a special blessing because we suffered a cruel tragedy early in our marriage. We had both wanted children from the very start and Christine was soon pregnant. But Christine lost the baby five months into her pregnancy. That was a bitter blow, but fortunately, Christine was soon expecting Jenny. Then we knew our luck had turned.

Apart from my own youngsters, playing Mike Baldwin keeps me young, When I step into the part I feel I'm still just a lad, which is pretty incredible as I also have four grandchildren and two step-grandchildren and keep in touch with them all. But I don't worry about being a grandfather for one moment.

I still *think* I'm just a grown-up teenager anyway. And when I look at Jenny I think she *can't* be that age. I'm only 20!

I realise that it has been difficult for Mark and Karen since my first marriage broke down. Sadly, Mark's first marriage didn't work, but he has three wonderful children from it: Claire, who is 12; Samantha, 9; and Jonathon, 6. Mark has now remarried and has two stepchildren: Leigh, 15; and Kerrie, 12, by his second marriage to Susan. I am very proud of him and am delighted that he is putting a real sparkle into people's lives as he carves out a very successful career as a jewellery designer and diamond setter.

Karen's marriage didn't work either and she is now divorced. She has a lovely little girl, Emma, eight, but I am very, very disappointed in Karen's behaviour. Earlier this year, police decided to take no action after she was arrested in a drugs bust — and she criticised me for not being there for her. She said that after the break-up of my first marriage, she only saw me on television. You don't want to speak ill of your children, but this was not the first time she had sold me down the river to the press. On the day of my father's funeral, she had a newspaper photographer waiting when I went to pick her up, and I can't help thinking, 'Where does the forgiving stop?'

These public criticisms are terribly hard to to take and when my daughter Jenny read the stories she phoned me every six hours to see how I was and told me, 'Daddy, I am only a phonecall away. If you want me I will be up that motorway.'

And I thought, 'How lovely of her,' because she is at university and has her own life to lead.

I know that one of Karen's criticisms was that she found my absence hard to cope with, but that is a lie. She was always welcome in our home, and Christine welcomed her until she disgraced herself and was sick all over the bed and took one of Christine's suitcases without asking. She was about 12 at the time and the case was part of a set that Christine received for her 21st birthday. But instead of asking if she could borrow it, Karen assumed that she could take it. So, rather than upset Christine any more, I said, 'OK, she won't come here again.'

When Karen was in hospital I was told she was suffering from anorexia, but I have been told since that her lung collapsed from drug addiction. Why couldn't her mother turn round and tell me the truth? Why couldn't someone tell me the truth, because, eventually, the truth will always out.

How can a woman blame her behaviour on something that happened when she was eight? It is just an excuse.

I didn't receive any letters and I would have thought that if someone felt like that they would have written to their father and explained it. But there was no correspondence, apart from a plea for money — and I didn't know that what she asked for would be put towards her drug addiction. If I had known, I would have had her in an institution and done something about it. It is like me, at the age of 62, saying I am doing this because my father hit me when I was eight.

My son Michael, of whom I am very proud, is doing psychology and is reading to become a criminal psychologist. I am sure his view of the situation would be the same as mine.

I have been offered dope, marijuana, the lot, since I was 16. But I was taught by my parents that it was bad for you and would lead to other things, so don't do it. And I haven't. What really turned me off was the film about the horrors of drug addiction, *The Man with the Golden Arm*, with Frank Sinatra, and I thought I couldn't go through the 'cold turkey' withdrawal bit. I think that film should be shown in every school in Britain and America. People would surely realise that, considering how difficult it is to give up smoking, giving up something like drugs must be five times more difficult. So if you don't start, you don't have the problem.

I used to smoke 15 cigarettes a day before I joined the Army, but when I found I could sell them to the Germans for five times the price I paid for them, I stopped smoking and started making money!

Christine and the family are my rock, the stabiliser that keeps my feet on the ground. When I have rushed home from *Coronation Street* after a truly momentous day, like when the Queen and Prince Philip visited the set, Christine remains a sea of calm and rapidly brings me back to earth. On that occasion, I burst into our mock Tudor home in the West Midlands full of excitement. With my words pouring out like a torrent, I gushed, 'The Queen came to see us today and spoke to me and asked me about Baldwin's factory.' Then, barely pausing for breath, I raced on, telling her that I had also chatted to Prince Philip. Christine looked up and, with a polite half-smile, said, 'How lovely, I'm so pleased, but can you please take the dustbins out. I can't lift them and tomorrow's dustbin day!'

She was just as cool — and equally practical, one Friday when I finally got home after a particularly long, hard and trying week. To cap it all, my usual 90-minute drive home had been turned into a four-hour marathon crawl with the rain cascading down in torrents. I finally got in at 9.30pm, sat down in the lounge and said, 'It has taken me four hours to get home in this weather.'

Christine murmured sympathetically and I heard this tinkling sound behind me.

'Ah,' I thought, 'she is pouring me a drink. Just what I need.'

Suddenly, I felt this liquid splash all over my head.

'What the heck!' I shouted, leaping to my feet, and frantically thinking, 'What on earth have I done for Christine to sling a drink over me?'

'It's all right,' Christine smiled, 'you have just been nitted.' As I looked at her in total amazement , she went on to explain that there were nits in the kids' school and everyone had to be treated for them. 'That's blooming charming,' I thought, but it showed me that there is more to life than *Coronation Street*.

The children can be just as cool. I was talking to Christine one day when Stephanie interrupted, 'Daddy!'

'Stephanie,' I chided, 'I am in the middle of talking to your mother, can you hang on a minute? Don't be so rude.'

So I carried on talking to Christine and once again Stephanie interrupted,

'Daddy!'

Starting to get a little cross, I said sharply, 'I told you not to interrupt when I'm talking to your mother.'

Stephanie then fired back a killer of a response.

'You may think you're famous, but I don't know your name!'

Apart from Stephanie, the children don't show any inclination to go into the acting profession, which I'm rather pleased about. I would never discourage them from anything they had really set their hearts on, but I hate children who go into acting on the basis of their father's name. I think these dynasties, like the Redgraves and the Foxes, are all wrong. It may work for those families but I am uncomfortable with it. I could probably get my son or daughter into acting because of my name, but I am reluctant to do so.

I remember chatting to Robert Mitchum once when we were having a drink in the Compleat Angler at Marlowe and the conversation got around to acting.

'Are you any good,' he asked me.

'I don't know, ' I replied. 'I don't like watching myself.'

'Yes, I never watch myself either,' he said. 'The only film I have been in that I have watched is *River of No Return*, and that was because Marilyn Monroe was in it — and she *was* worth watching. I don't watch myself because I don't think they will ever give me another job!'

And that's the problem with acting. There aren't enough jobs for all the actors, and you need a lot of luck as well as a lot of talent.

I'm convinced our marriage works so well because Christine knows me better than I know myself. She is always two jumps ahead of me.

She swept me off my feet when we first met; I thought she was the most beautiful thing I had seen in a long time — fresh, young, unspoilt. And, let's face it, she has to be someone special to put up with me for more than 23 years.

Now I live for Christine and our four children and am most relaxed when we jet off to our home in the Florida sunshine. There, I can unwind away from all the stress of being a television celebrity. Nobody knows me over there, particularly as my home is on the Gulf of Mexico side of the Sunshine State. We don't get many English visitors — they tend to go to Orlando — but, even tucked away in our non-tourist part of Florida, you can be surprised.

I was playing golf with a neighbour, the baseball hero Hector Lopez. When we came off the course we ran into a party of Canadians who swarmed around me grinning with delight.

'Give me your autograph, Johnny, ' they chorused, while others were saying, 'Great to see you,' or 'Oh God, John, I never thought I'd see you here.'

I was amazed, but I knew from a visit I had made to Canada that *Coronation Street* is very big in Toronto and that made me a big star in their eyes. But they hadn't a clue who Hector was, so he just stood to one side, being totally ignored, grimacing up to the skies and smiling.

When the Canadians left, Hector asked me where I was going, and I told him I was heading for the shopping mall to get some batteries. As he was also heading that way, he offered me a lift and as we walked into the mall, we passed an ice cream parlour where a dozen American teenagers were hanging out.

The moment they spotted us, the shout went up, 'Oh my God, he's here!' and they rushed towards me. Thinking, 'I really am popular today,' I put out my hands to take their books, and they raced straight past me to Hector, who caught my bewildered eye and, with a shrug, grinned, 'That's showbiz!' It was wonderful. I stood there with egg all over my face.

Once again, I was just a face in the crowd ...

But that is the joy of America. I would love to live and work there. If I had done in America what I have done in England for the last five years I would be a multi-millionaire. American Equity looks after its artists, so they are not exploited, while over here Equity is a waste of time. What is the point of having a union if your profession is allowed to be an open shop? Every day, 90 per cent of actors are out of work, only the lucky ones are working. Unfortunately, even for the lucky ones who are working and for whom everything goes well for several years, there is still no guarantee that it will last. I am 62 and have been acting for 50 years. For most people, if they had been working for 50 years, they would expect to be at the top of their profession, but in acting you can be right where you started, or alternatively, you can become an overnight success. It's just a question of who gets the lucky break.

I admit that I have been lucky. In this profession you have to have ability, but you also need luck. I have been terribly lucky. I don't know who my guardian angel is, but if I ever meet him, I will break open the Dom Perignon. Anyone who says you can only get to the top in acting through hard work is talking a load of rubbish. You have to have luck and ability — and then it's down to what you can make of it.

The public don't want to see celebrities effing and blinding and making problems because they are drunk. You have to live up to the public's expectations. You can't roll up to a place drunk and awful. I wouldn't like one of my daughters to bring a Gallagher home.

What these so-called stars forget is that it is the public who put them where they are. If you appear at the Albert Hall and no-one comes to see you, you are not a star any more. You can soon be forgotten in this business, because the public are very quick to change their minds. So you must always remember, you are only there because the public wants to see you.

I remember walking down the King's Road with my ex-wife Caroline, when we spotted Albert Finney, whom she was wild about after his success in *Saturday Night and Sunday Morning*, even though he had pushed my nose out of joint by getting the role. He said 'Hello, Johnny,' and I introduced him to Caroline. He was scruffy and in jeans — and she was bitterly disappointed. Then Diana Dors swept up in her pink Cadillac. That was star quality — and I have never forgotten it.

I like the American way of life and object to the way we

are ripped off back in Britain. You realise just how ridiculous prices are when you spend time in the States.

It's the standard of living there and the way of life that attracts me. I have been wildly enthusiastic since I went over there in 1990 with some friends to play golf.

One day, after a boisterous lunch and half a glass of red wine, we went looking at some houses for sale and I put a $1,000 deposit on one in Lakeland, just south of Orlando, in Florida.

When I got home and told Christine, she went beserk, accusing me of doing it on a drunken impulse, she furiously told me, 'Get your money back. I don't like America. I have seen it on television.' I tried to argue that she had only seen a Hollywood version of the States, insisting that where I was buying the house was quite different. But she wouldn't listen to reason, so in the end, I said, 'You are such a tough lady, why don't you go over to America with me and get the money back?'

'All right, I will,' she said, much to my surprise, and a couple of week's later we drove to the show home of the real estate agents who had sold me my house. I could see that Christine was impressed by its appearance and size and she said to the agent, 'Just a minute, isn't this two houses knocked into one?'

'No, madam,'he replied. 'This is identical to the house your husband has chosen. It is called the Pinehurst.'

Christine then pointed at a huge hole they were digging out in the grounds and asked, 'What is that area over there?'

'That,' said the agent, 'is the pool area.'

By now, Christine was seriously interested and we went to see the site I had picked. But she still wasn't completely happy with the deal.

'I don't like this very much,' she told the agent, adding, 'Do you have any nicer plots?'

'Not here,' he replied, 'but we have some over on the west coast in a place called Hudson.'

'Oh,' said Christine, 'is it far?'

The agent told her it was about half an hour's drive, so

we went to Hudson on the Gulf side of Florida and after looking at various plots, Christine chose one with a $3,000 premium on it because it was not overlooked.

'Oh, this will do, this is lovely,' said Christine, before stunning the agent by telling him she wanted the pool situated so that it was in the sun all day.

'Americans don't like their pools in the sun, they want them in the shade,' the agent started to argue.

But Christine swiftly retorted, 'Well, we're British and I want my house built so it is facing such and such a way and I want the pool in the sun all day!'

The astonished agent then protested, 'Well, madam, your drive will be curved, instead of straight.'

'Well, curve it,' Christine flashed back.

The next thing I know, Christine is heading for the furniture store.

'Hey,' I protested, 'I thought you were going to get my $1,000 back?'

'Johnny,' she said with a winning smile, 'if you are going to get a house you must get it right!'

It's my dream home with the pool and large grounds and we wouldn't swap it for the world. And our lifestyle is fabulous. I have a Cadillac and Christine has a Chrysler Seabring convertible to run around in. Now we go there as much as possible. Once you have been to that side of Florida, you wouldn't ever go to Spain, or anywhere else, again. I don't like California, and I'm not too keen on New York, but I like Hudson, Florida. Michael calls it 'God's Waiting Room'.

The weather is perfect, everything is so much cheaper and the service is superb. Petrol costs me 64p a gallon, an oil and filter change for the Caddy is just £8, and food and booze are less than half the price in Britain.

I get up early — between 4.30 and 6.00 every morning — and am on the golf course by seven. I then get back home by 11.00am and go for a swim in the pool. We will then go bowling, karting, fishing or simply go out for lunch at one of the great restaurants. We even have an English pub. And in the evenings, Christine and I leave the children arguing over what they want to watch on TV as we retreat to our bedroom to watch a video. It is pure bliss.

I just love the freedom. I haven't been able to walk around freely in Britain for decades. I'm not complaining, but it can be rather restricting always having people stare at me.

When I met 120 of the most beautiful girls in the world earlier this year, as a judge at the Miss Hawaiian Tropic beauty contest in Las Vegas, along with Donald Trump, tough-guy actor Joe Pesci and the woman editor of *Playboy*, Jenny fixed it so that I couldn't get too friendly with any of the girls and concentrated on my golf instead.

Before I flew to Vegas, I went on holiday to Barbados with the family and Jenny started painting flowers on the family's toenails. She then painted the nails of Frank Bruno's wife and daughter, before turning to me and, with a wicked gleam in her eye, dared me to have my big toenail done, too!

I didn't think anything of it at the time, but when I was in Vegas, Jenny said to Christine, 'How do you think Daddy's getting on with that painted toenail? I have really screwed him down, mummy, because he can't get it off, and with that daisy, there's no chance he will take his socks off with anyone around!' And they fell around laughing at the thought of butch Johnny Briggs with a daisy on his nail.

We had a super family holiday, but a giant shadow was cast over it just as we were leaving. Anthony was a bit sluggish and I said, 'Come on, buck yourself up and help Mummy.'

As I spoke, I caught hold of his arm and he went, 'Aargh!' and collapsed on the floor.

I said, 'You are a better actor than me ... get up.'

Anthony then said, 'Look,' and rolling back his sleeve showed me an enormous boil type of thing on his arm.

'How long have you had that?' I asked, started to feel alarmed.

'About three days,' he replied.

Christine immediately rushed him to the nurse at our holiday complex, who said it was a spider's bite. She dressed it and told us we should take him to hospital as soon as we landed after our flight home. When we got back to England, I could see why they took it so seriously, as by then Anthony had a livid red line running right up his arm and the hospital staff told us that if we hadn't caught it in time, he would have had septicaemia. Poor old Anthony had to have his arm in a bandage and underwent three weeks of treatment. The bite was so bad that, at first, the antibiotics didn't work. So when you go to Barbados beware of spiders!

Christine, as usual, handled it marvellously. But then she is always at her best in a crisis. Whenever I am working, she tries to keep problems away from me, and while it is very good of her, I accuse her of hiding things from me. I know I shouldn't, but I think it is a form of guilt because I am not there. Other fathers are there in the evening, but I'm not. I leave Sunday evening and arrive home again the following Friday night.

I haven't been as good a father as I would have liked because I am never home — I am usually in Manchester working. But I couldn't move to Manchester because it's too wet and cold and all my wife's friends and all my children's friends are in the Midlands. I couldn't cause all that upheaval and move them to Manchester while on a year's contract that could end tomorrow.

I certainly couldn't cope like Christine does — running a home, bringing up four children, and working as a teacher. She is now a supply teacher, but for the first 15 years of our marriage she was a full-time teacher, handling 36 children. I couldn't do it. If she leaves me with our four children for four hours I am a nervous wreck!

It has worried me to be away from the family so much, because I have not been there to help bring the children up, and to discipline them. Now, if one of the children loses their temper they turn on me and say, 'Oh, Daddy, go back to Manchester!'

Just how cool Christine can be in a crisis was really

brought home to me three years ago when we were caught by a huge wave while sailing across the Atlantic on the QEII. And what made it even more remarkable was that Christine was absolutely terrified, as she found herself living her life-long nightmare.

Ever since she was a girl, going to school by the sea at Torquay, Christine has been haunted in her dreams by this premonition of being engulfed by a gigantic tidal wave — and in the early hours of 11 September 1995, she came face to face with her demon as hundreds of thousands of tons of water hit the Cunard flagship head on and crashed over the bows. The wave, whipped up by the 130mph winds of Hurricane Luis, was 95ft high and 400ft long. It was so huge that the skipper, Captain Ronald Warwick, was at eye level with the monster wave as he controlled the liner from the bridge. And to add to the terror, we had our white-knuckle night of terror off the Newfoundland coast — where the Titanic had sunk!

When Christine first heard that we were heading for really bad weather she wanted to be airlifted off the liner. But she conquered her fears, calmed down and, amazingly, has never had that nightmare since our night of terror.

The first we knew about the atrocious conditions was at lunchtime on Monday 10 September, when we went into the liner's shop, where the saleswoman was taping the cosmetics to the counter. When we asked why she was lashing everything down, she explained that we were heading for a Force 11 storm. Christine, her eyes widening with fear, visibly paled as she gasped, 'This is my nightmare,' before going on to describe the huge wave in her dreams. Everyone laughed and we went to the bar for a little steadying drink. But Christine was still uneasy and, by evening, she was starting to get really worried, as she had lived with this premonition for so long. And I realised we were in for a bumpy ride when the captain failed to appear in his quarters for the cocktails to which we had been invited, because he was too busy on the bridge. The liner had by now slowed down to five knots as it battled through the mountainous seas but, as Christine and I had had injections against seasickness, the rough ride didn't bother us and we went in for dinner. Eventually, we were the only people left in the dining room, so I suggested we went off to bed.

We had been warned not to go on deck as it was so dangerous, but I wasn't bothered and, despite our date with destiny, I went off to sleep, much to the annoyance of Christine, who reckons I snored the storm away. But no one could have slept through that mighty wave, which hit us with a terrifying judder and it felt as if the ship was scraping along the bottom of the Atlantic. The liner turned over on one side and hung there, before violently lurching back again.

As Paul Daniels was also on the liner, I reckoned we could have used a little of his magic, especially when we made a 16-mile detour towards the eye of the storm to answer a distress call.

But that was as spooky as Christine's premonition. We never found the source of the distress signal, and so resumed our course. There was no ship missing, so Christine reckoned it was a ghost of the Titanic.

Christine's dreams certainly have an uncanny knack of coming true. She dreamed about being on a plane that couldn't gain height and crashed into a block of flats — and a week later a plane flew into a block of flats.

Sailing away on the QEII, or going to our home in Florida, gives me a tremendous break from the pressures of being constantly recognised and it is because of those restrictions on my lifestyle that real friends are very important to me. My best friend is my wife — and I count two more women amongst those whose friendship I really cherish — Sue Davis, my accountant, and Marina Martin, my agent. They truly are more than just close business associates, they are people I would trust with my life.

Then there are the guys I have always been able to rely on: Captain Brian Wallace, who has stuck with me through thick and thin; Rodney Gabriel, who used to live next door to me in Ashford; another Ashford man, the clarinet-playing

Des Bolster; driving instructor George Harris; *Coronation Street* writer John Stevenson, who has always been very kind to me and with whom I still enjoy a drink; my great Manchester golfing partners, retired wrestler Alf Margette and Father Danny Canning; Anne Kirkbride's husband Dave Beckitt; Steve Williams, who got me into Mercedes cars; Alec Milnes, who taught me a lot about the rag trade and how to behave like a manager as Mike Baldwin, and who is Anthony's godfather ... I could go on a long time.

There are also the friends who sadly are no longer with us: Alec Ross and weightlifter and body-builder Roy Shepherd. Roy had a superb physique and I was convinced he would outlive us all, but at 47 he failed to survive a heart by-pass operation. I also have two wonderful friends in America, Steve and Sue Croft, who were both members of the Special Branch Royal Protection Squad. It is really funny when Steve and I go anywhere as people think he is my bodyguard! I also have one very special fan, Ernest Joynson, who lives in Toronto, where *Coronation Street* is extremely popular, and regularly sends me money for a drink. He recently sent me $55 with which I bought a very nice bottle of champagne to toast his health and wish him health, wealth and happiness.

There are also friends who have annoyed me. Anna Neagle's godson David Gregory, who was my pal at the Italia Conti, really let me down in 1965 when I loaned him the money I had put aside to pay my taxes, so that he could open a pub. He didn't pay me back and when times got tight for me I had to take him to court, where he was ordered to pay me £4 a month. But that dried up after a couple of months. I never saw it all back and it was because of that loan that I had to sell my Bentley when cash started to get really tight for me, too.

But the biggest let-down didn't cost me anything, although it was the worst snub I have ever received.

Anthony Newley had always appeared to lead a charmed life as far as I was concerned. When we were at drama school and in Rep together, he always pulled the birds and he got some very good breaks early on, but we had remained quite chummy until, early in 1982, when I went over to Hollywood to see what was on offer. Anthony was already there with Leslie Bricusse, so I wrote telling him I was coming over. He wrote back full of enthusiasm saying, 'Where is that skinny little fella I knew in drama school? Love to see you. My secretary's name is Annie. Call in, here is the address ...'

So in due course, I called at his office, and was given the cold shoulder. I was told he was in conference and when I asked when the conference was likely to end, the woman said, 'I don't know.' So I showed her the letter I had received from Newley and said, 'I am staying at so-and-so hotel, please ask him to phone me.' He didn't even have the decency to phone me to say 'Hello' — so I crossed him off my Christmas card list.

But I have been luckier with my family and realise that I am a very fortunate man ...

11

WHEN IT COMES TO BEING A HEART-BREAKER, Mike Baldwin's the man. And people who don't know me assume that Briggs and Baldwin are exactly the same. But while the cheeky smile's the same, the rest isn't.

I'm a family man from top to bottom, and always have been. Mike isn't and that twinkle in his eye always promises mischief. He gets a kick out of putting one over on people, and if that involves a bit of hanky-panky, so much the better.

In the 22 years I have played him, Baldwin has become the Bogeyman of *Coronation Street*, the street-wise charmer with a ruthless streak who always plays to win — no matter what the cost.

Over the years, the Romeo with a heart of flint has bedded the birds with the ease Jack Duckworth downs pints, and he's carved his way through the business jungle with the same iron will.

Alma may think she's tamed the biggest rat on television, but I wouldn't bet on it. Baldwin has always had an eye for the girls since I was brought into the show and made my début in a passionate clinch with Julie Goodyear — and that's the way I hope it stays. Baldwin is at his best when no lady is safe from his predatory eye.

The *Street* ratings went through the roof, and we won a major award with the famous Ken Barlow, Deirdre and Baldwin love triangle back in the Eighties and that rivalry hasn't mellowed with the years. The animosity is as potent as ever, with burning hatred only just below the surface, and they're still slugging it out. Baldwin has always got a kick out of putting one over on Ken since Mike first kissed Deirdre in his Jag, before tempting her back to his flat. It was wonderful stuff then and we have managed to keep that magic going through the years.

Ken eventually won her back then, after an explosive punch-up. But Baldwin was soon back for more, eventually whisking Barlow's daughter up the aisle, and the bitter Baldwin–Barlow feud has continued ever since. The brutal confrontation in the Rovers at the beginning of the Nineties, when Mike smashed Barlow for six, set the tone for another decade of mutual loathing, which was always waiting to be given a savage new twist.

And, much to my delight, it exploded again earlier this year in an even more sensational storyline, drama that was so intense that it gripped the whole nation as no soap has ever done before.

And, I must confess, I was thrilled the moment I first saw the scripts involving Deirdre in a new love triangle, with a bigger, though less successful, con-artist than Baldwin. I knew at once that this was the quality of drama upon which television history is made. We played it for all it was worth and even I was amazed at the way the nation turned fiction into reality. The potency of the Baldwin–Deirdre relationship was given a heart-breaking poignancy, while the feud between Baldwin and Barlow was exploited to the full. The feud has always been a ratings winner and I've loved every minute of it.

You see Barlow on screen and you can't imagine anyone liking him. Baldwin and Barlow are like chalk and cheese. Mike is everything blokes want to be, while Barlow is everything they want to hate and never want to be. Mike doesn't like Ken at all. He thinks he is a complete and utter drip, and makes it perfectly plain at every possible opportunity. Barlow, in turn, despises wide-boy Mike and all his tricky ways, and hates his effortless success with the ladies, although Barlow has had more than his fair share of babes over the years.

They have had eight punch-ups over the years. In the first two, Barlow got the first punch in while Mike wasn't looking, and Barlow again sent Mike spinning early in 1998 when he sent him flying on to the cobbles when Mike wasn't expecting it. But Mike landed the best punch of the lot when he smashed Barlow for six in a sensational sequence before the shocked regulars in the Rovers in one of their most bitter fights at the beginning of the decade. In that fight, Ken thought he was going to get in first again, but Mike said, 'Oh no,' and I felt fantastic as I smashed Barlow straight over the table.

And the rivalry is still there. In one of our three furious clashes this year, the for once not-so-boring Barlow sent Baldwin crashing on to the *Coronation Street* cobbles. And that really hurt — for real. In my long career, I've been lucky to have been barely scratched over the years, despite all the action roles I've played, including sword-fights, punch-ups with villains after hair-raising car chases, and even mad dogs. But this time Bill had me heading for the doctors in real life.

The production crew had put a thin strip of foam on top of the cobbles to cushion my fall for the confrontation in which an angry Barlow shoved me unexpectedly and, catching me off balance, sent me crashing to the ground. But those Coronation Street cobbles are very unforgiving and the foam wasn't thick enough to protect me. As I hit the ground, I caught my elbow and the pain shot right up my arm. It was really sore as you are hitting solid stone when you crash to the deck on the most famous cobbles in the world. At the time, however, I just picked myself up and brushed it aside, laughing along with the rest of them at the way hard man

Baldwin had had the wind literally taken out of him.

But the pain grew progessively worse and eventually I decided to go and see the doctor, just to make sure I hadn't broken anything.

Fortunately, I hadn't, but by then my elbow had blown up like a football and my arm was every colour of the rainbow. The doctor wanted me to rest my arm and use a sling to ease the pressure on it. It looked so bad when I was in his surgery that he drew two lines on my arm with a special marker ink, above and below the multi-hued injury, and told me that if the bruising spread beyond the lines I was to go and see him immediately. He warned me that if that happened I would have to have my arm drained. I didn't fancy that very much, and told him so. I also told him that the sling was out. I explained that I was in the middle of a crucial storyline and we couldn't suddenly have Mike Baldwin walking around in a sling. So I went back to work, with some tablets from the doctor to ease the pain. The really annoying thing was that it sparked off a twinge of gout! Barlow definitely owes me one for that!

In the other two confrontations in the Deirdre trial and jail drama, I, or rather Mike, and Barlow squared up to each other and had to be pulled apart — once in the Rovers and, on the other occasion, outside the courtroom after Deirdre was sentenced to 18 months for fraud. Mike certainly came off best in those clashes — I actually tore Bill Roache's lapel with the intensity of my grip in the court clash.

So I reckon it's time Baldwin and Barlow had another punch-up — a real vengeance bout. I enjoy doing those. And, hopefully, the feud will continue until we are hitting one another with our Zimmer frames. Maybe it will end with me pulling out Barlow's hearing aid!

People are always amazed when they see Bill Roache and me off screen. We get on very well together.

Viewers tend to believe that the famous animosity between us is real, that we truly do hate each other's guts. But we get on very well together and are pals. I play in his golf tournaments, and he plays in mine. When people see us

together they say, 'Oh, I thought you two were enemies!'
And we smile and reply, 'Yeah, we are. We hate each other,
really.' And then we just have a good giggle about it.

I genuinely like Bill very much. There is nothing to
dislike about the bloke. He is a very intelligent, quiet,
reasonable, well-mannered guy.

He is not big-headed, doesn't throw his weight around
and is a genuinely nice guy. He has a very successful son,
Linus, of whom he thinks the world. Bill is all right. And the
only time I want to smash him for six is on the golf course.
Now there really is rivalry there and I get a special thrill if I
can put one over him then.

I have to admit, though, that I enjoy the feuding and
womanising, along with the wheeler-dealing. Baldwin is a
guy on the edge. Just when you think it's safe to swim, the
shark is back ...

In Weatherfield terms, flashy Baldwin would be quite a
catch, but it isn't just the money that enables him to bowl
the girls over. Girls go for him because he is a loveable
rogue, and I don't think he really hurts anyone. Well, hardly
anyone.

He did hurt Susan Barlow when he dumped her when he
found out that she had had an abortion. He even called her a
murderer, but the fans didn't mind that at all — and she
deserved it!

The day Baldwin walked down the aisle with Ken
Barlow's daughter, Susan, was my worst moment in the
Street. When I heard what they were planning, I was spitting
mad. I was so angry that I went straight to Bill Podmore, who
was then the executive producer, and complained bitterly.
'What the hell are you doing to me?' I protested, as I felt it
spelled disaster. It was the worst thing that had had ever
happened to my character, and it was the last thing I thought
should happen to Mike Baldwin. I had had an agreement
with Bill Podmore since I first joined the show that
Baldwin wouldn't marry and would remain the wide-boy,
womanising rogue he had been since he first sweet-talked
Bet Lynch into bed in his earliest scenes. So when the show's

executives decided to marry me off to Susan Barlow I was furious. I felt betrayed, and let Bill know it.

It was Baldwin's first marriage and, after my protests, the bosses promised me that it wouldn't last long. But it went on for more than a year — and that was too long as far as I was concerned.

If ever a marriage was made in hell, that was it.

Mike only wed young Susan because, subconsciously, he wanted to upset his arch-rival Ken Barlow. Susan was just an unsuspecting pawn in their bitter game and it was bound to end in tears. The unlikely couple were divorced when Susan went ahead with an abortion, despite Mike's strenuous objections.

The whole business was a really rotten period for me. Wendy Jane Taylor, who played Susan Barlow, and I didn't get on at all. She behaved like she was a star and wouldn't listen to any criticism.

She would be told things, but they would go straight through her. She took absolutely no notice at all.

It drove me wild and I plotted ways to make her life as miserable as she was making mine.

I pride myself on being able to get on with any actor or actress, particularly if you have to do intimate scenes together. It makes it so much easier to be convincing before the camera. But I found Wendy very difficult to cope with. It got so bad between us that I would deliberately eat meals laced with garlic the night before we were to film a passionate scene, just to wind her up. I know that sounds horrible, but it was the only way I could get through those days working with her. It was so bad I have tried to blank that period from my mind.

A lot of women have fallen for Baldwin's smooth charms and most of the affairs have ended in tears. And that goes for the weddings, too.

I must confess that I also arrived in Manchester with a bit of reputation as a lady-killer, sharing Baldwin's passion for a fast shilling, fast cars and even faster women.

After the collapse of my marriage to Caroline, I was a bit

shell-shocked at first and spent a year very anti-women. I used to lie in bed and ask myself how it had happened. Perhaps, I reasoned, it was because I was too young when Caroline and I married, as I was only 26. Anyhow, I decided to keep away from women altogether, and just go out with the boys.

I did for a while, but I have always been a bit of a flirt and, as a single guy, I could see no reason why I shouldn't enjoy some female company. And I did.

Brunettes, blondes, red-heads ... I dated them all, and had a marvellous time. It was wonderful. But, apart from Christine, none of the romances were serious.

Until I fell head over heels in love with Christine, I had been described as 'a jet-setting, love 'em-and-leave 'em heartbreaker' with my high-speed bachelor lifestyle. Well, it was pretty good, and I have to admit I loved every minute of it. But a reputation like that can spell trouble.

So I shouldn't have been surprised when Julie, with her opening breath on the day we met, decided to warn me off from trying to add her to my list of conquests, particularly as we were about to embark upon a passionate screen love affair and that very first scene together — our long kiss.

When Julie told me that she could be a great friend, she meant it. And that's what she was throughout all the years we were in the *Street* together. We used to have lunch together almost every day and she was very good to me when I first joined the show. She mothered me! And there were never any temper tantrums or anything like that. She was very nice to me — and also very protective. Too protective, as I was to eventually to discover.

If I was talking to someone of whom Julie didn't approve, she would swiftly move in, give them a short , sharp burst of her tongue, and they were off!

She liked it even less when I was talking to girls. Christine was the only one of whom she approved — she used to get rid of the rest. Very swiftly.

And that happened quite often.

I had had a fantastic time as a free, single guy with a high profile. It was perfect. I always reckon a guy shouldn't get married until he is at least 35 so that he has basically sowed his wild oats before he even thinks about settling down. Because, by then, if you meet the girl about whom you think, 'Right, this is it!' you are mature enough to be able to try and be faithful to her and make it work. By then, you have experienced enough of life and had enough girlfriends so that you don't worry about what other women might be like. You don't think you are missing something, because you realise you have experienced something similar before and know that while every girl is different, sex is pretty much the same.

I have known guys who have been with girls they haven't liked, just for the thrill of going to bed with someone else. I couldn't do that. I couldn't make love to a girl I didn't really fancy in a million years. It beats me how guys can make love to someone they don't want ever to see again. And, let's face it, if she is ugly and fancies you, but you don't fancy her, that can be a real pain and lead to a lot of problems.

I have always felt that if you are going to go to bed with someone, you have to have some genuine feeling for her. Then making love to her is OK, even if it is a one-night stand, but I could never go to bed with someone just for the sake of it. I would rather leave it until I found someone I did like.

When people ask me my advice for a married man who is embarking on an affair, I say, without trying to be holier than thou, 'If you can avoid doing it altogether, that is the best policy. But if you are going to have an affair, make sure it is with a girl with whom you are prepared to spend the rest of your life — in case the affair wrecks your marriage.' The girl has to be really special. Because if you are going to have an affair with someone about whom you couldn't really care less, you are being totally stupid.

I have never been one for ego trips and in the days when I was pally with Tom Jones, I was always the one trying to keep the girls away, as opposed to trying to pull them. All my mates would be desperately trying to get off with the girls and I would be saying, 'No. It's awfully sweet of you, darling, but no.' I'd realised that they didn't want me for myself, but for my image. They were attracted to the image I had had since *No Hiding Place*. If I had been ugly they would still have wanted me. Not because I was Johnny Briggs, but because I was a glamorous television personality. And it was like that in my early days on the *Street*. I had more girls after me than anyone else. They used to monitor the mail at Granada, and I used to get loads. And the offers would make your hair curl.

Julie was well aware of this and was determined to protect me from predatory girls, fans or otherwise. She also liked Christine and was determined that I should give up my bachelor life and marry her. Julie would ruthlessly pile on the pressure, telling me, 'Yes, Christine's the one for you. I think she is the girl you should marry.'

I wasn't too keen on having Julie run my life, particularly my love life, and I would swiftly reply, 'I'm not thinking of anything like that.' But there was no putting her off and she would swiftly retort, 'Well, it's about time you settled down!'

We had a running joke in which I would say, 'Julie, when I came up here to *Coronation Street*, I was footloose and fancy free and had an MG. After you finished with me, I had a mortgage, a house, a wife, insurance policies — the full catastrophe!'

She would just laugh and say, 'Well, you need them.'

In those days, of course, although I was very close to Christine, I was still fancy free and so when girls came milling around, Julie would see them off with the same iron will she was later to employ with such impressive style as landlady of the Rovers. She would whisper in my ear things like, 'You don't want to talk to her darling.'

'Why not?'

'Oh, split ends. Not good enough for you, darling. I will tell you when the right one comes along.'

I wasn't too keen on being bossed around like that and would argue, 'Well, this one is alright. She's a good-looking bird.'

But Julie would sweep aside all my objections, declaring, 'Oh no. No. No.'

She would get rid of any girl she thought was making a play for me. Julie would wait for the girl to go into the toilet, then she would follow her in and say something to her — and the girl would just go. She would suddenly disappear. I used to wonder why all the girls did a runner the minute Julie said she didn't like them, but I never realised at the time that it was Julie who was giving them the elbow.

She was very protective, but she liked Christine, which is just as well or she would have tried to give her the heave-ho, too. But Julie realised right from the start that Christine was special.

And, looking back, I can see why Julie was so protective.

From the moment I joined the *Street*, I was set up as the Jack the Lad, Cockney wide-boy who was always out to score with the girls, when he wasn't pulling a fast one on everyone else. And that worked wonders with building a big fan following.

Chris Quinten was the young heart-throb, but I, as 'The Man You Love To Hate', drew big crowds of fans, too. And a lot of the girls who crowded around whenever I did a personal appearance, made it quite clear they wanted more than an autograph. And, to be honest, the offers might have tempted me a few years earlier. It sounds dreadfully big-headed, but hundreds of women used to write in saying that I was their favourite fantasy. They would say they would love to go to bed with me, going into the most intimate details. Some would even go so far as to say that I could call on them — and make them pregnant — any time I liked! It was incredible.

But you have to take it with a very large pinch of salt. I suspect that if I had turned up at their front door when their husband was out they would have run a mile. But I never wanted to try, and I have always been very careful not to fall into that trap all through my career. I had had similar adulation in *No Hiding Place* a decade before and you have to be very careful not to start believing in your own publicity.

More importantly, I had Christine. And our marriage has been such a blessing, although, when we wed, some people cynically maintained that it would never last five minutes.

Christine and I share the same zodiac sign — Virgo — which is supposed to be a recipe for disaster, according to star-gazers.

Nowadays, I don't chase girls because I have got much better at home. The only snag is that my work takes me away from home and during the week I live alone in a flat at Salford Quays. It is a superb development and only a few minutes from the Granada studios.

But, much though I love my family, I would never move our home to Manchester — there's a lot to be said for a chap being away from home during the week.

My mother-in-law says that it means that Christine and I have a 'continuing honeymoon', and I think she has something there. Also, deep down, I know that this 'different' sort of married life really suits me temperamentally, however lonely I may get sometimes. Often I think that Christine and I get on so well because we don't see each other all the time, like most married couples do!

When I joined *Coronation Street* Julie was a very important member of the cast. She, and my great friend Pat Phoenix, were the Queen bees. And, of course, Julie was very pretty.

She may have made her name as the mouthy, busty blonde always giving blokes the come on-over the bar of the Rovers, but that was just her screen image. That great beehive hairstyle was a wig — and when she finished filming that came off, along with the yard-long earrings and the gloriously over-the-top clothes with the plunging necklines that left the guys gasping.

Her real hair was quite nice and she was quite attractive. She was so different in real life to the character she played. She loved the outrageous earrings she wore as brassy Bet and had hundreds of pairs that had been sent in to her by fans, but she seldom wore that sort of thing off-duty. True to form as Bet, however, she did make a bit of a splash when the

Queen and Prince Philip opened the new set in 1982 — sporting a pair of 'royal' earrings with cut-out pictures of Prince Charles and Princess Diana.

Julie spent a fortune on clothes for herself and dressed very smartly, but her own clothes were subdued. She also had, of course, the most fabulous legs! I was very fond of Julie.

But while she was very keen on running my life, particularly as far as women were concerned, she didn't confide in me about her own fairly spectacular love life.

Julie had already been married twice when we met on *Coronation Street*, and both marriages had ended in disaster, with the fellas walking out on her. But you wouldn't have known that Julie had ever had a care in the world.

She was always very secretive about her romances and she played her cards so close to her chest that the first a lot of the cast knew about her passionate romance with hotel manager Andrew McAllister, whom she met on holiday in 1980, was when she declared her love for him before millions of television viewers on the hugely successful show *This Is Your Life*. There, before the world, Julie grandly announced that she planned to wed McAllister after she had made a Leap Year proposal! But that romance was over within a week of her making the programme, with Julie dumping McAllister, and throwing him out of the semi-detached home in which she then lived in Heywood, Lancashire.

Well, we all knew that Julie had a reputation for loving — and leaving — her men as fast as Bet, so the rest of the cast carried on as if nothing unusual had happened.

The affair that really startled the cast, however, was Julie's romance with top Granada director Bill Gilmore in 1983. Julie kept that affair secret, not only from the fans and cast, but also from American businessman Richard Skrob, whom she had also been dating since they met on a flight from Los Angeles in 1981.

Skrob, apparently, had proposed to her three times since he first fell under her spell, but the first he knew of Julie's romance with Gilmore was when, once again, Julie's latest love was trumpeted to the world. Skrob realised he was being left out in the cold when Julie and Gilmore's marriage plans were announced in the newspapers. Skrob flew back to Britain to plead with Julie to call the wedding off. He really was in luck that time, as Julie had already broken off her romance with Gilmore.

Julie's affair with Gilmore really set the tongues wagging in the Green Room, where we used to relax between filming. In those days, the cast was much smaller as we only made two episodes a week and we spent a lot of time socialising with each other. People would sit around playing cards or just swapping the latest gossip — and you couldn't get a piece of more prime gossip than Julie's fling with Gilmore. But she didn't confide in anyone, not even me, although we were such good mates. She rightly regarded her business as strictly her own affair and no-one else's.

Julie announced that her wedding to Gilmore was off and while she didn't tell me the reason, I later read in the tabloids that she claimed it was because of his boozing. She eventually went on to marry Skrob in a huge blaze of publicity on the sunshine island of Barbados on New Year's Day in 1985. That, however, didn't last either, and the marriage ended in divorce in 1987.

It was quite bizarre that while Julie had an unerring eye for spotting the right person for me, and knew instinctively from the moment they first met, that Christine and I would be wonderfully happy, she couldn't find the same magic herself. But she was always a great mate of mine.

I have a very soft spot for Julie, and our chummy relationship lasted throughout her time on *Coronation Street*. If we ever went anywhere special, like at Christmas, with the rest of the cast, she always latched on to me, and we went together.

After Julie left *Coronation Street*, Amanda Barrie took her place. Now, if we have to go anywhere as the cast, Amanda latches on to me and we always go as a couple!

My on-screen romance with Julie was a sensational way to enter such a big show as *Coronation Street*, and it worked wonders, not just for the ratings, but also for me. But it had never been designed to last. It was originally only meant to be a three-month wonder, so the writers had to come up with the perfect reason for flash Mike to dump the leggy blonde. And they came up with a corker: Brassy Bet became too sloppy for smoothy Baldwin.

We did a wonderful scene where Baldwin came downstairs one day to find Bet sitting around in her rollers, reading the morning paper, with a fag in her hand. She looked a right mess and just didn't fit in with Mike's image. To make matters worse, she hadn't even had the decency to cook his breakfast! So, I'm afraid, she just had to go.

To make the break-up even more plausible, the writers gave the Weatherfield Romeo an even more pressing reason for getting rid of her. Baldwin had someone else lined up to take her place. So without blinking an eye, Baldwin told Bet she would have to move out of Number 5, which he had bought, because his 'wife' was coming to stay. Needless to say, Mike's 'wife' turned out to be another girlfriend, Anne Woodley, who was played by Carole Mowlam.

But Bet wasn't going to be dumped without a fight.

Our final scene in that affair was to prove a real tear-jerker — but not in quite the way that the producer Bill Podmore had imagined.

It was then that I discovered that Julie could serve up a wallop that packed a lot more punch than anything dreamed up by Corrie brewers Newton and Ridley. In fact, she almost knocked my block off!

In the scene where Baldwin announced that he was throwing Bet out because she didn't measure up, Julie had to slap my face before storming off. In the rehearsals Julie did everything in the scene, except the slap. But when it came to shooting the scene, she hit me so hard she fair rattled my teeth and really brought tears to my eyes.

That really was a whack, but Julie, despite appearances, didn't do it on purpose. It was literally a case of nerves.

In those days of union power, it was even more imperative that you didn't run a second over time, or it would cost the company hundreds of pounds in overtime for just a few moments. And that was the case the day we filmed this highly emotional — and very explosive — scene. The director, Quentin Laurence, told Julie and I, 'We have got a three-and-a-half minute scene, and I've got just four minutes in which to film it. If we don't get it in, I don't know what we will do. So we have got just one go at this — and it has got to be right.'

This put the pair of us under a lot of pressure and I think that for Julie, it was just a case of getting though the scene and making sure it worked. She was so nervous of making a mistake that when it came to the slap she went for gold, giving me that real teeth-rattler.

But she had no option. She had to make it look good, for in those days when they said 'Cut' it was literally just 20 seconds before the lights went out and you were plunged into total darkness. The unions had such a stranglehold that when you ran out of time you were out of business, unless the company was prepared to start paying out large sums of extra money, which would have added massively to the costs of the show. So I never complained, and it certainly looked good. So good, in fact, that Podmore was soon signing me up as a regular cast member. And I guess that Julie has to take some of the credit!

Julie respected me as an actor. I don't think she had been up against someone who had had so much acting experience, and she learned a lot from me. Although we were good pals, she was also wary of me — wary that I could upstage her at any particular time. At rehearsals she just took a deep breath and said her part. She respected me because I didn't want to make her look silly. I wanted her to look as good as I did — and she did.

When I returned to the show the following year, the writers soon had Baldwin up to his old tricks and, with romance in mind, the rogue moved Terri Clayton (Jenny Edwards) into his warehouse as a trainee. But he had reckoned without Ivy Tilsley, played by my old mate Lynne Perrie, who threatened to strike over Terri's preferential treatment. So that was the end of Terri.

But Baldwin was just starting to get into his stride. The girl he had his eye on next was another blonde bombshell, Suzie Birchall, played by Cheryl Murray. It was hardly one of Baldwin's great romances, and for once he got as good as he usually dishes out, but it was a lot of fun.

Baldwin bet Eddie Yeats, the Ogdens' bin-man lodger, played by Geoffrey Hughes, that he could get a date with Suzie — and she agreed. But then some snitch told Suzie about the bet and she stood Baldwin up. So Mike had to plead with her to give him another chance and, naturally, she fell for Baldwin's easy charm, and the winning smile.

But for once the smile wasn't enough. After just three dates, Suzie became bored with the relationship and told Mike he was too old for her. Too old! What a cheek!

I liked Cheryl, she was full of fun and very bubbly, but Suzie was a bit too flirty for Baldwin's liking. He likes women who have eyes for him alone. I don't think he could have trusted Suzie for long. And Baldwin couldn't have coped with that. Baldwin likes to do the dirty on people — not to have it dished out to him.

I was lucky when I joined the *Street*. Not only did I have the advantage of having been brought in by Podmore to boost the ratings, I also had the good fortune to have a set of writers who enjoyed creating terrific situations for my character. The *Coronation Street* writers were not used to writing for a Londoner, but they learned fast. And I must admit that if they hadn't picked up on the Baldwin character, I wouldn't be in the show today.

John Stevenson — the main writer — Peter Whalley and Julian Roach all latched on to Baldwin, especially John, who had just joined the show, and Baldwin was their baby. They wrote superb stories which the bosses liked, and so did the public. Podmore would feed in ideas and they turned Baldwin into a must-watch character.

Bill and I became good buddies, but the fact that we were so close created difficulties for both Bill and myself. I couldn't be granted favours or people would say, 'Oh well, you know why!' So Bill was quite strict with me, as I expected him to be. I liked him. He was a very, very clever man and was in complete control. He started as a cameraman on *The Army Game* and knew the business inside out. So, for instance, if a cameraman said, 'Oh, I don't like that shot, can we do so-and-so,' Bill would say, 'Why not?' And if there was any argument, Bill would then come down on to the set and do it himself. No one could pull the wool over Bill's eyes.

I socialised a lot with Bill, and went all over the place with him. We used to go to quite a few Variety Club sportsmen's nights and had a great time. Bill enjoyed a drink and we had some fun times, but I had to be careful because I didn't want the rest of the cast thinking I was crawling, although that never came into it.

Through my friendship with Bill and another Granada executive, John DeCoverley, I joined a wonderful society called The Mates of Malawi. John knew John Brown of the giant Australian wine producers Brown Brothers, and was Head Mate of the 20-strong society. We used to meet once a year and, while top wine waiters have an elegant tasting spoon around their necks, we used to have a bit of rope and a wooden jug! Every Christmas, John Brown would send us boxes of the finest wines and it really is a splendid and most exclusive society.

And there was plenty of action on screen for Baldwin, too.

In November 1978, he was trying it on again when he was impressed with the looks and talent of buyer Carole Gordon, played by Louisa Rix. Mike took her out and offered her a job, but she got a better offer from another firm and turned him down.

That same year Mike was to embark on what was to become round one of the most famous affair in *Coronation Street*, the incredible love triangle between Mike, Deirdre and Ken Barlow.

But neither Anne Kirkbride or myself had an inkling of what was to follow years later when back in 1978, Mike was there to give a comforting shoulder to the then Deirdre Langton (Anne) when her former Borstal boy husband Ray (Neville Buswell) ran off to Holland after an affair with Janice Stubbs, a waitress in the newly opened café on Rosamund Street.

Neville's departure came as a huge shock and completely threw the writing team. And Bill Podmore, I know, was really concerned that Neville wanted to leave. They certainly couldn't kill him off following the spectacular death of Ernie Bishop, played by Stephen Hancock, in an armed robbery earlier in the same year.

I know there have been multiple slaughters of key characters in other soaps, with plane crashes and similar devices, but *Coronation Street* has never been like that. There may have been plenty of deaths over the years, as there would be in real life, but the *Street* is rooted in reality, with a strong dose of morality, behind the high jinks and carrying-ons. And two violent deaths in the same year just wouldn't have been right for Britain's favourite family show.

Personally, I thought that the death of Ernie Bishop was an absolutely wonderful episode and it still stands out in my mind as one I particularly enjoyed. I was sorry to see Stephen leave. At the time we both drank Guinness and there would always be a pint waiting for me when I walked into the club. So I liked him very much. But that was sensational television and Stephen played the part so well he made me feel really sorry for him.

But Neville's decision to quit was a real shaker for the production team. And just as Stephen's departure, in a dispute over contracts, had at one time put Eileen Derbyshire, as his wife Emily, at risk, so Neville's bombshell put Annie in the firing line.

In fact, the first time that Annie knew that Neville was quitting the show was when Bill Podmore told her, and informed her that she would have to be written out too, because there were already too many single girls in the show. Luckily for all of us, as it eventually worked out, Neville finally persuaded Bill to let Anne stay. Neville successfully argued that it wouldn't be fair to axe Annie just because he wanted to leave the show. Bill took some persuading, but, in the end, he decided she could be a real asset as a single mum.

Following the collapse of his fling with Carole Gordon, Mike had a fairly lean time and the closest he came to romance was when, in 1979, he gave away the illegitimate Gail Potter (Helen Worth) at her marriage to young Brian Tilsley, played by Chris Quinten.

Chris, who was a former real-life apprentice fitter in a shipyard, was a good-looking lad and a big hit with the girl fans. But I used to tease him about the length of his hair, which cascaded down to his shoulders. It was quite fashionable in the Seventies, but I took to calling him Christine. One day, I yelled across the set at him, 'Hey, Christine, you're wanted on the phone.' That narked him, but he could see the funny side and had a go back at me, riposting neatly, 'All right, Joanna!' The strange thing was that despite his reputation as a bit of a Romeo, he never filled the set with a lot of stunning girls and, at the risk of sounding too big headed, there were plenty of times when I seemed to have more fans chasing me!

By March 1980, Baldwin had started an affair with Pauline Stringer (Patricia Browning), who was a buyer from a rival firm. Mike eventually persuaded her to move to his firm as a supervisor, but like all Baldwin's early adventures, the romance didn't last.

That, however, was the lull before the storm.

The following year was to signal the real beginning of the Deirdre, Mike and Ken drama with its record ratings and major awards for Anne and myself ...

12

LIKE SO MANY SPECTACULAR EVENTS, it all started very gently and neither Anne Kirkbride, Bill Roache or myself realised just what it would lead to.

As a seasoned pub man who enjoys a drink with the best of them, I never thought I would ever get on the wrong side of the nation's landlords. But I did. For when the story started to build towards its climax, we found we were emptying the pubs all over Britain. Now that is quite a feat and I have to confess to being secretly rather proud of it. Not because I don't like a drink myself, but because that was the measure of our success.

But it was a slow build. It began on screen in February 1981 when, one evening, Mike met Deirdre in the Rovers, where she had been waiting in vain for Barlow, who was wooing her at the time. True to form, Mike was in there like a shot and was soon dating her. But although he took her out a few times, Deirdre was soft on Barlow, and she eventually ended the romance with Mike. But Mike would be back.

That March, Mike nicked one of Barlow's girls from right under his nose, but Mike was really the loser. It happened when Mike threw a house-warming party and Barlow brought along Sonia Price (Bridget Brice). Barlow, however, was soon making a bee-line for Deirdre. Irritated that Barlow was getting on so well chatting up Deirdre, Mike tried to put one over on Barlow by taking Sonia to a club.

We didn't think the *Street* could pull in many more viewers than when Deirdre, cashing in on the Royal wedding fever that year, following the marriage of Charles and Diana, dramatically removed her glasses to marry Ken Barlow in a church ceremony that pulled in a staggering 21 million fans. Bill Roach was particularly pleased with the chemistry between himself and Anne, but that was nothing compared to the chemistry the three of us were to make in the not too distant future.

Meanwhile, having lost out to Barlow in that round, Mike had greater success the following December when his father Frankie, played by Sam Kydd, turned up in Weatherfield to borrow some money. And Frankie had a young friend, Sylvie Hicks (Debbie Arnold), who caught Mike's eye, even if she was with his dad!

Filming the Baldwins' reunion was one of the most dramatic events in my career because Sam was taken very ill with emphysema while we were filming. It was a terrible blow as I had a very soft spot for Sam, and it also threw the whole production into a spin. With Sam in hospital, the writers had to come up with a plausible excuse for his absence, which they managed. But it really put the pressure on me.

In the plot line, when Mike refused to lend the money, they had Frankie storming off back to London, and I had to play all the scenes we should have played together talking into a telephone, supposedly to Sam.

And we had to work on the tightest schedules of my life. I was brought up on live television, but this was even worse. As no one had anticipated Sam's illness, the writers were having to rewrite the scripts on the run. So they were upstairs doing fresh scripts, which were then being brought down to me to learn and act. I would be filming one scene, while they were still writing the next! And I had to convey all the drama, and explain exactly what was happening, in a series of bogus phone conversations. That really was a bit of a stretch as I had to do 12 minutes on the phone telling the viewers the actual plot that should have taken place before Sam was rushed off to hospital. It was the only way we could get round it.

Sam eventually died, as have so many of the people I have known and worked with over the years. And I got a nasty jolt only last year when I was reminded of my own mortality while doing a photo shoot for the glossy women's magazine *Elle*. While we did the pictures, the photographer said, 'You were in so and so... and why did you do such and such?' I joked that he knew more about my career than I did, and it was then that he let me in on his secret. He told me that he had got all the details from his sister, who did the obituaries for the *Daily Telegraph*!

'Oh, thank God, that has made me feel much better,' I said, forcing a wintry smile. 'It's really great to know that they have done my obituary,' I half joked. But he tried to reassure me by explaining that they prepared the obituaries for all the celebrities once they reached a certain age.

'Oh thank you, that has really cheered me up,' was all I could reply.

Before he became ill, however, there was another very good reason why Sam's stay at *Coronation Street* is burned into my memory; he nearly bankrupted me.

Sam liked a flutter on the horses and encouraged me to join him. He bet every day, and persuaded me to do the same. Sam seemed to have a magic knack for picking the winners.

'Ah,' I thought, 'this should be an easy way to make a bob or two.' The trouble was that every day I lost. It got so bad that I thought the only way to recoup my losses was to double the amount I was gambling. Wrong again! I lost a lot of money, while Sam just went on winning. It cost me hundreds, before I decided enough was enough, and quit.

I only got back into the winning saddle when Amanda

Barrie joined the *Street*. She has completely changed my luck. Amanda knows more about horses than I could ever even hope to and, wonderful woman that she is, she gives me tips. The other person whose tips I treasure is Bill Waddington, who plays Percy Sugden. Bill owns race horses and every horse he has tipped has come up.

But Sam's exit from the show gave Baldwin a chance to date another babe when he took Sylvie out. But, for a renowned womaniser, he didn't do very well then, eventually losing out to his dad when she decided to return to London to live with Frankie.

In May 1982, Mike had a perilously close call that nearly cost him his much-prized freedom when he became involved with Maggie Dunlop, the career-girl boss of Eddie Yeats' girlfriend. The affair with Maggie, who was played by Jill Kerman, became serious and she moved in with Mike, to the horror of his cleaner Hilda Ogden. Hilda, played by the marvellous Jean Alexander, was shocked at such goings on, but the relationship eventually turned sour when Mike refused to loan Maggie £3,000 to expand her business.

As a parting shot, Maggie revealed to Mike that she was pregnant by him, but , really turning the knife in an act of monumental spite, she refused to marry the normally love-'em-and-leave-'em rogue. That was a real blow for Baldwin as she later married Harry Redman and gave birth to Mike's illegitimate son, Mark, in May 1983.

Before Mark was born, however, Maggie had been swept from Mike's mind as he embarked on the love triangle that was to give me one of my moments of greatest glory.

It hadn't taken long for the shine to rub off the Barlows' marriage and by, December 1982, Deirdre was ripe for Mike's plucking.

Mike moved swiftly to rekindle his romance with Deirdre, now very much a disenchanted wife, taking her for a romantic meal. And for a while it looked as if Deirdre's marriage to Ken Barlow was over. Mike and Deirdre's affair galvanised the nation, with the press and fans arguing about how it should all end.

I had been around long enough to know you just run with the plot. Your character is created by the writers and while I and the writers all feel intuitively about how Mike would react and what he would do in any situation, I would never try and call the shots. So I was happy to go along with the love triangle and give it all my best shots as Mike attempted to entice Deirdre away from Barlow. And working with Anne and Bill made it easy.

But I know that Bill was very concerned about this steamy love triangle. He didn't like the idea of Deirdre having an affair with anyone, let alone my boisterous, devil-may-care character. Bill was very protective of the characters, but I thought the whole set-up was magnificent and was delighted that the then producer, Mervyn Watson, had come up with such an audience-puller. Let's face it, the whole nation was locked into the plot and I thought it was a wonderful piece of writing that enabled us to produce such magnetism on screen.

The minute that Deirdre, very wisely, I thought, declared her love for Mike and continued to see him behind Barlow's back, all the national papers latched on to the fact that this was *Coronation Street's* most explosive storyline and the television event of the year.

The readers of the *Daily Star* sensibly came out for Mike, declaring that Deirdre should go ahead and have her fling with the Weatherfield Romeo, as did the *Daily Mail* columnist Lynda Lee Potter, who, with excellent taste, urged Deirdre to leave boring Barlow and go for the exciting Baldwin! Others were not so supportive and, to my dismay, I even had my greatest fan, Sir John Betjeman, who would never miss an episode and adored the Baldwin character, lining up against Mike, arguing that Barlow deserved better. Needless to say, I think the *Daily Star* readers were nearer the mark.

But that was not what the scriptwriters wanted. And it made for much better television when, after two months, Deirdre confessed the affair to Barlow. That scene was absolutely tremendous — simply mesmerising television —

with Bill and Anne ranting and raving until I, as Mike, was supposed to arrive at their front door to find out why Deirdre was in such a terrible state. That was one of the occasions in the long-running feud between Baldwin and Barlow that Ken got one over on Mike, with a little help from the director Brian Mills.

Originally, I was to have been thrown out of the house by the enraged Barlow, but after the first rehearsal Mills was worried that there was not enough passion being displayed. But to give credit where credit is due — and Bill also won an award for his performance in the drama — Bill had a trick up his sleeve which he didn't reveal to me or anyone else. Anne was expecting to deliver her lines to me inside the house, as we had rehearsed the scene. But Bill had other ideas, as he was convinced that in a real-life situation, Barlow would never allow Mike inside the house. He used his instinct — and he was absolutely right.

As Anne opened the front door to me, Bill took over and, completely unrehearsed, grabbed Anne by the throat and slammed her against the door — which was then slammed in my face. The emotions were so raw and the violence apparently so real, it caused an outcry, with Barlow even being accused of wife-bashing. That scene was so intense that Anne later admitted she thought Bill had gone mad. She was totally unprepared for Bill's violent action and at one stage was fighting for what she thought was her life!

Deirdre and Barlow were finally reconciled in the next episode, when they kissed and made up after she begged Ken to let her stay, and promised never to see Mike again.

So many people were by now on tenterhooks that the result of the drama was actually flashed up on the scoreboard at Old Trafford, where 56,000 soccer fans were watching Manchester United play Arsenal. As it flashed out 'Deirdre and Ken united again' there was a mighty roar, with screams, boos and shouts. What a result.

Not for Mike, unfortunately, but at least people started going into the pubs again in the evenings and the publicans stopped hating me. That was a relief as it had got to the stage where I hadn't dared go near a boozer for fear of being lynched by an irate landlord!

We had pulled in the biggest viewing figures ever, in excess of 21 million, and I won the Pye Male TV Personality of the Year Award, while Anne won the Female Personality of the Year award.

Back in *Coronation Street*, Deirdre and Ken flew off to Malta for a second honeymoon — and poor old Mike was left to lick his woulds.

I have to confess that I never really expected it to have such a sensational impact. I had known all about high profile in *No Hiding Place*, but this was something else again. But when we came to do the scenes they felt good, so I wasn't that surprised.

And working with Anne was a dream. She is always quite superb and I invariably enjoy our scenes together.

They say that men seldom make passes at girls who wear glasses, but Anne is the exception. She was dubbed 'Sexy Specs' by the media and with those big eyes, magnified by those big glasses, she certainly lived up to her nickname.

During the big romance between Deirdre and Mike, I had a letter from a young lady who wore glasses saying how lovely it was that I was having an affair with someone in glasses.

And then I was asked if she took them off in bed! To that I gallantly replied, 'Oh, that would be telling ...'

In real life, Anne and I are great pals. She is lovely and, in fact, she is married to one of my very best friends, Dave Beckitt. Dave and I became pals when he was in *Coronation Street* in 1990, playing one of Deirdre's lovers! As maintenance man Dave Barton, he rescued Tracy Barlow from a chip pan fire at Number One, and later fell for Deirdre and they started an affair, when he decorated her house.

In the *Street*, Barton broke up with Deirdre when she refused to commit herself to him, but away from the cameras they fell in love for real and she ended up marrying him. It really is a small world.

Anne is quite phenomenal. She is one of the few actresses

I have ever worked with whom you never see with a script. She just knows her part, perfectly. She arrives knowing all her lines and never needs a script, no matter how long the scene. It is incredible she has mastered every word and gesture and action before she even steps into the studios.

All our big scenes together have always been easy to do because if you are with someone who really knows what they are doing, there are never any real problems. And Anne can do it.

At the height of the love triangle we were always being stopped in the street and I remember one classic occasion when we were filming in Manchester's Oxford Street at 10.00pm one night. Anne and I were sitting in a car waiting to film when this fella walked past. 'You don't want to mess about with him, luv, you would be much better off if you came with me,' he told Anne.

'Where are you going?'she asked.

'I am going to this club just up the road,' he replied.

'Oh, alright, I will join you,' said Anne, climbing out of the car.

'What?' gasped the man.

'I said, I'll come with you.'

At which, the man ran off up the road, shouting, 'No, no, no. I was only joking.'

And there was Anne running up the road after him shouting, 'Hang on a minute. I will come with you.'

He just kept running, calling back, 'No, no, no,' over his shoulder. Anne and I fell about laughing.

Anne has always been a great sport, and she needs to be with me. I adore garlic, and while I used that to upset Wendy Jane Walker when we did our love scenes together, I have always tried to be very careful not to make life difficult for Anne because of it. So if I was going out for a meal, or knew that I would be eating it at my flat, I would phone up Annie and tell her, so that she could also eat garlic, and then she wouldn't be able to smell it on me. But it didn't always work out as I had intended. Sometimes she would have been out when I phoned, or I would have eaten garlic unexpectedly and when I arrived for work the next morning she would gasp, 'Oh God!' So she used to carry this spray to kill the smell and in the morning she would say to me, 'Open your mouth' — and squirt away at me.

Annie really is great fun, but she also has a very, very deep voice and can sing in an even deeper voice. And whenever she looks likely to burst into song, I will plead, 'Anne, please don't sing.'

'Why not?' she always asks.

'Because it makes me feel ill when you sing.'

That always stops her in mid-note — and she falls about laughing.

But I have never succeeded in getting Anne to organise breakfast for Dave and myself when we set out on our early-morning golf matches together. They live really close to a golf course, with only the River Mersey between their home and the greens so, naturally, Dave and I play there a lot. In fact I am beginning to think that all the money he wins off me is helping to pay their mortgage! We start playing at 6.30 or 7.00am, and I keep saying to him, 'Wouldn't it be lovely to see Annie on the side of the course with some bacon sarnies?' Dave, in turn, keeps suggesting it to her, but I fear it is falling on deaf ears!

But if we thought the Eighties love triangle was an unbeatable ratings buster, we excelled ourselves early in 1998 when the country was electrified by the jailing of Deirdre for fraud committed by her slimy con-artist lover who first pretended he was an airline pilot and then convinced her he was going to marry her.

Even after all these years, I was astounded at the way the Deirdre case produced a week of national outrage with the Prime Minister and the Leader of the Opposition pleading for her release. Tony Blair's official spokesman declared that while the Prime Minister was not allowed to intervene in such cases, as a member of the public he was entitled to a view and 'his view is, it is clear to anyone with eyes in their head she is innocent'.

It was incredible. Mr Blair's spokesman went on to say

that the premier not only had family links with the show — his wife Cherie's father, Tony Booth, married the late *Street* star Pat Phoenix — but he carried fond memories of achieving a life-long ambition of pulling a pint in the Rover's Return, before the last election. Not to be outdone, William Hague went on the record as saying, 'The whole nation is deeply concerned about Deirdre, Conservatives as much as everyone else.'

And there was Mike right in the middle of it all, getting slapped around the face by an outraged Alma after she found out he had coughed up £10,000 for Deirdre's defence. As if he didn't get enough violence in his confrontations with Barlow! I am used to the tabloids reporting the *Street*'s dramas in great detail, but this time we made the front page of *The Times*, while the *Daily Telegraph* devoted its top leader to the case. Taxi drivers threatened to go on hunger strike and all the popular papers ran campaigns to 'Free the Weatherfield One'. It was a staggering outpouring of emotion.

Even before the verdict, viewers were ringing Granada asking, 'Where is the court? Because we want to come up and speak up for her and tell the jury that she has been conned by this man.'

Annie couldn't go anywhere at the time she was having the affair that eventually led up to the fraud charges, without being told, 'You ought to know dear, that this man is a con-artist.'

Annie would then say, 'I can watch it, too. It is only a TV series. But I am glad it has got you thinking about me.'

After the first 100 or so it gets irritating, and Annie found that she couldn't go anywhere without people saying, 'Leave him, the man is a swine.'

In the same way, I found that everywhere I went people were obsessed with the whole affair. When the world fell in on Deirdre, I knew how Annie felt because I had been trolleyed in Sainsbury's because Mike had been a real swine to Hilda Ogden and the viewers didn't like it. People take these things so seriously that they completely blur the line between fact and fiction. Tina Hobley, who brightened up the Rovers as Samantha Failsworth, told me that people were forever coming up to her asking what Des Barnes (Philip Middlemiss) was like in bed. They would then ask how Chris Collins, played by Matthew Marsden, compared, and she would turn on them and say, 'Excuse me, this is a television series. We are actors — we haven't been to bed together in real life.'

But the impact of any storyline involving Baldwin, Barlow and Deirdre is always phenomenal — and long may it remain so.

Back in the Eighties, in a bid to get over Deirdre, Mike fell for interpreter Eileen Hicks (Helen Rappaport) when she visited his factory with a Russian delegation in July, 1983, but little came of it.

But Mike didn't have to spend too long crying into a large scotch and he soon swept Rovers barmaid Goria Todd (Sue Jenkins) on to his arm. I think that affair w as very much a case of being caught on the rebound. Baldwin's ego had been badly dented when Deirdre went back to Barlow, and he needed a pretty girl to prove he hadn't lost his pulling power. Gloria, however, always came over as a victim as far as men were concerned — and she never really stood a chance of hanging on to someone as nimble-footed as Mike.

Baldwin was always too keen on trying it on with anyone he fancied, which is what happened when designer Christine Millward (Julie Shipley) brought her designs to the factory in January 1985. She made quite an impression on Mike and although she told him she was happily married, a little detail like that wasn't going to deter him. They went on a business trip to London together and saw each other frequently, but Christine's husband finally put a stop to the affair.

Then in 1986, Mike made the worst mistake of his life when the producer and writers dreamed up his marriage to Barlow's daughter Susan (Wendy Jane Walker). It came across as a classic piece of revenge, but, as I have said, I hated the whole business. It also brought yet another punch-up with Barlow, who was beside himself with fury that the man he most hated in the world was bedding his daughter. At first, it seemed a brilliant stroke to Baldwin, who detests Barlow for his snobby attitude and the fact that he hung on to Deirdre.

To make matters worse, the continuing row between Mike and Barlow flared again and Barlow ended up thumping me in my own factory.

Baldwin had to wait four long years to get his revenge, when he smashed Barlow for six in the Rovers. Fortunately, the marriage, at least, didn't last too long, and in 1989 Mike fell for Dawn Prescott (Louise Harrison), who worked as a receptionist at Alan Bradley's security firm. Bradley tried to rape her and Dawn tipped off his lover Rita about his dishonest dealings, which should have sent the alarm bells ringing in Rita's ears.

Mike fell for Dawn in a big way and it was an excellent storyline as it ended with Mike down — and almost out — after being turned over by an even craftier rogue than himself. Dawn was just what Baldwin wanted after the disaster with Susan, but he made the mistake of mixing business with pleasure. Dawn's brother Robert conned Mike out of a small fortune with a dodgy land deal in Spain. Mike just couldn't stand the thought that someone had turned him over and made a right mug of him, so that was the end of that affair.

But if Mike was down on his luck, he was determined to bounce back and prove he was still the king of the *Street*. After losing all his money in the land deal, Mike was faced with the indignity of having to take a salesman's job for textile tycoon Peter Ingram. There were plenty of silver linings there, however, and that little set-up soon saw Mike once again mixing business with pleasure. It also led to another doomed marriage — one that only lasted a week!

At the time, Mike was sharing a luxury dockland flat with Alma Sedgewick, my present screen wife played by Amanda Barrie. But when Ingram dropped dead from a heart-attack, Mike saw his chance and smoothly moved in to comfort the grieving widow — and line his own nest. After advising her on how to run the business, Mike was soon given the job of running the plant. Baldwin was on the way back.

By now, however, Mike was also heading for another tangled love triangle, only this time there were two women. Alma feared she would lose out to the younger, wealthy Jackie (Shirin Taylor). Once again, the fans took that triangle very seriously and, in real life, Alma received letters from viewers warning her that Mike couldn't be trusted, while others were telling Shirin that Mike was only after her money!

Mike could certainly see the main chance and finally manoeuvred Jackie into bed. At the time, I thought Jackie was the ideal woman for Baldwin, especially as the bosses were so keen on marrying him off again. She was intelligent and rich and just the sort of bird Baldwin would stick with, in as much as he can stick with anyone.

You could say that Mike was attracted by her beauty, her money and her jewels, but not necessarily in that order. At first, Alma turned a blind eye to the affair, but when Mike moved in with Jackie, Alma headed back to her flat over the café.

That provided the writers with the perfect opportunity to set up Mike for the next round in the bitter feud with Ken Barlow. While Mike thought he was heading back to easy street as he and Jackie prepared to tie the knot, Barlow moved in on Alma. Mike's marriage to Jackie, however, was the most disastrous of the lot. Mike had barely swallowed the celebration champagne when Jackie announced she was selling the business so they could spend more time together. Mike almost choked on the bubbly for that was the last thing he wanted, which was hardly surprising as he had used company money to buy the lease of Alma's café. Jackie went wild when she found out, particularly when she heard of Mike's technicoloured past and, in my favourite *Coronation Street* scene, she proved that she was one tough babe. She threw Mike's wedding ring at him and reached for her double-barrelled shotgun ...

That really was a stupendous scene — absolutely

unforgettable. She threatened me with the gun and stuck it in my mouth. But Baldwin, macho to the end, sneered, 'Go on then, pull the trigger. Pull the trigger. It isn't loaded.' And then I swung it out of her hand and looked into the barrels — and, to my horror, saw that it was loaded. With two shells!

It was good working with Shirin and, apart from Amanda, she is one of the people I have liked working with best. She had done other things and was a bloody good actress. It really was a joy to work with her.

Shirin also thoroughly enjoyed that scene. She believed that Jackie was fundamentally a strong modern woman who had lapsed into weakness when her husband died and had let herself fall for the predatory Baldwin. So she felt totally betrayed by Mike — and then used all her strength to get herself back together again.

But there wasn't a great deal of joy for Mike. She ordered him out of her life and filed for divorce.

Mike, however, always comes up smelling of roses and he did it again, even in that bleak hour. Jackie gave him a £10,000 pay-off, and he used part of it to open his garage, MVB Motors. Baldwin's luck had changed again.

Better still, Mike also once again got the drop on Barlow. On Christmas Day, 1991, in the second of two special episodes, Mike lured Alma into bed, after getting Barlow off the scene by coaxing Tracy to persuade Deirdre to have Ken over for the day in the hope they would get back together.

It didn't, however, go quite as smoothly as Baldwin planned. Alma was disgusted when, after they had gone to bed together, Mike boasted to her how neatly he had got Ken out of the way.

Alma later, foolishly, told Ken when they were staying at a smart hotel on New Year's Eve and, true to form, Barlow walked out on her, making it easy for Mike to woo her back.

There were three weddings in *Coronation Street* in 1992, but the one that really stole the headlines was Alma and Mike finally getting hitched. But even crafty Baldwin had his work cut out persuading Alma not to ditch him at the last minute.

Alma accepted Mike's marriage proposal after he conned her into believing that he had managed to persuade Jackie to drop her name from the divorce proceedings. But when she found out that it had been Mike's idea to have her cited, she was furious and it was touch and go whether Alma would turn up for the wedding.

It's been a bit of an up-and-downer since then, but Mike has generally been able to patch things up, probably because Alma has absolutely no illusions about Mike. She has known all along that Mike is a male chauvinist pig, so she was aware what sort of man she was marrying. But Alma has a will of her own and Mike can never take her for granted, although she dotes on him.

Amanda is a joy to work with too. She is a real pro and I knew her husband, Robin Hunter. I had known of Amanda from my *Carry On* days, when she was in a couple, including the title role in the 1964 *Carry On Cleo*, a wonderful send-up of the big Hollywood epics. And Amanda looked absolutely stunning as the bare-tummied Cleo. She had also been in other projects that I worked on, but, strangely, we never met until she joined the *Street*. She was a leggy Glamcab driver the year before in the black and white *Carry On Cabby*, but I joined the *Carry On* scene later, and in the other projects it was not unusual to avoid meeting anyone who wasn't in your actual scenes.

She is lovely, a smashing lady and, like myself, full of insecurities. But that is part of our success — we give each other strength. If she sees panic in my eyes she rallies round, and if I see her faltering, I rally round . We have this superb *ésprit de corps* and I adore her. She is a very good actress too.

I have even greater admiration for her because she is dyslexic, so sometimes she gets the line the wrong way round, and we all have a laugh. That is why I think she is superb and acts with such conviction, having overcome that barrier. Susan Hampshire is the same.

I take my hat off to all actors and actresses who beat such handicaps. Robin Ray and Clive Francis stutter off stage, but once the curtain rises they lose it completely, I can't understand it, but I admire them.

It's an amazing thing about acting. You can be standing in the wings with a terrible cold or 'flu with your eyes running and you are so congested you can hardly speak, but the minute you go on stage it vanishes. Then, when you come off, you start coughing and sneezing again. It's a funny old business.

As with all Mike's marriages, I was worried when they decided that he should wed Alma, but now I'm sort of stuck with it and it doesn't bother me any more because I think they are suited to each other. And Amanda is such a good actress. I love the bits where Mike, as the hard businessman, comes home full of himself — and she takes the mickey out of him mercilessly, with a little twinkle in her eye.

And Mike can still be roguish. Don't forget that old saying about the leopard ...

13

I WAS VERY LUCKY WHEN I JOINED *CORONATION STREET*, for just as in *Crossroads*, where I knew Noele Gordon, so at Granada I knew Pat Phoenix, who as Elsie Tanner, was *the* female lead. She was the biggest star and, more importantly as far as I was concerned, she was an old mate. And, just as Julie looked after me, so did Pat. Miss Phoenix, as she was known everywhere she went, carried enormous clout and her friendship was worth its weight in gold. Woe betide anyone who was nasty to her Johnny because they would then have the wrath of Pat Phoenix to deal with.

But while Pat wielded a lot of power, she didn't throw her weight around. At that time Pat and Violet Carson, as the incomparable Ena Sharples, were the big two in the show, but Pat never played on it. Such behaviour just wasn't in her nature.

Yet, although I frequently spent the night at her home in the country, we were just the best of friends, and neither of us wanted to change that relationship. I might have had a big reputation as a ladies' man, and Pat, fundamentally, may have been a lover who just wanted to be loved, but it was friendship that was the key to the superb relationship we enjoyed. She treated me like a brother. She also used to worry about me, and she was always trying to mother me. I used to chuckle at her concern for the welfare of Johnny Briggs, but there are worse fates than having Pat Phoenix looking after your interests, I can assure you!

I first met her in 1960 when I spent a year working at the Granada studios in Manchester making *The Younger Generation* series with John Thaw, and she was very different then from the *femme fatale* she was to blossom into in *Coronation Street*. To be brutally honest, in those days Pat was quite hubby and, I thought, rather plain, really. She was certainly nothing to get excited about. Pat, however, was one of those women who became more beautiful with every year that passed. And, even in 1960, she had a tremendous personality that transcended her looks, and still turned her into a winner. Pat had heard of me because she had been around a fair while as a jobbing actress, and when I first ran into her she was carrying a tray of tea in the Granada canteen. I asked her what she was doing as it was obvious that she was terribly excited about something.

That 'something' was *Coronation Street*, but, along with some other members of the cast she was worried in case it was axed. The then brand-new show had been savaged by a respected critic, the *Daily Mirror*'s Ken Irwin, who said it would only last six weeks. So Pat was over the moon when the show went national. Originally, it had only been shown in the old Granada franchise area, which then covered most of the north from Mondays to Fridays. But, despite the criticism, the bosses of the other ITV companies soon heard that the show was proving a huge success and they wanted to cash in on it. So they eagerly picked up the show, and started to screen it right across the nation. The cast breathed a sigh of relief, and Pat, a chronic chain-smoker, no longer had to puff on her fags quite so nervously!

I frequently returned to Granada on other projects, like *Inspector Rose* and *It's Dark Outside*, and would always say 'Hello' and have a natter in the canteen with Pat, as she devoured cigarette after cigarette over her coffee. She was always bubbly and great to be with, but I never dreamed that one day I would join her on the *Street*.

When I did join the show, Pat had slimmed down and looked absolutely stunning and a fantastic friendship was born. Pat was a wonderfully generous person. She would do anything for people she liked and could surprise even her closest friends by her spontaneous acts of kindness, as I discovered in my early days on the show.

I had the most terrible digs in Fallowfield, a student area of Manchester, and so couldn't wait to leap into my MG sports car to race back to London, or the Midlands to see Christine, at the first opportunity. One weekend, after I had been to London, as I set off back north, the sun was shining, the daffodils were in flower and it was so warm I drove back in my shirt sleeves. A bad mistake. I had forgotten the big difference in temperature between the north and the south. As I drove through Birmingham, I noticed that the daffodils were only in bud — and when I reached Manchester they were so far behind they were still just green leaves! So the next morning it felt absolutely perishing cold as I stood around the set the in my short-sleeved shirt.

'You look absolutely freezing,' Pat greeted me, concern flashing across her face, as she swept into the Green Room. 'Why don't you put on a sweater?'

'I haven't got one,' I said with a shrug. 'It was lovely when I left London and I didn't think I would need one.'

'What will you do all week?' asked Pat, now starting to look really anxious.

'Don't worry, I'll get something from wardrobe,' I replied, smiling to stop my teeth from chattering.

I thought no more of it, but after lunch Pat came up to me and, handing me a package, said, 'There you are, put that on — you still look bloody freezing.'

I opened the package and inside was a magnificent pale blue cashmere sweater. Pat had been so worried about me, that she had left the studios and bought me the gift from the exclusive Elite Dress Agency, where she used to buy her frocks. For once, I was speechless. It was a wonderful gift, and typical of Pat. She was the most generous person I have ever met, apart from Lynne Perrie, who played 'Poison' Ivy Tilsley, later Ivy Brennan after Ivy's marriage to Don Brennan. I was so thrilled with the gift that, after I eventually found out from where Pat had bought it, I raced around to the Elite to see if I could buy another. But, like Pat, it was a one-off.

'I'm sorry, sir,' the assistant told me, 'Miss Phoenix had the only one.'

If that action was typical of Pat, so was the reaction of the shop assistant. No matter where Pat went, she was always addressed as Miss Phoenix. And she didn't put on airs. She just had this incredible aura about her. When she opened a supermarket, she would draw more people than the Queen.

She had this incredible presence and charisma. People were fascinated by her and everywhere she went she was the centre of attention. She was a wonderful, wonderful girl and I loved her. She was superb.

She also did everything in style. After a technical run, which in the Seventies used to finish at about 4.00pm in the afternoon, she would say to me, 'Do you fancy a cup of tea?'

'Yeah,' I would reply, 'I wouldn't mind, Pat.'

I would then carry on chatting to other members of the cast until Pat would come bustling back up to me, declaring, 'Right, the taxi's here.'

'Taxi!' I would say. 'Where are we going?'

'Cup of tea,' she would reply.

'Where?'

'In the Midland, of course,' Pat would retort.

And I must confess that is my idea of the way to go for a cup of tea. The Midland was then *the* Manchester hotel, a magnificent Gothic pile in red stone and tiles by the old Central Station, which is now the G-Mex exhibition centre. And tea was an elegant occasion — hot tea cakes with expensive jam, dainty smoked salmon and cucumber sandwiches, pastries ... and all served on the finest china by a waiter in black tie and tails. It certainly beat the Granada canteen.

She obviously felt I needed feeding up. She would frequently say to me at the end of the working day, 'What are you doing?' And if I said, 'Oh, nothing really,' Pat would then enquire, 'What time are you in tomorrow.'

'Nine o'clock,' I would say.

'So am I. Would you like to come home for a meal and a few drinks?'

There was always only one answer to that. And we would go to her home where her housekeeper Kitty would cook us a steak, accompanied by a splendid red wine. They were always great evenings. Sometimes a friend would drop in, but there was nothing more to those visits than friendship. We were just chums.

But one morning when I had stayed overnight after a splendidly boozy evening, the famous Phoenix cool was badly dented. I was downstairs having a spot of breakfast when Pat, who was running late, came sweeping down the stairs in a hurry, and as she turned the corner on a small half-landing she caught her little toe on a stone angel, which stood in the corner.

'Kitty,' Pat roared in a mixture of rage and pain, 'when I get back tonight I want that fucking angel OUT!'

And the angel was chucked out because Pat had stubbed her toe on it.

Why she worried about me I will never know, particularly as I used to nag her constantly about her smoking. I was worried at the amount of cigarettes she puffed away at and often used to give her a right bollocking.

'You're killing yourself, smoking,' I told her, emphasising the point by adding, 'I don't want to talk to you if you smoke.'

Surprisingly, she took that to heart and one day she said she would quit. Great, I thought. But I obviously didn't know Pat as well as I thought. For the next day she came into the studios puffing away as usual, but the smell was different.

'God, what are you smoking?' I asked, twitching my nose at the stink.

'Herbal,' Pat told me proudly, convinced that they were

the solution to her smoking problems.

She was convinced that switching to herbal cigarettes was the equivalent of quitting.

'Well, they smell like burning leaves in the garden,' I said, adding, 'I don't know which I dislike the most.'

'Oh, all right,' said Pat. 'I'll quit. I'll just finish the packet — I've only got 18 left!'

Sadly, she just couldn't kick the habit and started smoking again three or four days later — and eventually died of lung cancer in 1986, aged just 62.

Because she had this incredible air about her she seemed larger than life, but, in reality, Pat was quite small. She was only about 5ft 3in or 5ft 4in tall. She was considerably smaller than me and I'm only 5ft 7in. But she has to be amongst the most memorable people I have ever met and it was great working with her, although she kept you on your toes. You were frightened of getting it wrong when you were doing a scene with her because she would slay you with a glare — but it was only in fun.

I had my own little moment of triumph with Pat when we went with Bill Podmore on a promotional trip to Singapore in 1980 for some special photographs. Pat and I were in the lift of this superb hotel when an Englishman thrust an autograph book at me. Naturally, I obliged, delighted to be recognised so far from home and thinking, 'That just goes to show the power of *Coronation Street*.'

As he turned away, Pat, as the uncrowned star of the show, also offered to sign, adding with a smile, 'I'm in *Coronation Street* as well.'

'Never heard of it,' said the bloke, 'but I remember this lad playing the copper.'

It turned out that he had left England before *Coronation Street* went nationwide, but had seen episodes of *No Hiding Place*, which had been exported .

People thought that Pat was vampy, but she wasn't at all; she was just loveable. She just needed lots of loving, did Pat. She was a lover and she liked people to love her.

Alan Browning was the big love of her life and, just as

Elsie Tanner married his *Street* character Alan Howard, so Pat and Alan Browning married in real life too. Alan Browning liked a drink and that was a fairly tempestuous relationship, but Pat was far too professional ever to bring it to the studios, where Pat and I remained the best of chums. Pat even bought a pub, the Navigation Inn, at Chinley, which was Alan's idea of heaven. Alan, who played a businessman, had joined the *Street* in 1969, and left a couple of years before I moved to Weatherfield, and during his five year-stint as Alan Howard he became Elsie's third husband! But then the fans were used to Elsie having a new man on her arm — she had 21 different fellas, including a couple of high-profile romances with Len Fairclough (Peter Adamson) in her years on Britain's most famous show.

Elsie's marriage to Alan was different, however, as he moved into her home at Number 11 and stayed for three years — the longest time Elsie ever spent with a man. When the marriage went through a bad patch, the couple moved to Newcastle, which was the opportunity for Alan to leave the show — and Pat went with him. Although she wasn't written out, Pat was desperate to return to the theatre and she and Alan had a spectacularly successful tour with *Gaslight*.

In 1976 Pat was back on *Coronation Street* when Elsie returned alone from Newcastle, and was soon once more back in business as the woman who could always get the fellas, even if they treated her badly. She had similar heartbreaks in her own private life and in 1979 Alan Browning died of a liver complaint, aged just 53.

Pat stayed on in the show until 4 January 1984, but the then producer, Mervyn Watson, and the studio bosses had been bracing themselves for the blow since the previous autumn, when Pat had suddenly announced she planned to quit the show, just after the newspapers had been full of the sacking of Peter Adamson for breaking his contract with a series of revelatory behind-the-scenes articles.

That was a shattering blow, She was the queen of the *Street* and a lot of people thought it would affect the ratings. But it didn't.

And, to be honest, much loved though Pat was, I wasn't surprised. At the time, Pat was still the most glamorous female in the show and commanded great respect wherever she went. She only had to say, 'How are you doing, chuck,' to someone and they were hers for life. She engendered a sort of servitude amongst people, who were ever so pleased to do anything for her. And when you watch old episodes you can see how clever she really was. She had a fire, a bite about her, and the older she got the better looking she became. But I have always known that the public switch on to see the *Street*. They may have their preference for one or two characters, but I don't think they specifically turn on the television to see those characters, or you would find that in the weeks when those characters were not on the screen the ratings would fall — and then go up when they returned. But that isn't the case. People switch on to see what is happening in the *Street*.

I wasn't that surprised, either, when Pat announced she was quitting. She had left the show three or four times before to go and do other things and had always come back. Although we were pals, the announcement came as a big shock to me. She had never said a dicky bird to me about leaving. But I knew that she wanted to do another stage show. And that is what she did — touring with *Limelight* to packed theatres every night. You couldn't get a seat. Pat loved the immediacy and intimacy of the theatre. She loved the applause, the bouquets of flowers, the curtain calls the instant adulation.

Surprisingly, as we had been so close, I didn't see much of Pat after she left. I bumped into her once when she came into Manchester shopping and she said she didn't regret leaving for one moment because she loved the theatre so much. And the door was always open for her to go back, but she just did her stage shows and then it was too late as she became ill.

I think the end was very sad and I'm only glad that she found happiness with Tony Booth — and that, near the end, she was granted her wish and they were able to marry. She was dying in the Alexandra Hospital, near Manchester, but the specialist felt that she had improved sufficiently to be able to cope with the strain, and so she and Tony were given permission for the bedside ceremony on 10 September 1986. Pat was not expected to survive long after the ceremony, but, fighter that she was, she survived for another week, before dying at 8.00pm on the 17th, as Tony knelt beside her, holding her hand.

One of the worst days of my life was going to her funeral in Manchester. Thousands turned out for it and it was a very sad occasion. Pat had tried to lift our spirits by having a traditional jazz band play, but nothing could stem the tears flooding from people's eyes. It did seem the end of an era.

Pat, as I have said, was the most generous person I have known in my life, apart from Lynne Perrie, who, unfortunately, got some very bad publicity when, as Ivy Brennan, she had plastic surgery to her lips. I thought Lynne was super. I like her very much and she was a very good actress. She was very generous, too, but she was more of a variety artist and didn't really understand the discipline of television. All my life I have never been late. As an actor you just cannot ever be late. I explain to my children that if I am half-an-hour late it can cost the company £10,000 with technicians just hanging around waiting for something to do. Even now, my journey to Manchester from my home in Stourbridge can take between one-and-a-half and two-and-a-half-hours. So, if I am filming, I allow three hours. This was something that Lynne didn't seem to understand, and was occasionally late. But Lynne was lovely. An adorable woman and she is my daughter Stephanie's godmother. I felt sorry for her because people took advantage of her generosity and ripped her off left, right and centre.

Lynne was a great mate and when I first, with a Baldwin-like flourish, started buying property in Manchester — I now have four luxury flats near the city centre — she rented one from me. Eventually, Lynne decided she wanted to buy this flat, which was very near the studios, so I sold it to her. She later bought a bigger property in the city — and I bought my flat back!

I have always tended to get on well with the ladies, which is just as well in the case of Doris Speed. As Annie Walker, Doris ruled the Rovers for years and she used to expect us to fall into line in the same way.

In those days we used to play a lot of cards in the Green Room and I was always Annie's partner at bridge. And she used to get livid if I wasn't there. One lunchtime, shortly after she was awarded the MBE, I told her I couldn't play as I had to go to the bank.

'No you are not,' she said in her most imperious manner. 'You are playing bridge with me.'

I said, 'Doris, I'm sorry, but I really have to go to the bank.'

But Doris wasn't having that. Drawing herself up regally, she declared, 'If you do, I'll have you beheaded!'

Only Doris would have had the neck for that — but I still went to the bank.

Doris was a wonderful character and could be very easily pleased. Fans were always giving her little gifts, which she was only too happy to receive. So, knowing how much she enjoyed receiving presents, I brought her back two packs of playing cards when I returned from a holiday abroad. It was only the smallest gesture, but I thought she was going to make a proposal of marriage to me, she was so pleased. 'Of all the presents I have had this year, no one could have thought of anything better than two packs of cards. Johnny, you are a darling,' she gushed. 'I am so thrilled I won't let you be dummy so much.' But I still ended up as the dummy (the non-playing partner in bridge), for Doris would always out-bid me to make sure she played.

The only time I generally played was when she got up from the table to go to the lavatory. She would then grandly announce, 'You can play this hand, darling, I am going to the toilet.'

In the end, I became so fed up with being her dummy, that I teasingly told her, 'The only way I am going to play two or three games on the trot is if you get diarrhoea!'

Her face was a picture of outrage as, pulling herself up to

her full height, she acidly retorted, 'Don't be disgusting, we have just eaten! '

Doris had a put down for every occasion. One day a huge fella came in to play a car salesman and, during a scene they had together, he kept obscuring Doris with his head. This really infuriated Doris, who finally could stand it no more and in her most autocratic tone told him, 'Oh, darling, please stop wiggling your head. It's hard enough trying to remember the lines without having you stand there waving your head about.'

The guy was very contrite and explained, 'I am sorry, Doris, but I am trying to get the shadow off your face.'

'Very wise, darling,' she replied. 'The Labour Exchange is full of actors who cast shadows on my face!'

Doris was simply wonderful. She used to walk into make-up, sit down and, pointing to her face, say to the make-up girl, 'In here are two eyes and a mouth. It's your job to find them!'

Doris finally left the Rovers, and the show, in 1983 and after that nothing seemed to go right for her.

She was admitted to hospital suffering from a mystery stomach illness. Then, after suffering the indignity of having her real age of 84 revealed in the press, she was poorly again and, to add to her misfortunes, thieves broke into her home one night while she was there. Terrified and fearing for her own safety, Doris ended up inside her locked bedroom calling the police on her phone as the villains ransacked her home. It was dreadful shame and a far cry from her life at *Coronation Street*.

It was wonderful in those days; the cast was much smaller and there was a terrific team atmosphere. If anyone was in trouble, the rest would gather round.

And sometimes you need that, because I was knocked sideways when I heard that Peter Adamson had been accused of indecently assaulting two young girls in a swimming pool. As Len Fairclough, Peter had been one of the biggest stars in the show for more than 20 years when that bombshell exploded. And he had been jolly good company. We all used to spend a lot of time together and as actors are by nature very sensitive, you tend to get the measure of a person. When I first joined the show, Peter, Brian Mosley (who plays the wonderfully pompous Alf Roberts) and I would go to the Granada club and share a bottle of wine together. Peter later gave up drinking completely, but that didn't stop him playing gags. And while Peter tended to keep himself to himself, he had a wicked sense of humour.

Every Wednesday, Brian Mosley, Fred Feast (who played Fred Gee), Adamson and I used to go out for a steak and when we split up afterwards, Peter used to bait the police. As he was stone cold sober, he used to tease the police mercilessly by pretending he had had one over the eight. If he saw a police car while he was driving home in one of his flash cars, he would deliberately start to drive erratically. The police would immediately spot Adamson and then swoop on him, believing he had been boozing. When they pulled him over and asked if he had been drinking, Adamson would then secretly delight in leading them on by telling them he had been out for the evening, They would then breathalyse him and be totally dumbfounded when the result came out negative.

The next day, Peter would breeze into the studios and, grinning wickedly from ear to ear, come up to me and say, 'It happened again last night.' He would then give me the full story. 'I was going up the road and I saw this police car and I thought, "This is it." So I braked when I shouldn't have and indicated to go right — and turned left. The police pulled me over and asked me if I had been drinking. "Well," I told them, "I have had a drink or two."

'"When was that, sir?"

'"Oh, about 25 minutes ago.'

'"Would you like to breathe into this, sir?' they asked as they got the breathalyser out.'

You should have seen their faces when they looked and said, "But this is negative!"

'"Yes, I've been drinking tea," I would explain. They were furious.'

Peter loved winding the police up and they got really fed up with it. In the end he was warned that if he didn't stop, he would be charged with wasting police time.

Peter — whom we called 'Choy' for some reason which I never discovered — really could be a hoot. Adamson, Geoffrey Hughes, the fella who used to play Annie Walker's son, and I used to invent an owl hoot for a giggle when we were filming. The director would say, 'Quiet, we're going for a take,' and one of us would nip behind the scenery and go 'Oow, oow,' and the sound man would call out, 'Stop, there's an 'Oow, oow' sound.'

And the director would become livid, shouting, 'Shut up. Where is that blasted owl? Can anyone see it?'

Soon, the production crew were out with binoculars scanning the studio roof, looking for this 'owl'. It was hilarious. We would be behind the set wetting ourselves with laughter. I loved gags like that, but I have to admit, that it was the other three that caused the mayhem for the simple reason that I couldn't get the sound right, no matter how hard I tried. I just couldn't get the pitch high enough, but the other lads were totally convincing.

It was the most magnificent hoax. In the end, the studio bosses called in the RSPCA to find this owl and get it out of their hair. And that is when it became a bit hot for the four of us. When the RSPCA didn't, literally, find a dicky bird, the bosses became suspicious, and we thought we had better stop or we would be sacked.

But, by the most incredible coincidence, just as we went to earth, the studios were genuinely invaded by real live pigeons! It was incredible. I could scarcely believe it, but it's true. The pigeons built a nest in the gantry, and started calling 'Coo, coo'. Having finally realised that they had been fooled over the owl, the bosses were incandescent with rage as the bird calls continued. And they threatened dire retribution against the people they believed were still playing the prank. So every time a pigeon cooed, the director would roar, 'If I catch the bloke who is making that noise, he will be sacked on the spot.'

The pigeons, naturally, didn't take a blind bit of notice and continued to coo. With mounting fury the director would bellow, 'Whoever is doing that is going to get the sack.'

'Coo, coo.'

'I'm telling you, I'm warning you ... a joke is a joke, but ...'

'Coo, coo.'

So once again they sent for pest control and a bloke arrived telling them, 'I've got an air rifle, I'll soon pick them off.' This horrified the make-up girls who chorused, 'Oh, no, you can't do that. That's cruelty to animals. It will be in the papers.' There was chaos until one of the girls said, 'Let's get the RSPCA,' which they did, and the RSPCA finally cleared out the nest and the pigeons ... but I still can't make that owl hoot.

Peter was quite pleasant, but he did some odd-ball things, like the time he bought 100 washing machines when he was boozing in a pub in the days when he used to enjoy a drink.

'Why did you do that?' I asked, when he recalled the nightmare incident.

'I don't know,' he said.

'What do you mean, you don't know?' I asked, beginning to suspect that I was being sent up. But I wasn't.

'Well, it was like this,' Peter continued. 'I woke up one morning to find some guys delivering 100 washing machines to my home. At first, I thought the guys were crackers, but then I remembered being in a pub and buying 100 washing machines.'

'Flipping Nora,' I said, 'what were you going to do with 100 washing machines?'

'I don't know. I honestly don't know,' he said. 'I am as bewildered now as I felt at the time. There they were in my garage, all 100 of them, in their packing cases ...'

When I again asked him where he bought them, all he could say was that he was in a pub and didn't really remember much else. And he wasn't even able to send them back. When they were delivered, he had said to the men,

'Take them back, I'm not paying for them,'

They told him, 'You paid last night. In cash.'

'Where did you get the cash to buy them?' I asked, but again all Peter could do was shrug his shoulders and repeat, 'I don't know ...'

I never did find out what he did with those washing machines.

I kept an open mind about the court case and Peter was cleared of assaulting the eight-year-old girls, but he and his family were devastated by the experience. He was sacked for writing a series of controversial newspaper articles and his wife Jean died a year later, after suffering for years with crippling arthritis.

Although I used to go and have a steak with Fred Feast, I never really took to him. He used to come into the club, buy himself two pints and then sit in the corner and drink them. I suppose he was frightened that if he joined us he might have to buy one back.

But that has never been my style, nor of any of my real mates. This type of penny-pinching attitude really gets me down, and reminds me of the saga of Mike Baldwin's car, although there was more than a few bob at stake that time.

I used to always drive a Jaguar XJS, and we used my car in the show as it was perfect for Mike Baldwin's go-getting image. But when the Queen visited *Coronation Street* in 1982, two Japanese car manufacturers, realising the commercial advantage of having their car on display before millions of viewers every week, approached me separately, asking if I would use one of their cars in the show instead of the Jaguar. But being pro-British, before I agreed to a deal with either company, I approached Jaguar and told them of the deals I had been offered. Jaguar were only too keen for me to continue to use one of their luxury cars and offered me the same deal, whereby I could have a top-of-the-range Jaguar for my own use if I also drove it in the *Street*. I was delighted, and the producer gave the scheme the go-ahead, saying, 'Johnny, you have to have a car as Mike Baldwin, so if you can use it as well, that's fine by me.'

Well that deal worked well for years — until Ford took over Jaguar. They then tried to change the rules. They were delighted for me to continue to drive a Jag in the show — but they wanted me to fork out £400 a month for the privilege!

I couldn't believe the Americans' cheek. They wanted me to pay them to promote their car in a worldwide show. Naturally I told them to 'bog off'. So they said they wanted their car back and I told them to come and fetch it. They then made a fresh attempt to persuade me to use the Jag, but they still wanted me to pay the £400. So again, I said 'No'. At that point, they tried to persuade the producer to make me keep the Jaguar, but the producer told them, 'I can't tell Johnny what to drive in his private life.' And in the end they had to fetch it themselves — as the tax had run out!

Infuriated, they then put out a statement saying that they had taken the car back because Mike Baldwin was broke and couldn't afford such a prestigious car. I was livid, and put out a press statement of my own, giving the true facts.

Then I had a real stroke of luck. I was playing golf with the managing director of Lexus and when he heard that Baldwin needed a new set of wheels, he stepped in offering me one of his magnificent cars. So Baldwin now drives a Lexus, supplied totally free by the manufacturer, and it is a brilliant luxury car. Unfortunately, I can't use it for my private driving — because it is too long to fit into my garage at the flats where I live in Salford Quays. It's a marvellous development, but the garage is just 12 inches too short, and I don't feel it would be right to leave such a top-of-the-range car out at night. It would be asking for trouble. So it is kept at the studios — and the only time I drive it is when I'm filming. But you can't have everything in life. So, instead, for my private use I now drive the Saab convertible.

14

THERE HAVE BEEN SOME MAGNIFICENT CHARACTERS IN THE *STREET*, and just as Peter Adamson would wind up the police with his non-drunk antics, so Jack Howarth used to torment the Manchester taxi drivers.

Jack played pensioner Albert Tatlock, who needed to take extra jobs, such as being a lollipop man and the caretaker at the mission to earn a few extra bob in his *Street* role. But away from the show, the dapper Jack lived in style in a suite in the elegant Midland Hotel and took a taxi to the studios every day. But he could be irascible and he annoyed the cabbies by never tipping them, yet still being very demanding. He used to bang his silver-topped walking stick against their bumpers to get their attention.

'Come on, come on,' he would shout at them, while he banged on their cars with his cane.

The cabbies would turn on him, 'Don't you bang my bloody mudguard like that with your stick, mate. You'll dent it,' they would shout back, adding with real venom, 'Now bugger off.'

In the end, they wouldn't take the old campaigner at all

and Jack was reduced to catching the bus to the studios, until one of the production staff spotted him waiting at the bus stop one morning and offered to ferry him to and fro.

I got on very well with Jack and, and as he was a very old man when I joined the *Street*, he didn't socialise. But he was a great charity worker and although he was 88 when he died in his sleep in 1984, he used to travel the length and breadth of Britain raising money for the Stars Organisation for Spastics. And if you were doing a personal appearance at, say, Llandudno, he would con you into picking up cheques for him.

In real life, Jack was clean-shaven, and that landed him with a very red face the day he encountered a new make-up girl. Every morning he simply walked into make-up, sat in the chair, and they stuck on the moustache. As he didn't have any other make-up, it normally took only a few seconds of his time. But not this particular day. The new girl had been told all she had to do was get out his moustache and stick it on, but when she went to the moustache box there were three or four different types, and she didn't know which one was his.

Jack marched briskly into the make-up room, plonked himself down in the chair and, as usual, closed his eyes.

'Come on then,' he said briskly, expecting immediate attention.

Flustered, the little girl said, 'Your moustache?' unsure which one to use.

'Yes, my moustache,' said Jack, eyes firmly closed. 'Get on with it.' As the girl hovered indecisively, Jack rapped out, 'Come on. Come on. Come on. Get on with it. Stick it on.'

So the girl thought, 'Oh, I don't know!' and, taking a chance, took out the middle one from the box. Unfortunately, it was an Hercule Poirot-style moustache, which she then stuck on the upper lip of the increasingly agitated Jack. Everyone collapsed laughing and a flustered Jack immediately looked at his flies, but of course it was the moustache. He was not amused.

Some people thought he was grumpy, but it was his sense of humour. He would say, 'Move out of the bloody way,' but he didn't mean it to be nasty, it was just his way and his humour. He was all right and I liked him. And he had a lovely sense of fun, too.

We were standing at the bar one day, after he had had a major operation which meant that he had to use a catheter, when he suddenly beamed at me and, with a wicked twinkle in his eye, said, 'I'm doing something you can't do! I've just had a pee ...'

Another great character was Bernard Youens, who played the magnificent Stan Ogden, who was the Rovers' most valued customer for 20 years. Just like his screen character, Bernard was very fond of a drink and we often had one or two after work. So I wasn't surprised when one afternoon he said to me, 'Are you having one after rehearsals?'

'Yes,' I said.

'Good,' he replied, 'I have just got to go and see the quack and I will see you in the bar at 5.30pm.'

I went into town to do a few things and got to the bar at 5.45pm to join Bernard, whose normal tipple was half a beer and a whisky chaser. I was astonished at Bernard's appearance. He looked shocking and, trying to hide my worries, I asked, 'How did you get on at the quack's?'

'Oh, he gave me a right bollocking,' said Bernard. 'He said I mustn't drink beer and whisky.'

With that he asked, 'What are you having?'

'Oh,' I replied, 'I will have half of lager,'

Turning to the barman, he said, 'Half of lager, half of bitter and a brandy.'

'Who's the brandy for?' I asked.

'Me,' said Bernard.

'I thought the doctor said you had to cut it out,' I said, raising an eyebrow.

'He didn't mention brandy,' said Bernard. 'I've cut the whisky out!'

'That is even worse,' I told him, but he wasn't having it.

'No,' he said, 'and you can shut up. He said I mustn't have a whisky chaser with my beer. He didn't mention a bloody word about brandy ...'

So I thought, 'Oh God, forget it.'

He had something wrong with his foot and went into hospital. I went to see him and he was fine. He recovered but, sadly, in 1984, 69-year-old Bernard suffered a fatal stroke. I was very fond of him and he was a good pal. In his younger days, he was a very good-looking guy; he looked like Clark Gable.

Strangely, despite Baldwin's tough, wheeler-dealing, womanising image, and all the rogues I have played, the only time I have ever been attacked by an irate fan was over Bernard's screen wife, Hilda Ogden, played by the superb Jean Alexander. Hilda used to be Baldwin's cleaner and my problems began when Mike sacked Hilda when he found out she was cutting the bristles off the brush so she could have a new one.

I was shopping in Sainsbury's one day when a woman hit me over the shoulder with an umbrella, screaming, 'You are a mean pig. Hilda has every right to earn a living. Give her back her job!'

I was laughing my head off thinking, 'Right, my character is really getting across.' But in the end I had to do a runner to the car park as this woman kept chasing me, wielding her brolly, and obviously determined to do me some real mischief. The shop was in uproar with customers standing open-mouthed witnessing nasty Mike Baldwin getting his come uppance and a taste of his own medicine. As I fled the shop she continued to run after me, screaming abuse and yelling at the top of her voice, 'She is a human being like you; she has a right to earn a living ... cutting bristles off a brush ... I'll give you another brush if that is all you are worried about ...'

It just goes to show that some people thought Mike was so ferocious they didn't realise the business with the bristles was a slice of classic *Street* humour. I was sad to see Jean go when she left in 1987 after 23 years and I still miss her a lot because I used to do a lot of comedy scenes with her and I miss them.

Baldwin is so real to many people that I get a lot of mail from men and women asking me to give them jobs. They send me their CVs and ask if there is an opening in either the factory or being my driver. It is quite amazing.

Yet I don't normally get into a fracas with some one looking for a fight, because the characters I have been playing for the past 30 years have tended to be loveable rogues. The guys seem to like that. They like the idea that I am a bit of a rogue, but am quite a nice guy underneath who shouldn't be taken advantage of. And they like it when Mike gets one over on people. They probably see themselves as that sort of person. So I never get any problems at all from fellas.

I used to go out quite a lot with Jean Alexander because, as she had a house in Southport, she also used to stay in the Midland Hotel during the week and was quite a loner. She was a lovely, charming lady and we had a lot in common, talking about various places we had worked. She looked completely different without the curlers and I wasn't surprised when she finally decided to call it a day. She used to say, 'I am such and such an age. I've only got me so I might as well enjoy my money and start spending what I have been saving all these years.'

Geoffrey Hughes could never resist a gag, the saucier the better, and he found his perfect opportunity for a bit of mischief when a stray cat came to live in the studios and was as much of a nuisance as the pigeons. It used to hide everywhere and no one could catch it. So the administrative staff decided they were going to poison it — until Julie Goodyear found out.

She was horrified and tore into them, declaring, 'Don't be so bloody cruel.' Julie saved the cat, but it really was a pest, leaving little poos and puddles all over the place. This gave Geoffrey his opportunity. He used to buy fake cat's poos and put them down everywhere, much to the anger of Julie, who became more and more annoyed with every day that passed.

Inevitably, Julie and I were going for a take one day when I said, 'Julie, Julie, don't step too far back, because there's some some cat's mess just behind you.'

She glanced over her shoulder at this neat little pile of cat's mess, then, turning back to me, said, 'Oh, I'm so bloody sick of it.'

At that moment, there was an announcement over the tannoy, 'Come to studio in 30 seconds.'

Without any more ado, Julie bent down and picked it up — and it was a real cat's poo!

'Studio in ten seconds,' boomed the tannoy, and a furious Julie, her fingers covered in cat's mess, glowered at me.

'You rotten , filthy …'

'I warned you,' I said, grinning from ear to ear. 'Yes, but I thought you were kidding. What am I going to do?'

'You had better get a tissue or something,' I replied — and Julie had to do the scene with cat's mess under her finger nails.

But I always thought that Geoffrey was a typical Liverpool taker. For instance, if someone sent in some shirts for the cast and they were a size 15 collar and he was an 18, he would still take one. I would say, 'Why are you taking that, you are an 18?'

He'd reply, 'Well, I'll give it to … I'll have four.'

If it wasn't my size, I wouldn't take one. On another occasion, a guy came in with loads of records for the cast. But they were all obscure pop groups I had never heard of. But that didn't stop Geoffrey. He took the lot. Mind, if it had been Frank Sinatra or Andy Williams, I might have been interested. Geoffrey said he was giving them to charity.

When I first joined the *Street*, we not only had a far smaller cast, we also saw a lot more of each other as we all tended to be on screen at the same time more frequently than now with *Street*'s phenomenal four-times-a-week output. But the humour is still there, both on — and off — screen.

A classic example of that was when the McDonalds

moved in to Number 11 in December 1989 after research showed that teenagers were more tuned in to youth-orientated Australian series like *Neighbours*. So Mervyn Watson brought in a new family with two good-looking teenage sons, twins Andy and Steve McDonald, played by Nicholas Cochrane and Simon Gregson. The boys were an immediate hit, but Nicholas was always moaning in his early days on the *Street* that he didn't have a girlfriend in the show. So Beverley Callard, who plays the boys' screen mum Liz McDonald, and a couple of the others, told him that he was going to have a girlfriend — a beautiful blonde who was a little bit older than himself.

When he heard this, a delighted Nick raced around the studios shouting with joy, 'Yes, yes ... I'm getting a girlfriend, yes, YES ...'

Beverley and the others in on the gag even persuaded the casting director to go along with the joke, which went on for a month before Nick's 18th birthday. Eventually, he was told to go to casting, where, just as Beverley had hinted, he was told that a woman was coming in to the show to give his character some sex interest.

And while it was true that she would be a little bit older than him, nevertheless, she was going to be sexy. Nick lapped it all up, saying, with an eager gleam in his eye, 'Yes, yes ... I'm getting a girlfriend.' It really was a classic wind-up because they had got one of the writers to produce a special script to make it even more convincing. Nicholas was then told, 'She is coming in now with the casting director to read the script over with you on the set.'

That morning, Nick was on tenterhooks looking at every bird who came along thinking, 'Oh gee, is this the one!'

Well, they had got a 'girl' all right — one of the extras who was 50 and wore horn-rimmed glasses. She came over towards Nick as he sat, all expectantly, on the set.

'There she is,' said one of the gang in on the joke. 'There she is with the casting director.' And Nick's beaming smile slowly faded and his face dropped as this woman got closer. The poor lad suddenly went white as he was introduced to the 'love interest' who was coming into his life.

'Oh yes, great, wonderful, yes ...' he mumbled apprehensively as the casting director said, 'Would you like to read the scene?'

So, with the camera running, he started to read and, suddenly, we all sang, 'Happy Birthday to you ...' It was a magic moment as he blurted out, 'You bastards ... you rotten lot ...' as he realised just how well and truly he had been had.

People say to me, 'Why have you stuck in that show so long?' I tell them, 'I have done it. I have done all the major things — movies, touring the London stage, television plays and series that have been Number Ones and now I am in the top show in the world. Where do I go from here? If I stopped working in the *Street* tomorrow, whatever other television I did would be second to *Coronation Street* — a step down.'

'Wouldn't you like to do a London show?' they ask. Well, I've done it. You can't do anything all day. You do the show at night and all the luvvies come round, 'Oh, darling, you're wonderful ...' and you're trying to get rid of them to get to the pub for a quick one before closing time. Then you get home, go to bed and start all over again. I've done it.'

They say, 'What would lure you away from *Coronation Street*?' And I tell them, 'An American series. ' I would do it for a year; I would be a millionaire and then I would have my 'goodbye money.' Then, if I was to have a stroke or I was to be ill, I would have enough to keep me comfortable — until I could be a burden on my children!

As long as I can do what they want me to do and can deliver the goods, I am in the top television show in the world. All the other people who have left to do other TV series; where are they now? Arthur Lowe is the person most people mention. Well, Arthur, who died from a heart-attack in 1982 when he was 67, was a bloody good actor and he had something else lined up before he left.

As draper Leonard Swindley, who was jilted by Emily Nugent at the altar, he was such a hit that he is the only *Coronation Street* character to have been given his own spin-off series, *Pardon the Expression*. So it was no surprise that Arthur went on to star as the pompous Captain George Mainwaring in the brilliantly funny *Dad's Army* — one, I suppose, of the great classic television comedies. But Arthur had done a lot before he joined the *Street* in 1960.

All those people who left and think they are great big international stars are living a delusion. Because the way the system works in *Coronation Street*, is that the producer and casting director generally get someone unknown who then becomes a worldwide television personality because of the show. That doesn't mean producers and directors are going to give them the opportunity to do other things because they haven't got a proven track record. I have done everything as far as the arts are concerned, apart from a one-man show, which I wouldn't particularly want to do. I am not that egotistical.

Now I speak to respected actors and actresses I have known for the last 30 or 40 years and they think that *Coronation Street* is marvellous. Even Sir Laurence Olivier wanted to be an extra in the Rovers, and they wouldn't let him. He wanted to dress up in tramps' clothing and sit in the corner, but the bosses said 'no,' in case someone recognised him. And at the time the Granada boss David Plowright was his brother-in-law! It was the same when Dustin Hoffman wanted to stand in the Rovers because of the show's huge reputation. He was desperate to have a walk-on part, but again the bosses said 'no'. If you are lucky enough to be in a show that your peers revere and then leave, to my mind, you are only taking a step downwards.

The cast has more than doubled from about 20 to something like 44 since I joined, as the number of shows we do has also doubled. So it is no longer as intimate, but they are still a nice crowd. You would think that among

44 people there would be one rotten apple, but, luckily, there isn't.

I think that Brian Park, the current producer, has done an excellent job. He had an unenviable task because, naturally, when you are changing a show and bringing in new faces, you have to terminate people's contracts. He has been criticised and called the Axe Man, but just look at the ratings!

Thelma Barlow's decision to leave after the axing of her screen husband Derek Wilton, played by Peter Baldwin, shook a lot of people. Thelma first came into the show as Emily Nugent's friend Mavis Riley in 1971 and after more than 25 years she felt she had had enough. She has always been terribly interested in gardening and she had been saying for years that she wanted to do a gardening programme. Her children were educated and off her hands, which meant no more expenses, and there were other things she wanted to do which she couldn't if she was committed to the *Street*. Whether you like it or not, it is a 24-hour-a-day commitment — and if it isn't, you might as well leave. It has been very good to me and the only way I can repay it is by giving 100 per cent. Like Jean Alexander, Thelma wanted to do her own thing.

As wonderful as *Coronation Street* is, people sometimes decide they want to go their own way. I was very friendly with Thelma and I liked her very much — she was another one with a working background and you could talk about other projects you had both been on.

I also knew Peter Baldwin from way back. He had been in *No Hiding Place* and we had done *Softly, Softly* together. I had quite a long association with Peter between 1964 and 1966. I was also very friendly with Peter. He could talk about other theatre projects and the people we both knew. He also had his shop in London's Covent Garden which sold miniature theatres. I found chatting about making those miniature theatres fascinating. Peter also knew a hell of a lot about wine and we used to compare notes.

Some people thought that the departure of Ken Morley,

as the irrepressible shop boss Reg Holdsworth, would have an effect on the *Street*'s ratings. Ken had become a great comic asset to the show and his screen antics with Sherrie Hewson, as his long-suffering girlfriend and then wife, Maureen,were very funny.

Their hilarious waterbed romp was a *Street* classic, a brilliantly written scene they both made the most of. But the powers that be know that even if three or four people leave the show at one time, it won't affect the show or the ratings one iota.

Where the series and the producer are so clever is in making sure the plots and storylines are never about one person or even one group of people. Instead, there are lots of little plots interwoven all over the place. In the old days you could say 'Oh God, I haven't seen *Coronation Street* for two months, but I'll be able to pick up on what is going on.' Not any more. Now, if you miss a single episode, things will have happened with the storyline that will throw you completely.

And that's the way it was when Ken Morley left. His departure had absolutely zero effect on the show or on the rest of the cast. We felt nothing. If he wanted to leave that was up to him. No one is forcing you to work on *Coronation Street*, but it is an honour to be asked. For goodness sake, it goes out to 18 million people a week in Britain alone, let alone the rest of the world. No other television programme in the world gets 80 million viewers per episode, or anything near that.

Violet Carson, who created the immortal battleaxe Ena Sharples, understood this only too well. If anyone suggested to her that the *Street* would die without her, she used to insist that the only star was the show itself. Vi became depressed after she retired in 1980 after 20 years with the show because people still associated her with Ena. But that was inevitable. She had created this wonderful character, but with a face like hers wherever she went she was Ena Sharples. And although she maintained that she could lock the character away and be herself, it was very difficult.

There are other people in the cast who appear very distinctive, like Anne Kirkbride, but the moment Anne speaks she is not Deirdre. Sarah Lancashire was the same. Because she wore a wig in the show to play Raquel, she could lose the character the moment she took it off and spoke in her own voice. Then she was Sarah Lancashire.

But even if, to some extent, the character does take over your life, for the rewards the show gives you that is just part of the price. You can't have it both ways. The show has made you. And, let's face it, Violet was quite an old lady, 82 in fact, when she left the show. And the show was very good to her.

When I first met her, she was playing the piano for Wilfrid Pickles in *Have a Go* on the radio. And when I ran into her again at the Granada studios at the beginning of *Coronation Street* in 1960, when it was still just a regional programme, she said to me, 'I just hope this runs. This is the best thing that has happened to me — no more playing that blooming piano!'

You certainly couldn't blame her. Wilfrid Pickles was a bit of a one-off, too. When he was staying at a hotel, the night before he was due to leave, he would go to reception, see the manager, and say, 'How much is my bill, landlord?'

The landlord would say, '£25,' or whatever the bill was, and Pickles would say, 'Right.' He would then sign a cheque for £25 and, along with a picture of himself saying, 'Thank you. How lovely it was staying here,' place it in a frame. The next morning, he would present it to the landlord to be proudly displayed!

My most memorable moments have literally been command occasions — the Royal Command show at the Palace Theatre, when I first met the Queen, and a Royal Command Performance at the Palladium, when I met the Queen again. But the highlight of them all was when the Queen and Prince Philip came to the *Coronation Street* set in 1982 and the Queen asked me how the factory was doing. She then, jokingly, said she would like a garment run off in the factory and I said I would be only too happy to oblige — as long as I got the royal crest.

There have been some unfortunate moments, too, such as my disastrous excursion into the pop world in 1983. That was when I made my first pop record, the love ballad, 'Warm', and it was a flop. What a shambles! The record turned out so bad that I asked for all the copies to be withdrawn from sale. It sounded as if I was singing from under a pile of blankets! Bill Podmore, the canny blighter, was right on the money when he bet me £50 that any record I made would fail to make the charts.

Then there was the time when I was 'stalked' by a teenage girl fan who bombarded me with gifts, letters and cards for weeks. I love getting a good response from fans — they are the people who make you. But this was totally over the top. I never met or encouraged her, but she telephoned me at home and even proclaimed her love for me over the phone to Christine. That did it. I didn't want to hurt the girl's feelings but, in the end, reluctantly, I was forced to call the police to ensure that my family were no longer pestered. I may be a public person and fair game, but Christine and the children aren't.

Normally, despite my high profile and the huge fan following I had from the moment I arrived at *Coronation Street*, I have managed to avoid any trouble, even from jealous boyfriends of girl fans. I used to go into the pub and the girls, who would be there with their boyfriends, would say, 'Oh, he's my favourite, I love him,' and come over for a kiss. But I never tried it on. I never did anything to encourage the girls, so the word went round, 'He's all right. He's not lairy.' But if I had said, 'Oh come here, darling. What are you doing tonight?' and all that, the blokes would have gone, 'Oh, hello, hello,' and there could have been trouble.

But I have never had any aggravation from blokes being jealous because I made it quite clear that I just didn't want to know as far as their girlfriends were concerned.

They couldn't understand it and must have thought, 'What's wrong with you?' The truth is that I just didn't want to get involved, because I am more of a bloke's bloke and would rather go out for a game of golf and a chat with the boys, than take some girl out. I have never wanted girls chasing me, but I got it and I still do. But it doesn't mean anything to me. It's not an ego boost, because I am a 62-year-old bloke and I have been in this business since I was 12. I have been doing it for 50 years.

I have bought the T-shirt, washed it, and shrunk it!

And the abiding joy of *Coronation Street* is that, just as in real life, it is forever changing. People come and go. They are born and they die. Some deaths, particularly of a young baby, are particularly harrowing, but that, unfortunately, is what life is about — and *Coronation Street* mirrors the lives we all lead.

Some people have grotty neighbours and there was a furious outcry when the Street introduced their own family from hell and the Battersbys first descended upon the cobbles. Newspapers ran hysterical campaigns to 'boot out the Battersbys', but they have now become a key element — and I'm delighted. Brian Park knew exactly what he was doing by bringing them in. More to the point, they are good fun and, as I have mentioned, Bruce Jones, who plays the skiving Les, is my best pal. Bruce is also a very good actor — he was the stripper who wouldn't peel off in *The Full Monty* — and beneath his rough veneer, he is a wine buff. Bruce has a friend who is a German wine importer, and he often asks, 'Do you want another case of wine, Johnny?'

Without hesitating, I'll say, 'Yes, please, Bruce,' and I'll get a case at a very reasonable price.

Jane Danson, who plays Leanne, is a lovely young woman, while Vicky Entwistle, who plays mouthy Janice, has been through the most appalling trauma off screen, having had bad stomach pains which developed into peritonitis. But that was only the start of the drama. When they operated, the surgeon found that it was turning to gangrene. Luckily, they operated in time and she pulled through fine.